Praise for *Apathy for the Devil*

"Fifteen years ago Kent published *The Dark Stuff*, a collection of his finest music journalism, a book to rank alongside Greil Marcus' *Mystery Train*, Nik Cohn's *Awopbopaloobop Alopbamboom* and Jon Savage's *England's Dreaming*; *Apathy for the Devil* might even be better than that."

—DYLAN JONES, *GQ*

"As an eyewitness account of the dangerous excesses of the 1970s rock scene, *Apathy for the Devil* is in a compulsively readable class of its own. . . . Almost every page contains an anecdotal gem. . . . It's a miracle, frankly, that Kent survived to tell this tale, but as anybody who romps through *Apathy for the Devil* will agree, we're all lucky that he did."

—ROBERT SANDALL, *Sunday Times*

"While *Apathy for the Devil* adds some backstory to his classic interviews, it's also a 'my-drug-hell' tale dispensed with a bleak wit and brutal candour. . . . Full of fabulous rock tittle-tattle but also some uncomfortable home truths, this is a book for anyone that's ever read a music magazine from cover to cover but still wanted to know more."

—MARK BLAKE, *Q* Magazine

"Kent tackles his autobiography, as he does his music writing, throwing himself headlong into it and re-experiencing every minute. . . . The magnetic open-heartedness that drew his subjects close lies at the centre of this work, drawing the reader closer too."

—LOIS WILSON, *Mojo*

9/23

Apathy for the Devil

A Seventies Memoir

Nick Kent

DA CAPO PRESS
A Member of the Perseus Books Group

Typeset by Ian Bahrami

Cataloging-in-Publication data for this book is available
from the Library of Congress.
ISBN: 978-0-306-81915-5
Library of Congress Control Number: 2010926741

First Da Capo Press edition 2010
Reprinted by arrangement with Faber and Faber Limited

Published by Da Capo Press
A Member of the Perseus Books Group
www.dacapopress.com

Da Capo Press books are available at special discounts
for bulk purchases in the U.S. by corporations, institutions,
and other organizations. For more information, please contact the
Special Markets Department at the Perseus Books Group, 2300 Chestnut
Street, Suite 200, Philadelphia, PA 19103, or call (800) 810-4145,
ext. 5000, or e-mail special.markets@perseusbooks.com.

10 9 8 7 6 5 4 3 2 1

This book is dedicated to the ones I love – Adrian and Margaret, Laurence and Jimmy

Contents

1970

When you get right down to it, the human memory is a deceitful organ to have to rely on. Past reality gets confused with wishful fantasy as the years march on and you can never really guarantee that you're replaying the unvarnished truth back to yourself. I've tried to protect my memories, to keep them pristine and authentic, but it's been easier said than done.

Music remains the only key that can unlock the past for me in a way that I can inherently trust. A song from the old days strikes up and instantly a film is projected in my head, albeit an unedited one without a linear plot line; just random scenes thrown together to appease my reflective mood of the moment. For example, someone just has to play an early Joni Mitchell track or one of David Crosby's dreamy ocean songs and their chords of enquiry instantly transport me back to the Brighton of 1969 with its Technicolor skies, pebble-strewn beach and jaunty air of sweetly decaying Regency splendour. I am dimple-faced and lanky and wandering lonely as a clod through its backstreets and arcades looking longingly at the other people in my path: the boys enshrouded in ill-fitting greatcoats and sagebrush beards and the bra-less girls in long skirts sporting curtains of unstyled hair to frame their fresh inquisitive faces.

It was at these girls in particular that my longing looks were aimed. Direct contact was simply not an option at this juncture of my life. Staring forlornly at their passing forms was the only alternative. This is what happens when you don't have a sister and have been sidetracked into single-sex schooling systems since the age of eleven: women start to exert a strange and terrible fascination, one born of sexual and romantic frustrations as well as complete ignorance of their emotional agendas and basic thought processes.

And so it was that – on December 31st 1969 – I found myself glumly ruminating on my destiny to date. I kept returning to its central dilemma: I had just turned eighteen and yet I had never even been kissed passionately by a lady. It was an ongoing bloody tragedy.

But then it suddenly all changed – just as everyone was counting out the final seconds of the sixties and getting ready to welcome in 1970. I was in a pub in Cardiff when a beautiful woman impulsively grabbed me and forced her beer-caked tongue down my throat. She was a student nurse down from the Valleys with her mates to see the new decade in, she told me giddily. She had long brown hair and wore a beige minidress that showed off her buxom physique to bewitching effect. She smiled at me so seductively our bodies just sank into each other. In a room full of inebriated Welsh people, I let my hands wander over her breasts and buttocks. So this was what the poets were talking about when they invoked the phrase 'all earthly ecstasy'. Suddenly, a door had opened and the sensual world was mine to embrace.

It was only a fleeting fumble. At 12.05 I unwrapped myself from her perfumed embrace for some thirty seconds in order to seek the whereabouts of a male friend who'd brought me there – only to return and find the same woman locked in an amorous clinch with a bearded midget. The door to all earthly pleasure had slammed shut on me almost as soon as it had swung open and yet I left the hostelry still giddy with elation. At last I'd been granted my initiation into fleshy desire. I was no longer on the outside looking in, like that cloying song by Little Anthony & the Imperials. And it had all happened just at the exact moment that the seventies had been ushered in to raucous rejoicing. I sensed right there and then that the new decade and I were made for each other.

On the train back to Paddington the next day – I'd been visiting old friends in Cardiff the night before, catching up on their adventures ever since I'd moved almost two years earlier from there to Horsham in Sussex, a mere thirty-mile whistle-stop from London – I felt further compelled to review my sheltered life thus far. Everywhere around me in the new pop counter-culture of Great Britain and elsewhere, young people were gleefully surrendering themselves to states of chemically induced rapture, growing hair from every conceivable pore of their bodies and cultivating sundry grievances against 'the man'. And yet I was still stuck at home with my parents, who'd brainwashed me into believing that my adult life would be totally hamstrung without the benefits of a full university education and degree. As a result, most of my time was being spent furtively spoon-feeding ancient knowledge into my cranium until it somehow stuck to the walls.

It wasn't a particularly easy process. I cared not a fig for Martin Luther or his Diet of Worms. But I had three A levels to sit – English, French and History – in May and had to somehow cram all the arcane details of each syllabus into my consciousness in order to get winning results. In retrospect, it wasn't all a pointless procedure. The French I was studying would hold me in good stead when I came to live in Paris in my late thirties. My English A-level studies involved poring briefly over the poetry of both Yeats and T. S. Eliot, and both had a forceful impact on my own burgeoning literary aspirations. But then there'd be long mind-numbing sessions of having to grapple with the lofty moral agenda laid out in the collected works of John Milton.

In *Paradise Lost* Milton spelt it out to the sinners: 'temperance – the golden mean' is what humankind needed to adopt as an all-embracing lifestyle if they truly want to get right with God. Wise words, but somewhat wasted on an eighteen-year-old virgin just counting the days before he can catapult himself over to the wild side of life.

My father was a great admirer of John Milton also. His all-time favourite poem was Milton's 'On His Blindness'. He'd often quote the final line: 'They also serve who only stand and waite.' It fitted his overall view of an all-inclusive humanity. My father was a thoughtful man who'd had his young life thrown into tur-moil first – as a child – by his own father's bankruptcy and then – in his early twenties – by having to fight overseas throughout most of the Second World War. He returned in 1945 with the after-effects of undiagnosed malaria and severe rheumatoid arthritis partly instigated from falling out of a moving truck and landing flat on his back on a dirt road in North Africa.

He and my mother, an infant-school teacher born and raised in the North of England, had already met two years earlier in a wartime canteen and had begun an ardent correspondence. They married in 1945 at war's end and moved into a two-storey house in North London's Mill Hill area that same year. At first they were told by various doctors that my mother would be unable to conceive, but in April of 1951 she discovered she was pregnant. I

4

arrived on Christmas Eve of that year after a long and complicated birth. My parents couldn't believe their good fortune and – rightly sensing that I would be their only offspring – showered me with affection.

So often these days people tartly evoke Philip Larkin's damning lines about family ties – 'They fuck you up, your mum and dad. / They may not mean to, but they do' – as if it sums up the whole parental process in one bitter little sound bite. But my parents never fucked me up. They didn't beat me or abuse me. They loved me and fed me and encouraged me to think about everything, to develop my own value system and stretch my attention span. Above all else, they introduced me from a very early age to the sensation of having one's senses engulfed by art. Classical music streamed through our living room constantly. Much of it – particularly Beethoven and Richard Wagner – I found unsettlingly bombastic but the works of Debussy and Ravel were also played often and their enchanted melodies wove into my newly emerging brain-span like aural fairy dust. To this day, Debussy's music can still stimulate within me a sense of inner well-being more profound than anything else I've ever known. It is the sound of all that unconditional love pouring down on me as a little child.

My father liked to lose himself in music. He was often in physical pain and relied on its healing properties to keep him emotionally buoyant. He was a professional sound recordist – one of the best in the business. When Sir Winston Churchill – at the very end of his life – was persuaded to read extracts of his memoirs for recorded posterity, my dad was the one invited to Chequers – Churchill's stately home – to set up the equipment and tape-record the great man's every faltering utterance. He told me later that Churchill was in such bad health they had to employ an actor to replicate his gruff tones on certain passages.

At the outset of the fifties he was a staff engineer at EMI's Abbey Road Studios – George Martin was another new recruit at this juncture – but the pay was so abysmal that when I appeared, he was immediately forced to look for more financially advantageous avenues of employment. This he found in 1952 at Radio Luxembourg, whose London-based recording studios he basically ran for several years. The outlet then required a daily cavalcade of live entertainment to fill its airwaves – its transformation to a DJ-centric pop music format was still some years off – and so my father spent his days setting up the sessions and then recording everyone from George Formby to Vera Lynn.

Vera Lynn and him became first-name pals: she always had a good word for my dad. But he didn't like her music. In fact, he couldn't stand his job. He didn't like 'light entertainment' – he found it all offensively simplistic. And as a devout Christian, he was thoroughly appalled by the loose moral conduct he often encountered in the industry: the sexual favours and rampant alcoholism, the fly-by-night agents and managers with their predatory ways, the shrill-voiced, pill-addled post-war prima donnas careening from one private catastrophe to the next. When I'd become a teenager, he told me just how flawed these people were in his eyes. His most unforgettable reminiscence involved a much-loved actress of the era who'd become something of an English institution for her sympathetic, matronly portrayal of a farmer's wife on a popular radio broadcast. According to him, she'd once bitten a man's penis off whilst performing oral sex on him when the car they were both travelling in was involved in a sudden head-on collision with a wall. He tried to instil in me early his belief that most popular entertainment was – at best – smoke and mirrors and that behind its bejewelled curtain lurked a tainted and predatory kingdom.

Both my parents viewed what passed for popular culture in the fifties with a ferocious disdain. Elvis Presley they considered like some degenerate hillbilly sex maniac, the musical equivalent of Robert Mitchum in *Cape Fear*. Frank Sinatra they called a 'smarmy little gangster': my father already knew all the insider scuttlebutt (gossip) on his Mafia affiliations and leg-breaking routines. When I suddenly fell under pop's giddy spell, it was a shock to both of them.

The first time was when I heard Elmer Bernstein's 'Theme from *The Magnificent Seven*' on the car radio during a family outing when I was nine going on ten. Staccato violins suddenly stabbed out a turbulent mariachi rhythm over which a hauntingly exuberant melody was being articulated and every atom of my being was suddenly activated by its impact on my ears. I'd never before heard or felt anything as thrilling as this. Every detail is still vivid in my mind: my grandmother's fierce eyes looking at me from the front seat, my father's aching back as he drove, the rank odour of cheap petrol that permeated the back of the family car. From that moment on, I was plugged into a new form of rapture that my parents could never understand.

The world of pop that I found myself suddenly enthralled with was not one that bristled with danger and raw excitement. The early sixties were a slack time for musical daredevilry. Elvis had been neutered by the army and his hoodlum peers were publicly disgraced and slouching snake-eyed through their wilderness years. Their places had been taken by a markedly less disruptive breed of young entertainer – bland crooners with dimpled cheeks and puppy-dog eyes forever voicing their feelings of undying love to some sulky beehived harpy. It was mostly cloying stuff – musical Brylcreem that left you feeling sticky and light-headed.

But then, in October of 1962, I was listening to popular disc jockey Alan Freeman enthusiastically address the nation's 'pop-pickers' on the kitchen radio one Sunday afternoon when he introduced the debut single by 'a young combo from down Liverpool way' that he referred to as the Beatles. The song itself, 'Love Me Do', wasn't particularly groundbreaking – the harmonica refrain dominating the arrangement had been clearly inspired by Bruce Channel's recent mega-hit 'Hey! Baby' – but the robust blend of plaintive guitar strumming and playful Scouser vocalising made it infectiously easy on the ear nonetheless. No one could sense in that innocent moment that a musical and cultural revolution was about to blow up and that the Beatles would be its central motivating core, its leaders and all-purpose Pied Pipers.

How sweet it was to be ten years old when they kicked off: my whole teenaged experience was illuminated by their output and very existence. They never disappointed and each new musical plateau they ascended to left their audience delirious with a joy so contagious that it came to define the very spirit of the decade itself. The better world their songs aspired to was a universe that everyone was welcome to inhabit, one where notions of class and racial disharmony simply melted away, where being kind was infinitely more virtuous a pursuit than simply being cool and where the sophistication of high art could effortlessly be fused with the visceral impact of lowbrow pop. It was them and Dylan who kicked open the door that had formerly kept twentieth-century bohemian culture trapped in suffocatingly smoky nightclubs on the outskirts of town and let it come pouring into the high streets where young people were gathering to define a new sort of commercial mainstream for their own consumer urges.

Not forgetting the Rolling Stones of course. You can never overestimate their role in detonating the rebel instincts of my bright-eyed baby boomer generation. I should know. I was there in the front row when the deal went down. I felt the explosion full in the face. The force of it hot-wired my imagination, invaded my dreams and taught me everything I needed to know about the realities of youthful self-empowerment.

In 1959, my father – always on the lookout for better-paying employment – was offered a senior position in a fledgling TV company known as Harlech that was then poised to become the Welsh branch of the ITV network. He took the job even though it involved immediately uprooting his family from our relatively blissful North London home and hearth and relocating in Llandaff, a sleepy little village on the outskirts of Cardiff that was remarkable only for its lofty-spired cathedral, one of the largest centres of worship in all of the British Isles. I would come to know its interior well: my parents were weekly attendees and they obliged me to accompany them every Sunday morning until I reached the age of fourteen.

None of us were happy in our new surroundings. My father soon found himself in daily conflict with the higher-ups at the studio and the accumulated stress caused his various physical ailments to further flare up. My mother felt out of place, and I became lonely and withdrawn, uncertain of how and where to fit in with everyone around me.

The hearty 'welcome in the hillsides' that the Welsh were always promising to shower on all foreigners entering their borders had been mysteriously withheld from me. At school, I was mocked for my English accent, which I refused to modulate in order to blend in with the blocked-sinus cadences of the South Wales resident. I was useless at sports too – apart from cross-country running – and as soon as I'd entered grammar school at eleven, I found my place amongst the stragglers and the under-developed lurking in the shadow-dimmed corners of the play-ground.

One of my fellow outsiders at school was a youth with a facial defect who seemed at first glance to be ever so slightly mentally challenged. We got to talking one day and he mentioned that his father was a leading promoter of wrestling events and pop concerts in the South Wales area. I then talked up my dad's role as TV studio controller and the boy became excited. He immediately proposed a deal: if I could get my father to agree to take him for a guided tour around his studio, he'd coerce his dad to let me attend one of his pop concerts. He'd even take me backstage to meet the acts.

A few days later, I was formally invited to witness a concert that was booked into Cardiff's Sophia Gardens on February 28th 1964. It was a package tour of recent UK hit pop acts, headlined by an actor called John Leyton then renowned for his role as 'Ginger' in the TV series *Biggles* who'd also scored a no. 1 hit of late with his overwrought rendition of 'Tell Laura I Love Her'. The rest of the bill were similarly old-school Tin Pan Alley chancers and prancers with one marked exception: nestled well below Leyton's name and likeness on the marquee poster were five hirsute faces belonging to a Richmond-based quintet of young white R & B purists who called themselves the Rolling Stones. They'd already started getting publicity for themselves and had so far released two singles – the second, 'I Wanna Be Your Man', being a Lennon–McCartney composition – but neither had penetrated the top 10. They were still something of an unknown quantity outside of the South of England as a concert attraction and had been placed low on the bill in case their act failed to take off in the British provinces.

At around 5 p.m. on the evening in question, I entered the premises and was duly introduced to the acts that were already secluded in the backstage area. They were all surprisingly cordial with me, considering the fact that I was a pre-pubescent twelve-year-old dressed up like the quintessential spare prick at a wedding. Harold Wilson's Labour government had recently been brought into power after years of Conservative misrule and my parents being good socialist thinkers had celebrated by buying their only child an overcoat made in a material called 'Gannex' that one of Wilson's closest supporters and business cronies had begun manufacturing. It was supposed to be the fabric of the future but it looked and felt like a cheap bath mat with sleeves. It was a hideous material and was doomed to become extinct just as soon as Wilson had left power, but not before I'd been rendered sartorially challenged at this landmark occasion in my life.

Still, no one said anything untoward about my catastrophic fashion sense. The early-sixties UK pop breed were an approachable bunch if nothing else. They knew all about the devious nature of pop success and were fastidious about always presenting a smiling face and friendly word or two to any potential fan crossing their paths. Jet Harris – a hopeless alcoholic and one of UK rock's first-ever bona fide casualties who'd been booked on the tour even though he was so plastered all the time someone else had to play his guitar parts behind a curtain – was even nice to me. His girlfriend – a singer named Billie Davis – let me play with her dog. I felt accepted by all of them and liked being in their company. But as soon as the lights dimmed and each of them slipped under the spotlight to reveal their stagecraft, I could sense that they were all living in the past and only a few heart-beats away from becoming instant entertainment-industry relics.

All these acts basically looked the same. Thin lips, prominent cheekbones, pompadoured Everly Brothers hair, shark-white teeth clenched in winning smiles, tight shiny suits with spaghetti stains on the lapels, loud shirts and skinny little ties. They sounded identical also. Twanging guitars played at docile, non-feedback-inducing volumes, drumming you could gently tap your foot along with, singers clumsily attempting to reproduce the husky-voiced drama of Elvis Presley's recent recordings. In fact what we the audience were seeing that night was the timely ending of an era – the dreary watershed years separating the fifties from this new decade we were now living in and the beginning of true sixties culture as an oasis of unbridled hedonism. It occurred at the very moment the Rolling Stones entered the building.

The group had been delayed on the motorway and had arrived just in time to literally walk on stage for their spot. Suddenly the mood in the hall became more charged and disruptive. The pre-dominantly female audience had been polite in their reception of the other acts but now they were becoming distinctly agitated. Screams started erupting in the hall followed by a succession of adolescent females leaving their seats and rampaging around the building in fierce packs.

I was seated in the front row just as the lights went down to herald the group's onstage arrival and was suddenly confronted by a demented young woman who angrily demanded that I vacate my place for her. When I refused, she took off one of her shoes and positioned the stiletto heel against my neck like a shiv forcing me to acquiesce to her demand. One of the bouncers saw what was going on and pulled her off me, but by that time complete pandemonium had set in everywhere I looked. I was surrounded on all sides by young women in a collective state of extremely heightened sexual psychosis. They were touching themselves in inappropriate places and letting forth primeval howls. My eyes were popping out of my head.

This was the first time I'd ever come face to face with 'sex' – never mind raging mass sexual hysteria – so you can understand that the moment had more than a lingering impact on my naive little psyche. They were scary broads too but I instinctively understood the root cause of their dementia because the Rolling Stones' presence in the room had also sucked me into something equally life-scrambling. The Rolling Stones never smiled and physically they were the polar opposite of everyone else on the bill. No ties, no Brylcreemed hair slicked back to better define the young male forehead. The Rolling Stones didn't have foreheads. Just hair, big lips and a collective aura of rampaging insolence.

They slouched onto the stage and stared witheringly at the crowd before them as they donned their instruments. The house compère hastily announced them only to have his utterances drowned in screams. Then they began playing. It could have been 'Not Fade Away', the Buddy Holly song they'd release a week later, thus securing their first top-10 placing and their full-on ascension to the status of rebel-prince youth phenomenon.

All I can recall in my mind now is a vibrant, irresistibly all-embracing sonic churn – 'the very churn of sedition itself', I'd later come to call it. It was raucous and primordial and it sent young women into an instant state of full-on demonic possession. Something that had previously been forbidden in white culture was being let loose here: a kind of raw tribal abandoning of all inhibitions that held the key to a new consciousness still emerging. Within the space of their twenty-minute-long performance, my childhood's end was preordained and the door to adulthood held tantalisingly ajar. I remember it now like someone reaching into my brain and turning a switch that suddenly changed my fundamental vision of life from grainy black and white into glorious Technicolor.

They played 'Route 66', 'Road Runner' and 'Walking the Dog' and they were right at the top of their game. Brian Jones hadn't yet fallen by the wayside as a musical contributor and he, Jagger and Keith Richards presented a unique three-pronged attack as live performers. Jones – the most conventionally good-looking – minced menacingly on the left whilst Keith perfected a kind of big-eared borstal strut to his far right, endlessly winding and unwinding his coiled frame around the guitar rhythms he was punching out.

The two of them perfectly bookended Jagger, who at that point in time was one scary motherfucker to behold. No one had seen features quite like his before: the pornographic lips, the bird's nest hair. The Stones had a disturbing 'Village of the Damned' quality about their combined physical presence but Jagger had the most radically alien looks of the quintet.

And his was by far the most overtly malevolent presence in the house. At one point in the set, a spectator – I couldn't tell if it was male or female – rushed the stage and attempted to grab Jagger's legs in a sort of rugby tackle manoeuvre. The singer responded by calmly driving his mike stand into the interloper's face, causing blood and several teeth to arc across the spotlight. It was shocking to behold but also somehow perversely appropriate. We were all in the grip of something that was completely out of control, a sort of mass delirium, a voodoo ceremony for the white adolescent libido to come alive to.

By the end, all the barriers had come tumbling down. When they left the stage, they'd obliterated every performer and every note that had preceded them. I saw the other acts leaving the building with their instruments and suitcases at the end of the evening and they had to run a gauntlet of rabid female Stones fans outside the stage door who were only too willing to call attention to their various musical and image shortcomings.

The rules were all changing. 'Tame' was out. 'Audacious' was in. The Zeitgeist pendulum had moved to the other end of the culture spectrum, the one diametrically opposed to notions of conformism and bourgeois uniformity. And the Rolling Stones were at the centre of this cultural youth quake, its designated dam-busters.

I actually got to meet them that night too. The promoter took me and his son into their dressing room, which wasn't much bigger than a toilet cubicle, about a quarter of an hour after they'd vacated the stage. 'Why is that little cunt getting to meet them and not us?' screamed an enraged female, one of many being blocked from entering through the adjacent stage door. But hey, I couldn't help it if I was lucky.

At first glimpse the group looked utterly shattered, wrung dry by the exhausting routine of travelling around the British Isles in a cramped and underheated Transit van night and day. Keith Richards was stretched out on a makeshift sofa, eyes closed, mouth slightly agape, an open bottle of brown ale balanced precariously on his lower torso. Charlie Watts and Bill Wyman were towelling the sweat from their hair and necks and staring blankly at their dressing-room walls as if under hypnosis. They didn't exactly radiate approachability but when I timidly offered them a piece of paper to autograph, they obliged without complaint, even though I had to gently nudge Keith in order to wake him up.

Mick Jagger was the one I was wariest of. I'd just seen him literally smash someone's face in and now he was standing directly before me looking extremely angry about something or other. For an insecure second, I thought he might be experiencing an allergic reaction to my overcoat but then I noticed that his livid expression was aimed squarely in the direction of Brian Jones. Jones was surrounded by three young female fans, all of whom were clearly captivated by his genteel Cheltenham-bred manners and blond-haired pretty-boy insouciance. I could tell these girls were attracted by Jagger too – they kept shooting awed glances his way – but he frightened them with his contemptuous eyes and sullen expression so much that they never dared actually approach him. This set off a tense dynamic in the room: Jones swanning around these girls like the cat who stole the cream and Jagger staring at him with murder in his eyes.

Of course, Brian Jones had started out as the undisputed ringleader of the Rolling Stones and was certainly acting as though this continued to be the case. He was still physically strong and mentally focused: the drugs and alcohol hadn't yet diminished him. In fact, he was possibly at his all-time happiest at this precise juncture of his life. All his dreams were coming true and the Stones were still fundamentally 'his' creation. The Jagger–Richards songwriting partnership had yet to reach commercial fruition and so he could still kid himself that he held the reins and was directing the whole operation. It would take only two or three months for this to end all too dramatically. From then on, he was a lost boy, a dead fop walking.

In later years, I would talk at length to many of Brian Jones's closest acquaintances and they would almost always depict him as a ruinously flawed specimen of humanity. Some called him 'sadistic', others 'pathetic'. In his defence though I have to say – he was incredibly nice to me. He was the only member of the Stones that night who bothered to engage me in conversation. He wasn't condescending in the least; he told me he thought it was 'fantastic' that someone so young was coming to their shows. He said 'please' and 'thank you' repeatedly. He took his self-appointed role as the Stones' good-will ambassador so seriously it was almost quaint to behold. He was so clean, courteous and daintily expressive it seemed unthinkable that he might be harbouring dark intentions under all that golden hair. He had me smitten anyway. Suddenly I had my future adult agenda mapped out before me. This was exactly the kind of person I was determined to grow up and become.

It was providential indeed then that my parents hadn't actually heard of the Rolling Stones when they reluctantly agreed to let me attend the concert I've just described. If they had, I would never have been allowed near the venue. In the following months, however, they became aware of the group's existence and began loudly regretting the fact that I'd been exposed to their worrisome influence.

Things reached a head in early '65 when three group members were brought to court in order to answer charges that they'd urinated all over the forecourt of a garage somewhere out in the provinces. 'These people you seem to idolise – they're nothing but degenerates,' my mother scolded. My father went even further, invoking a word I'd never heard before. 'There's something decadent about that bunch of animals,' he said one evening as images of the group exiting their trial were broadcast on a TV news report. He was ahead of his time with that evaluation: the Stones' decadent phase wouldn't kick off for another four years.

There was one incident where my dad truly freaked out. We were both watching the television one evening in 1965 when *Ready, Steady, Go!*, the London-based weekly pop show, came on. That week, James Brown was the special guest: he and the Famous Flames performed live throughout its entire half-hour-long duration. It was Brown's first-ever TV exposure in the British Isles and he rose to the occasion with a performance that gave new meaning to the word 'torrid'. The cameras couldn't help but linger on the predominantly female audience, who were experiencing the same kind of shared sexual psychosis that I'd witnessed first-hand with the Stones. After about twenty minutes, steam started spouting from out of my father's ears. He bolted out of his chair, turned the TV off and told me in no uncertain terms that I was henceforth forbidden from watching *Ready, Steady, Go!* ever again. I still watched it though because it was usually broadcast at 6 p.m. on a Friday – a time when he was returning from work and I was alone in the house. Sometimes he'd arrive back just a minute or two after its conclusion and he'd always feel to see if the valves at the back of the TV were still warm. If they were, there was hell to pay.

In 1966, I saw Bob Dylan live backed by what became the Band on his seminal electric tour of Britain that spring. They played a single show at Cardiff's Capitol Cinema. A friend at public

school bought me the ticket so that I could tell him what transpired by phone the next day. It was the first time I'd ever seen
another human being under the influence of drugs. Dylan ram-
bled a lot between songs and his speech was seriously impaired.
And the music was so loud that it was impossible to take in on
any kind of aesthetic level. It was like standing in a relatively
small room whilst a jet-aircraft engine was set into motion.
'Tumultuous' doesn't even begin to cover it. I couldn't hear properly for a week afterwards.

In 1967, another epiphany: I attended a special 'psychedelic'
package tour – once again at Sophia Gardens – that featured the
Jimi Hendrix Experience, Syd Barrett's Pink Floyd, the mighty
Move from the Black Country and prog-rock pioneers the Nice.
Best bill I've ever witnessed. Four mind-boggling performances.
Seeing Syd that night ignited something within me that I've been
obsessed with all my adult life. The sense of mystery he projected
from that stage was something I felt an overwhelming compul-
sion to solve. His story – however it developed – was mine to tell.

He was also the second person I'd ever witnessed who was
clearly in a chemically altered state. He was so out of it he
couldn't sing or even play his guitar coherently. Jimi Hendrix –
who followed the Floyd ten minutes later – was the third. But
Hendrix was a pro. Being on acid didn't prevent him from
pulling out all the stops in his voluminous trick-bag of guitar wild
man theatrics – it only emboldened him to take the whole shtick
further until he'd incited mass hysteria in the house. There was a
sexual bravado about Hendrix live that night that was so palpable
it made my jaw drop. I was even more thunderstruck when I witnessed several young girls surrounding him at the lip of the stage
who had become so aroused they were trying to fondle his

genitalia whilst he played. I'd seen these same girls week after week timidly accompanying their parents to Llandaff Cathedral throughout my early teens.

In 1968, glad tidings. Harlech's contract with ITV expired and my dad moved us back to the South of England, close to London. I left Wales that summer with a spring in my step and nine O levels under my belt. My folks were well chuffed. And I was happy to be closer to the heart of the counter-cultural revolution. London was abuzz with magical concerts, many of them held for free in Hyde Park. I saw Traffic, Fleetwood Mac, the Pretty Things and the Move give great shows in an idyllic setting.

And then in August I got to go to my first extended gathering of the rock tribes – the Reading Jazz and Blues Festival, a three-day slog that I misguidedly chose to attend without bringing along a canvas tent. I spent the first night there sleeping on the side of the road. It was a fitful slumber. My big recollection of the audience was the preponderance of youths in greatcoats with 'Did J. P. Lenoir Die For Nothing?' stencilled on the back. It was a slogan that had been featured prominently on the cover of a John Mayall and the Bluesbreakers album called *Crusade*. Lenoir had been a hard-done-by black blues singer that Mayall was currently championing and so he was suddenly the new de rigueur totem of authenticity for the white middle-class blues-rock poseur.

Blues-rock was the sound of '68 and this festival became a kind of designated showdown for all the white guitar-slingers infiltrating the genre. Alvin Lee and Ritchie Blackmore made their fingers bleed to keep the crowd baying for more. Peter Green's Fleetwood Mac told dirty jokes and made a raucous fist of relocating Elmore James's Delta blues to the more sedate English suburbs. Jeff Beck dazzled everyone with his string-bending showmanship but his singer Rod Stewart was so shy he spent half the group's performance vocalising from behind a large amplifier.

At the climax of one evening, an unannounced Eric Clapton suddenly appeared – 'God' himself looking suitably messianic in a white suit and hair well past his shoulders – and plugged in to add fiery solo guitar accompaniment to a frantic drum battle being waged on the stage between his Cream acolyte Ginger Baker and Baker's drug buddy, the infamous junkie jazzer Phil Seaman. The hands-down winner though was Richard Thompson. His band Fairport Convention did a version of Richard Fariña's 'Reno, Nevada' that afforded Thompson the ample opportunity to stretch out and play an extended solo on the guitar that – for sheer inventiveness and musicality – put to shame everything else that had been ripped from a fretboard that weekend. He was seventeen years old.

1969 was another fine year to be a teenaged middle-class bohemian wannabe. That was when I read Kerouac's *On the Road* and started hitch-hiking hither and yon, mostly to Brighton. On weekends I'd use my dad's train card and travel to London, where I'd haunt One Stop Records in South Molton Street and Musicland in Berwick Street – the only two outlets for American imports in the city. They were also the first places to ever stock copies of the San Francisco-based fortnightly publication *Rolling Stone* in Great Britain.

Summer meant more festival-hopping: I first made it down to the Plumpton Jazz and Blues Festival. It was a glorious weekend marred only by reports that were circulating via the daily press available on the site that the actress Sharon Tate and several companions had just been sadistically executed in Roman Polanski's

Hollywood homestead. It would still be some months before the culprits – Charles Manson and his repellent Family – were caught and revealed to the world at large. The shock of seeing longhairs capable of cold-blooded murder would send a bullet ricocheting into the heart of hippiedom.

But that was all in the immediate future. For the moment, young people were still merrily uniting in benign displays of mass bohemianism centred around live music without fear of being ripped off and brutalised by their own kind. The Isle of Wight Festival that year was the key UK event of the season. The promoters had even snagged an appearance by Bob Dylan, his first paying performance in three years, and this was a most significant turn of events for we new-bohemians who'd been praying for his return to active music-making and getting only bad country music like *Nashville Skyline* as an occasional response.

When he finally arrived on stage flanked once again by the Band, he looked very different from the ghostly apparition who'd almost deafened me back in 1966. He was fuller in the face and wore a bulky white suit that made him look like a character from a vintage Humphrey Bogart gangster film set in Panama. He wasn't stoned either – at least, not so that you would notice. He looked more apprehensive than anything else. He had a right to be because it soon became apparent that he was a changed man vocally as well as imagewise. He sang every song in a whimsical croon that was light years removed from the amphetamine shriek of yore. You almost expected him to break into a yodel at any moment. Like the Band themselves, it was an exercise in old-school musical Americana that couldn't be faulted for its pioneering spirit and woodsy finesse. But it was about as sexy as kissing a tree.

I loved the Band's first two albums like everyone else but had issues with their collective fashion sense and penchant for extravagant facial foliage. They were just too hairy for my taste. Of course, this probably had something to do with the fact that I still couldn't grow facial hair to save my life. But the Band turned almost everyone in the rock milieu into budding Grizzly Adamses practically overnight. Look at photos of Paul McCartney during the *Let It Be* sessions. Or Jerry Garcia at the end of the sixties. You're confronted with more hair than face. These people were just disappearing behind a forest of their own testosterone. That's why the Stones were always the best-looking rock act of that era. Five members and yet no facial hair whatsoever. They always had their priorities well sorted.

Now it was 1970 and I was bored. Time weighed too heavily on me too often. I only felt grounded in the moments when I was listening to music or reading a worthwhile piece of literature. My mother had always made sure I was a reader. She made it her business to compel me to seek solace in books and enlarge my basic attention span in the process. I would have already started perusing the self-styled 'new journalism' tomes that had sprung up over the past ten years.

Truman Capote's *In Cold Blood* was the first – a great book. Capote had a marked influence on me – particularly his celebrity profiles. He truly got Marlon Brando and Marilyn Monroe to open up in print and give voice to their personal vulnerabilities. In a way you could sense Capote was also betraying their confidence by revealing their intimate bar-talk to his readers in such a naked light, but it was a warranted invasion of privacy, made with a flawless insight into the human frailties that lurk behind the surreal world of celebritydom.

I was certainly intrigued by Tom Wolfe's dandified upper-echelon hipspeak prose style and provocative choice of then-contemporary cultural fetishes to unleash it on. But the tome that really fired me up that year was James Joyce's *Ulysses*, the greatest book ever written. It was a tough nut to crack, involving at least six months of daily reading sessions and the added necessity of having to constantly consult two separate reference books that broke down into minute detail all the labyrinthine complexities lurking in each and every sentence of the text. *Ulysses* focused on just twenty-four hours in the lives of three Dublin residents at the turn of the last century, revealing their every hidden thought and impulse as they whimsically grapple with their destinies. Whilst writing it, Joyce found a way to penetrate the complex innermost workings of the human imagination and evoke them sublimely in the printed word. He ripped open the floodgates whence the whole 'stream of consciousness' aesthetic was sired. In a sense, it was a pioneering artefact of the psychedelic impulse because – if you only took the time to log into its many-layered meaningfulness – it was guaranteed to blow your mind and stimulate new insights into the world of artistic expression. To borrow a line that the *News of the World* – Britain's leading tabloid of the day – used to run at the head of every issue, 'All human life is there.'

My months spent doggedly digesting the full importance of *Ulysses* seemed to impress my English teacher, who then took it upon himself to persuade my parents that I should aim for a place at either Oxford or Cambridge University. This involved staying on at school for an extra term in order to sit a special entrance exam. It was probably just as well: my A-level results ended up being nothing to boast about.

In late October I took the test, flaunting my newly acquired

Joycean insights throughout one essay and attempting to pin-point the cause of Virginia Woolf's obsession with depression and boredom in her various novels in the second. Both were pretentious screeds unworthy of serious consideration. I sensed as much in early December when I was interviewed by a lecturer at Queen's College, Oxford, who wasted little time in further acquainting me with my shortcomings as a literary analyst. Those dreaming spires wouldn't be housing my sorry hide, I quickly concluded. I wouldn't be darkening the towers of higher learning in this exclusive neck of the woods. A formal letter of rejection was in the post heading towards my address before the year was out.

Was I sad? Not that I can recall. I was finished with kowtowing to the high-minded dictates of academia anyway. My brain couldn't take in another avalanche of useless information. The old ways meant nothing to me now. My mind was set on rambling, on striking out for parts unknown. My thoughts were all on how I could best project myself into the new wild frontier of London's brimming youth counter-culture.

What was I really like at this precise 'crossroads' moment in my life? A weird kid, certainly – moody, introspective, unsure of myself, girlish-looking, long-limbed, fresh-faced, a victim of bad posture. Puberty had been a hell of a long time arriving and I was still shyly adjusting to the new regime that had only recently invaded my body and hormones.

I was becoming something of a bedroom hermit, plotting out my future and fantasising the hours away behind drawn curtains. I had a lot in common with Tom Courtenay's escape-obsessed character in the landmark sixties film *Billy Liar*; my dreams had lately gotten so out of control that I needed to live them before they devoured me.

But what would happen if my dreams were suddenly revealed as a kind of living nightmare? Wouldn't it be somehow more sensible to opt for a life of quiet rural underachievement instead? That way at least my 'innocence' would still be protected. I wouldn't be soiled by worldly experience. But innocence has always been an overrated virtue in my scheme of things. It's a kissing cousin to naivety and being naive is only one small step from out-and-out stupidity. People who endlessly talk up its purity of sentiment usually turn out to be either morons or chicken hawks.

William Blake was right. You have to soldier on down that dank tunnel of adulthood until you arrive at the bigger picture. Otherwise you're just abandoning yourself to a world of small-mindedness, bitterness and regrets.

1971

Just as the sixties were tapering off into history, a dark vortex opened up in the era's rock culture. Hard drugs began knocking over musicians like ninepins. By 1971 many were hooked on heroin or burning out their nasal membranes and nervous systems with too much cocaine. Jimi Hendrix, Janis Joplin and Jim Morrison all expired within a few short months of each other, Joplin and Morrison from heroin overdoses, Hendrix from pills and booze. The West Coast rock scene was in utter turmoil. Once upon a time they'd been comrades-in-arms gently cushioned by the sweet scent of pot-smoke; now they were frantically pulling knives and guns on each other over cocaine deals gone awry.

Bad drug craziness was afflicting every nook and cranny of the youth music hemisphere that year. Young hard-rock hopefuls like Michigan's MC5 and the Stooges were being seriously side-tracked by their addictions. Down in Georgia, the Allman Bros. Band had to be forced into a rehab clinic by their record company just prior to a tour. The intervention didn't prevent their guitarist Duane Allman from dying in a motorbike crash just a few months later whilst stoned out of his gourd. Even the introspective US folkie brigade of the hour were tainted: James Taylor, the dulcet-voiced shy and retiring troubadour who'd lately become a bashful million-selling superstar the world over, was regularly on the nod throughout the period.

Over in England, it was just as bad. John and Yoko were both strung out. Eric Clapton had lately succumbed too. The fabled guitarist stopped playing in public in 1971 and self-medicated himself into temporary oblivion instead. He only left his country home once that year – to fly to the South of France in midsummer in order to attend Mick Jagger's wedding. As soon as he arrived at his destination he started experiencing acute heroin withdrawal. In great physical discomfort he phoned Keith Richards – who lived nearby – for something to tide him over. 'Tell him to go and find his own,' responded Richards curtly to the person who answered the phone and then transmitted the message. The caring, sharing sixties were dead and gone. Now it was every man for himself.

In such a cold and divisive climate, the Rolling Stones could only further flourish. They'd never made convincing propagandists for utopianism anyway. They were more inclined to view life through a dark prism of worldly cynicism. The inky black vortex was their natural habitat and so 1971 became their greatest-ever year, their sustained moment of true creative majesty. It saw the release of two mind-boggling Stones-related films – *Performance* and *Gimme Shelter* – as well as *Sticky Fingers*, the best album of their entire career. That same year, they toured the UK and then tax-dodged their way over to the South of France, where they lived whilst recording their last real masterpiece, *Exile on Main St.*, in Keith Richards's basement.

Performance had actually been filmed in the autumn of 1968 but an early edit had so mortified the higher-ups at Warner Bros., the project's backers, that it was initially deemed unviewable. After approximately two years of haggling and re-editing it was given a limited opening in the States, followed by a brief showcase at a plushly seated cinema in London's West End that began in early January '71. The delayed exposure would prove propitious to its acceptance. Late-sixties audiences would have found it generally too violent and disturbing to readily accept. It spoke far more eloquently to the uncentred, 'something wrong something not quite right' mood of the emerging seventies. The plot line starts out straightforwardly enough: a psychotically violent London gangland enforcer named Chas – unforgettably played by James Fox – gets too caught up in his bloodlust and incurs the wrath of his deeply scary employers. His life in jeopardy, he hides out in the basement of a Ladbroke Grove town house only to discover that his landlord is a reclusive rock star named Turner (Jagger) who shares his living quarters with two wacky female paramours and a prodigious supply of hallucinogenic drugs. The second half of the film revolves around an extended druggy mind-fuck confrontation between the gangster, the rock star and his witchy girlfriend Pherber (Anita Pallenberg). Turner wants to fasten onto Chas's ruthless self-confidence as a way to rekindle his own fractured career ambitions but only ends up reaping the whirlwind when Fox's character calmly shoots him during the film's final climax.

Essentially, it's a cautionary tale about corrupted souls toying with forbidden forces and then having to face the consequences, but that didn't prevent its mastermind, writer/director Donald Cammell, from also depicting the lives of his dissolute protagonists in a hypnotically alluring fashion. Seeing the naked Turner/Jagger smoking reefer in a bathtub surrounded by two exotic-looking naked European women certainly had a forceful impact on my easily stimulated late-teenage imagination. When I was only twelve years old, my dad had let me stay up to see *La Dolce Vita* on the telly and I'd experienced a similar tingling reaction. Fellini's film – like *Performance* – is a surreal meditation on the spiritual bankruptcy that lurks within the souls of those who ardently pursue the glamorous life. But that only became apparent to me when I saw the film again years later as a fully fledged adult. As a child, all I connected with was the endless cavalcade of beautiful available women, the dizzy flashing lights and wild all-night parties. It looked like heaven on earth. And the vision *Performance* conjured up of life in Turner's dimly lit Ladbroke Grove lair was equally bewitching.

The film still conveys an almost supernatural power whenever it's shown, but its lasting brilliance was clearly obtained at a steep cost to its key players. James Fox became mentally unhinged as a result of immersing himself in the film's disorientating script, suffered a personality meltdown and had to retire from acting for several years. Anita Pallenberg didn't act in a film again for some time. Cammell never managed to build a prolific career for himself in cinema after *Performance*; he committed suicide in the nineties. And Mick Jagger deeply estranged his soulmate Keith Richards during the actual filming when he and Anita Pallenberg, Richards's girlfriend, supposedly began an affair of their own. This would have perilous consequences as Richards chose to react to the perceived infidelity by introducing his bloodstream to the pain-relieving panacea known as heroin, thus setting in motion the Stones' true dark age and an antipathy between the two head Stones that exists to this day.

Both *Performance* and *Gimme Shelter* – which opened in London just a few short months later – focused down hard on the calamitous predicaments that tend to prevail whenever narcissistic would-be 'outlaws' come into direct contact with the infinitely more barbaric genuine article. But whereas the former was a many-layered work of fiction, *Shelter* was a flashback-driven documentary that chillingly captured the mayhem and carnage let loose at the Altamont Speedway on December 6th 1969, when the Stones headlined a free concert there only to be upstaged by the Oakland Hells Angels – unwisely chosen to provide security around the stage – who savagely beat up anyone in the audience they happened to take a personal dislike to. 'Altamont' was already being touted in the print media as the byword for the spiritual death of the sixties – that and the much publicised arrest in November '69 of hippie mass murderer Charles Manson – but prior to the film's premiere few had actually seen what transpired that fateful day and those that had all had different takes on whose fault it really was. *Gimme Shelter* didn't moralise or apportion blame; it simply replayed the nightmarish events as they occurred, leaving the stunned viewer to draw his or her own conclusions.

No one came out looking good from the experience. The onlookers resembled doomed sheep on bad drugs, the Angels acted like sadistic animals and the Stones seemed clearly out of their depth yet still numbly detached from the madness they were inspiring. Mick Jagger in particular is captured on film looking decidedly forlorn and fearful during his Altamont performance – a control freak suddenly confronted with dire circumstances way beyond his control. When the famous death scene is finally played out on screen – several Angels plunging knives into an eighteen-year-old black youth named Meredith Hunter during the Stones' live rendition of 'Under My Thumb' – the sense of mounting dread that the film has been building on from its opening scenes suddenly arrives at a harrowingly inevitable climax. It's amazing to think that this bloody debacle took place only six months after Woodstock's gentle-spirited bringing together of the massed hippie tribes up on the East Coast of the USA. The film made of Woodstock was one of 1970's biggest global cinematic earners – a three-hour-long love-fest mainstream blockbuster – but *Gimme Shelter* was generally for more acquired tastes, diehard Stones fans and art-house connoisseurs. The former's scenes of benign, beatific communal squalor were as pacifying to behold as the utter bedlam depicted in the latter was painful to even think about and yet the two events weren't essentially that different from the viewpoints of many who'd attended both. 'Woodstock was a bunch of stupid slobs in the mud,' opined Jefferson Airplane's strident vocalist Grace Slick. 'And Altamont was a bunch of angry slobs in the mud.' Grateful Dead manager Rock Scully – who'd been involved in the early stages of Altamont's genesis – was more specific still. 'Woodstock and Altamont are seen as polar opposites in a mass-media-generated parable of light and darkness but they were just two ends of the same mucky stick, the net result of the same disease: the bloating of mass bohemia in the late sixties.'

After Altamont, the Stones returned to England and Keith Richards promptly began shooting heroin directly into his veins. Suddenly he wasn't turning up to recording sessions any more or even answering the phone. The Stones had a lucrative new record deal with Atlantic to inaugurate, tiresome old contractual obligations with both Allen Klein and Decca to settle and a new decade to come to terms with. With no manager to guide them and a guitar player seemingly insensitive to their collective plight, Mick Jagger promptly become the Stones' de facto leader and business

brain. The Stones' two closest rivals – the Who and Led Zeppelin
– were both in the process of completing new albums for release
later that year – *Who's Next* and Led Zep 4 – so Jagger knew his
band had to deliver or die on the vine. *Sticky Fingers* was what he
came up with – the classiest, most self-assured collection of
Stones songs about wild sex, hard drugs and doomed love ever
concocted. Richards didn't even play on three cuts – 'Sway',
'Sister Morphine' and 'Moonlight Mile' – but managed to make
his maddeningly erratic presence felt on the other seven selections.

The record's young engineer Andy Johns would later recall a
telling episode during a session at Jagger's country home
Stargroves in 1970. 'We were doing "Bitch", Keith was very late
and Jagger and Mick Taylor had been playing the song without
him. And it didn't sound very good. I walked out of the kitchen
and he was sitting on the floor with no shoes, eating a bowl of
cereal. Suddenly he said "Oi, Andy! Give me that guitar." He put
it on, kicked the song up in tempo and just put the vibe right on
it. Instantly, it went from being this laconic mess into a real
groove. And I thought – Wow! That's what he does.'

When the Stones decamped to the South of France in spring
1971, they quickly became absorbed in recording the follow-up
album to *Sticky Fingers*. By this point they'd become so frustrated
by Richards's infrequent appearances at virtually any studio they
booked that they opted to record the thing in the one place they
knew he was always guaranteed to be, the house where he actually lived. It was an opulent mansion called Nellcôte that had formerly been the local headquarters for the invading Gestapo. Nazi
crosses carved into the heating system vents were still plainly visible. The dank basement the group used to record in had once

been the interrogation room. This became Keith's own dark realm in exile.

For his first month or so on the Riviera he was heroin-free but quickly returned to its soothing embrace after injuring his back in a go-kart accident. What happened next has already been well documented. Local drug dealers descended on the property, eventually alerting the local constabulary. The rest of the Stones, producer Jimmy Miller and engineer Andy Johns meanwhile wasted hours of each evening waiting for the smacked-back guitarist to descend from his living quarters and grace them with his presence. But – according to Johns – 'Everyone was too scared [to directly confront him]. Even Mick would never go up there. It was as if hell existed upstairs.' Then Keith had all his guitars stolen, unadvisedly pulled a gun on the local harbour master and also managed to alienate certain of his household staff, who promptly went to the police and denounced Richards and girlfriend Pallenberg as major-league heroin distributors and all-purpose degenerates.

The fallout was considerable: arrest warrants were immediately issued for the couple, they had to disappear from the country like thieves in the night in order to avoid incarceration and the rest of the Stones were also placed under investigation in the resulting messy legal brouhaha. One member's ballooning drug problem had managed to turn the ongoing odyssey of the world's greatest rock 'n' roll band into one potentially career-ending scenario after another.

Many supporting players in the whole Nellcôte saga soon fell by the wayside but the Stones still managed to turn adversity into sonic gold dust. *Exile on Main St.* – the record that mostly resulted from those troubled sessions in Keith's basement – took the whole sun-baked Riviera-on-hard-drugs languor of their day-to-day lifestyle and artfully moulded it to the hard-nosed horn-drenched American roadhouse rhythm 'n' blues sensibility that has always best suited their particular musical chemistry. Released in mid-1972, it would prove to be their last truly Zeitgeist-defining collection of new songs.

But we're getting too far ahead of ourselves here. Let's back-track a little. On March 10th 1971 the Stones played a concert in Brighton as part of a farewell-to-the-old-country tour of the UK just prior to *Sticky Fingers'* release and their move to the South of France, and I was there to cheer them on. The performance was prefaced by its share of backstage dramas. Keith Richards – arriving early for a change – found his group's dressing-room facilities still locked up and came close to pulling out a lethal weapon and braining the promoter in retaliation. Gram Parsons, Richards's ex-Byrd drug buddy who was travelling with him on all the English dates, became so chemically deranged as the evening progressed that when he attempted to find the stage the Stones were playing on he ended up instead staggering into a nearby cinema. But I'd only learn about those incidents many years later after reading an article by Robert Greenfield, an American journalist then on assignment for *Rolling Stone* who'd actually been in the group's designated touring party that night. On the evening in question, I was just another paying punter in a sea of faces and limbs come to pay homage to my dark-prince heroes and watch a truly stupendous live spectacle in an overcrowded provincial sweat-box of a venue named the Big Apple. It would be another two and a half years before I'd be granted direct access to their inner sanctum, and in retrospect I'm glad that fate didn't summon me sooner. The dark vortex could wait awhile before it claimed my young bones. Like Elvis, I still had a lot of living to do.

Did I tell you I'd finally located a girlfriend? She was a looker too with cascading blonde hair and a supple dancer's physique, a sweet sixteen-year-old suburban little princess for me to bottle all my overstimulated post-adolescent romantic fantasies up in. Her name was Joanne Good and we'd first linked up in December 1970 when I was press-ganged into being the side-stage prompt for a school play that she was acting in. Joanne's thespian skills would later bring her mainstream recognition throughout the British Isles: in the late seventies she'd become a regular fixture in the cast of *Crossroads*, the decade's best-loved UK TV soap opera (these days, she's a popular morning disc jockey on Radio London). But in 1971 we were both still soldiering down the treacherous path intersecting post-puberty with young adulthood. We both declared undying love for each other – our favourite courting song was the Temptations' heart-fluttering 'Just My Imagination (Running Away with Me)', a big hit that spring – but the love we really shared was closer to the tooth-achingly sugar-rush rapture expressed in a less sumptuous-sounding chart smash *du jour* – Donnie Osmond's 'Puppy Love'. We stared into each other's misty eyes a lot and held hands whenever in public. But physically speaking, we were an odd fit. I was 6 foot 1 whilst she measured 5 foot in her stocking feet. And temperamentally too we bordered on the incompatible. Joanne was vivacious, outgoing and gregarious whilst I was generally intense and prone to introspection.

Her family was Good in both name and nature, apart from her older brother Nigel, who was what they used to call 'a bit of a tearaway'. He was also Horsham's most notorious druggy, having lately been busted for pot-smoking in the town centre, an incident that saw his name subsequently splashed over the front page of the local paper. He and another youth named Rob Daneski, who looked like anyone in Black Sabbath, were the drowsy little commuter town's two resident heads. I met them through Joanne and we quickly became fast friends forever stalking the neighbourhood together in search of cannabis resin. Nigel and Rob liked to drop acid whenever possible, but I always refused to join them, as I sensed – quite rightly, I now realise – that I was still too emotionally and spiritually immature to react well to its lysergic lift-off.

Though I would later come to be perceived as one of the championship-level London-based substance-abusers of the late twentieth century, I started my journey into the world of chemical refreshment with tentative steps. I first smoked pot at the Bath Festival in summer 1970 when a fellow audience member passed me a droopy, hand-rolled cigarette and bade me suck on its soggy cardboard filter. Inhaling its fumes must have had some effect on me because the next thing I remember was descending from my instant reverie to be confronted by a hippie girl who was staring at me with an extremely alarmed look on her face. I felt like a door had been suddenly ripped open in my brain. Time no longer hung heavy on my stooped shoulders. Pot put me right in the moment, enriching my consciousness with the sensation of feeling simultaneously giddy and alive. From then on it became an integral part of my religion to consume as much of it as I could get my hands on.

But daily consumption only began in earnest once I'd moved to London later in '71. Drugs in general were hard to come by in the early seventies if you didn't live in England's capital or near one of its major cities that also doubled as a port. Forget heroin, cocaine and ecstasy. Crack had yet to be invented. All you could hope for was to befriend some long-haired ne'er-do-well in your region who sometimes purchased reefer from a connection in the big bad metropolis and pester him to sell you a small chunk. Doping up was still in its infancy as a British national pastime, particularly out in the suburbs, and those few who dared partake invariably became extremely paranoid due to the build-up of cerebral befuddlement and fear of getting busted.

In the early part of 1971, when I wasn't illegally stimulating my endorphins or belatedly experiencing first-hand the tumultuous joys and sorrows of teenage romance, I was sending my CV around to various universities in the hope that one of them would accept me onto their campus and postpone the day when I'd actually have to go out and find a job for a further three years. I was flat-out rejected by all of them, except for Bedford College, which was then part of London University. They called me down for an interview so I tied my hair back and hid the ponytail under my shirt collar, wore a suit that even an undertaker might call 'subdued' and somehow charmed them into taking me on board. I had good reason to feel elated by their decision. Not only would it mean that henceforth I'd be living in London but Bedford College was one of the only places of further education in Britain where the female student population sharply outnumbered the male. Like Jan and Dean's mythical 'Surf City', it functioned on a ratio of two girls for every boy.

In order to bolster my finances that summer in readiness for student life I went looking for any kind of legitimate work. Soon enough I got employed by a Sussex-based chemical plant and spent long days digging drainage ditches for a pittance. Later I manned the pumps at a local garage. Each job lasted roughly two weeks in duration, after which I got promptly fired for rank incompetence. I learned a lot from these experiences, the key lesson being that I was simply not cut out for the rigours of manual labour and should never consider it as a temporary career option ever again. Leave all that heavy lifting and sod-busting to the brawny lads with the muscles on their muscles. I was better off developing my brain and making a living from that.

Looking back through the misty veil of nostalgia, that summer of '71 now feels like a sun-drenched and special season of rampant carefree splendour. England's green and pleasant land never looked greener or seemed more pleasant to be a part of. Maybe it's just the pot I smoked back then playing tricks with my retroactive memory but I think not. It was indeed a golden age for middle-class floaters like me. Students still received grants. The world's biggest rock bands still performed to audiences no larger than two thousand at a time at venues that didn't cost an arm and a leg to enter. Records – my main expenditure – were reasonably priced. It cost nothing to hitch-hike whenever the urge for travel struck. Sex wasn't fatal. Only skinheads were to be avoided at all cost.

And the music being released that year was often outstandingly good. It was Tamla Motown's last golden year for example – starting with the Jackson 5's irresistible 'The Love You Save' and building to Marvin Gaye's transcendent 'What's Going On' – and you'd hear these singles constantly blaring out of transistor radios in public places, boldly lifting the spirits of the nation. On the white side of the tracks Rod Stewart – the rooster-haired, dandy-dressing Sam Cooke soundalike who'd left Jeff Beck's employment at the turn of the last decade to join the remnants of the Small Faces as their resident singer – was on constant rotation in pub jukeboxes throughout the country with his first-ever hit recording, 'Maggie May', a bitter-sweet smoky-sounding rumination on the perils of falling in love with an elderly prostitute. Everybody had mad love for the man sometimes referred to as Rod the Mod that year: rock critics swooned at the sound of his gritty self-deprecating voice, student drinkers were in seventh heaven over his habitual public displays of boozy camaraderie with the Faces whilst teenage girls were particularly smitten by his big-nosed cock-of-the-walk charm and tight satin trousers.

Another former sixties London 'face' making bold inroads into the mainstream pop landscape of the early seventies was a brash little hustler who called himself Marc Bolan. Three years earlier, Bolan could have been found sitting cross-legged on the wooden stage of any self-respecting UK hippie venue, strumming a cheap acoustic guitar and warbling arcane pseudo-Tolkien gobbledegook whilst an extremely stoned individual played bongos haphazardly alongside him. This quaint spectacle were known as Tyrannosaurus Rex and they quickly came to enjoy the patronage of several key underground taste-makers, most notably John Peel, who played their records ceaselessly on his Radio One broadcast and even contributed some dubious spoken-word snippets to one of their early albums.

But John Peel couldn't help Bolan achieve what he really wanted, which were big hit records and a shot at Elvis-like megarock superstardom. So 'the bopping elf' – as he was sometimes known – rudely brushed aside his DJ champion, sacked the stoned bongo player (who called himself Steve Peregrine Took), bought an electric guitar and started shaping his gauche, nonsensical lyrics around rudimentary riffs archly filched from old fifties vintage rock chestnuts like Chuck Berry's 'Little Queenie' and Eddie Cochran's 'C'mon Everybody'. His 'Queenie' rewrite – entitled 'Get It On' – became one of '71's national pop anthems and he and his new electric ensemble now known as T.Rex were suddenly on a serious roll that year with a succession of chart-topping singles and a hit album called *Electric Warrior*. At first Bolan seemed like a breath of fresh air: a new breed of rock star – haughty, androgynous and glamour-fixated – who was unapologetic about his thirst for fame and utter self-fixation. He was the first to cut loose from the late-sixties notion that rock was one big sharing, caring community where musicians and audience members stood together on equal footing. Bolan was more interested in creating an in-concert ambience that separated the two entities into 'the superstar' and his 'slaves'. T.Rex concerts in 1971 were actually the first public manifestation of the seventies 'me decade' consciousness in action. Bolan would primp and pose around the stage like a narcissistic guitar-strumming girl in front of a giant full-length mirror whilst his mostly teenage female fans would scream 'Me! Me! Me!' back at him hysterically from the stalls. Certainly it was a shallow and sometimes unhealthy spectacle but infinitely more entertaining than having to sit through yet another twenty-minute-long drum solo. Prog rock's halcyon days were suddenly numbered. The kids wanted vanity instead of virtuosity and Bolan was ideally suited to spearhead the new sea change – at least until his nemesis David Bowie swept in and stole his audience the following year.

Stewart, Bolan and Bowie were all flashily attired young fops who'd already tried to become superstars in the sixties only to languish in the musical margins of the decade. Their early failures had simply strengthened their resolve to make their mark on a new era. A similar case was Cat Stevens; in 1967 Stevens had enjoyed two UK pop hit singles – 'I Love My Dog' and 'Matthew and Son' which he'd written and recorded whilst still in his late teens. Ill health then dogged him for the rest of the decade and he fell off the pop radar for a while. But at the very outset of the seventies he bounced back as a bedroom mystic troubadour hippie Rod McKuen and by 1971 – when he had two new albums out, *Tea for the Tillerman* and *Teaser and the Firecat* – he'd become the new Messiah of the sensitivity set.

In early October I moved in to a dormitory overlooking Regent's Park, where Bedford College was actually located. The single room I occupied there became my new living quarters and my first home away from my parents' hearth. A month earlier I'd had my heart broken for the very first time: Joanne had chucked me. My first reaction was to feel like a victim in some maudlin country song about small-town cheating hearts but fortunately I didn't have the time or circumstances to mope too much. After all, I was one of maybe only three males living in a building with twenty-seven females, many of whom were soon inviting me into their rooms to get better acquainted.

That's when I experienced first-hand the hold Cat Stevens then had on young middle-class women throughout the British Isles. Practically all my female fellow students were head-over-heels in love with the guy and played his albums as though their lives depended on it. They were mostly nice girls from the provinces with lank hair and long skirts who were adjusting to their arrival in wicked old London by immersing themselves day and night in Cat Stevens's soothing airy-fairy blather until his discs became their own personal comfort zones. Sometimes their record-listening habits would stretch to superior musings like

Joni Mitchell's 'River' or anything by Leonard Cohen but they'd always return to the Cat-man piously proclaiming morning had broken. I couldn't stand it. His music was so drippy and saccharine it made my teeth ache. I quickly developed an irrational hatred of the man, which only intensified the following year when I started knowing several bona fide rock groupies in the biblical sense and all these women turned out to be dating Cat Stevens at the same time. One of them even phoned him up when we were together to tell him what she was up to. Now, of course, Cat Stevens is internationally known as a devout Muslim who left the lust-filled music industry to dedicate his life to his strict religious beliefs but back in the day the *Tea for the Tillerman* man was getting more pussy than Frank Sinatra.

Talking of pussy, I actually lost my virginity at the end of my first week there. Before that, I'd engaged in what can only be described as tentative oral sex but I'd never been inside a woman. I seem to recall being worried about actual penetration because so many of my school-going cronies had gotten their girlfriends pregnant and been prematurely forced into matrimony and a dead-end provincial job. But I'd finally escaped that sorry fate and was now free to make up for lost time and fumbled opportunities. A pretty, moon-faced Welsh girl named Ann – one of my student co-tenants at the dorm – latched on to me and wasted no time in inviting me to share her bed. God bless you, Ann, if you happen to read this. You set me free to roam freely in the world of adult pleasure and promiscuity – a great place to take up squatter's rights in when you're still only nineteen. I received a better life education from being in your carnal caress than I ever did from attending any lectures.

The only problem I had as a student was the actual course I'd enrolled in: linguistics, or the study of the English language. For some reason I'd envisioned reading and discussing mostly modern literature and so was deeply underwhelmed when I discovered I had to decipher the original texts of Geoffrey Chaucer instead. Chaucer is rightly renowned as one of England's first book-writers but that doesn't automatically mean he's one of the best too. His original *Canterbury Tales* is like a bad *Carry On* script written by a halfwit and having to translate it into a modern-language idiom was a task I couldn't work up the remotest inkling of a desire to pursue. When we weren't focusing on Chaucer's silly texts, we were getting bombarded by lecturers hopelessly in thrall to the ancient words and thoughts of my old pal John Milton. One old biddy who taught us would even occasionally break down and weep when discussing his timeless magnificence. Meanwhile, I was weeping invisible tears of utter stultifying boredom.

Soon enough I stopped turning up to these lectures altogether and spent my time instead furtively exploring current London-based culture. The city had some great live venues like Finsbury Park's Rainbow Theatre and Camden Town's Roundhouse: Sunday afternoons at the latter were a real poseur's paradise. The artsy cinemas had special late-night showings that were always instructive to attend and the hip bookshops regularly put on literary happenings and poetry readings: I saw Patti Smith boldly reciting some early texts of hers without the aid of musical accompaniment – her first-ever public performance in Europe, I believe – that winter to an audience of no more than fifteen people. I knew there and then she'd go on to become one of the decade's creative players. I'd already been impressed by her work because her poetry had lately been published in a Michigan-based periodical called *Creem* which you could only buy here in the UK from one source: Camden Town's Compendium book-shop. One issue I bought that year featured a review by staff writer Dave Marsh of a Question Mark and the Mysterians reunion concert in which the term 'punk rock' was first coined. A new genre was making its first tottering baby steps courtesy of the international rock press.

Meanwhile, *Creem*'s rival *Rolling Stone* was going from strength to strength – like its namesakes, the journal enjoyed its all-time creative peak throughout 1971. That year, Hunter S. Thompson's seminal gonzo screed *Fear and Loathing in Las Vegas* got published in its pages, months before it appeared in book form. John Lennon laid his soul bare to editor Jann Wenner in an extraordinary two-part interview. A freelancer named Grover Lewis – assigned to cover the Allman Bros. on a draining US tour – almost got beaten up by the group and retaliated by writing a wonderfully observed warts-and-all exposé of their charmless lives and nasty habits. And another freelancer, Tom Nolan, turned in a mesmerising extra-length feature on Brian Wilson and the Beach Boys, the first article ever to pull back the curtain on the madness and dysfunctionalism that reigned behind their rugged all-American image. This was new journalism at its very best. The writers weren't blandly observing their subjects from a respectful distance any more, they were right there in the scrum as wilful participants soaking up the essence and then channelling it into an art form of their own. That's exactly where I wanted to be. That's exactly what I wanted to do.

It wouldn't be long now. I could feel it in my bones. Being back in London had started a fire in me. The city was mine again – and it owed me a living. Destiny would take care of the rest.

1972

It was in January of 1972 that my future destiny as the Zeitgeist-surfing dark prince of seventies rock journalism actually started to experience lift-off. The year began inauspiciously enough. I returned to my student digs in Regent's Park in readiness for a new term at university only to discover I'd arrived several days too soon and everything was still boarded up. I decided to hitch-hike up to scenic Barnsley deep in the northernmost bowels of England on the off-chance that I'd encounter two friends, Nigel Good and Chris Roddick, who'd lately moved up there to work on an underground paper called – if memory serves – *Styng*. At 8 a.m. one grey January morning I stood at the North London entrance to the M1 motorway with my thumb outstretched. Five hours later, a large articulated lorry and its obliging driver had deposited me in Barnsley town centre. There was only one draw-back: I had no address or phone number for the people I was searching for. Not to worry, though: long-haired youths were few and far between in this neck of the woods so I just had to describe their appearance to some locals congregated in a market square and they gave me exact directions. 'Try the nearest pub' was their advice, and of course they were right. It was a joyous reunion. My pals couldn't believe I'd temporarily abandoned swinging London to spend time in their sleepy little backwater. And I was just happy to not be spending the night alone sleeping in a bus shelter.

In due course they took me back to their communal homestead – a two-storey house with minimal furniture and no central heating – and I got to meet the rest of the Barnsley counterculture. There were only five conscripts at this juncture – Nigel, Chris, a fellow called Roger Hutchinson who was very much the man in charge, his pal, a bespectacled youth whose name now escapes me, and his pal's girlfriend – so it was hardly a thriving community; but they approached their role as rabble-rousers to the drowsy North with great zeal and commitment. Partly, this commitment involved publishing from time to time new issues of their broadsheet stuffed with features detailing the latest conspiracy theories and calling for a full-blown social revolution. Mostly, though, it involved sitting around a smouldering log fire, smoking copious amounts of pot and passionately voicing their drug-drenched dreams for the future. In this regard, we were very much kindred spirits. Well-read, streetwise druggies with a vague work ethic were my kind of people, I was quickly discovering.

I only spent some forty-eight hours in their midst but those hours would prove to be deeply significant ones for me personally. I got to take speed for the first time – a black bomber – and felt my brain suddenly rushing through my skull like a locomotive train ablaze with thought. Twenty-four eye-popping hours later, the comedown began, leaving me distinctly drained and disorientated, and yet I had no regrets. The drug had freed up something in my cerebellum and offered me a more intense way of perceiving the world. It was an experience I was determined to try again at the earliest opportunity.

On my last night there, I managed to broach with Roger Hutchinson – *Styng*'s nominal editor – the subject of maybe writing some articles of my own for his periodical. Not about politics per se, but about music. He appeared enthusiastic but duly noted that – as I was then resident in London – I'd be better off contributing to that city's more prolific underground network. Roger then mentioned that he was in contact with *Frendz* magazine, a fortnightly journal based in Ladbroke Grove that he claimed was often in need of new writers. He encouraged me to visit its Portobello Road premises upon my return. 'Speak to either Rosie Boycott or John May. Tell them Roger Hutchinson sent you.' With these words still ringing in my ears, I hitch-hiked back from the North just in time to reconvene with the rest of my fellow students for the unveiling of London University's spring 1972 term.

A few underwhelming days after my return to academia, I actually got up the nerve to travel by tube to the address I'd been given back in Barnsley. I stepped out of Ladbroke Grove tube station on an overcast weekday afternoon and made the short walk under the motorway to where the butt-end of Portobello Road intersected.

Standing before me as I reached the street was a young man clearly in an advanced state of chemical refreshment. I recognised him almost instantly: it was Paul Kossoff, the guitarist from Free. Eighteen months earlier I'd been one of over half a million attendees at the 1970 Isle of Wight Festival and had witnessed Kossoff on stage there coaxing forth a series of barn-burning guitar solos out of a battered Les Paul alongside his three colleagues and being greeted with a mass standing ovation for his efforts. Free were at their absolute peak right at that very instant – their anthem 'All Right Now' had recently made no. 1 in the UK singles charts – and they were also Britain's best-loved up-and-coming outfit of the epoch.

They were also incredibly young. Kossoff and the others had been professional musicians since 1968 and yet he was only one year older than me. I'd just turned twenty and he was twenty-one years old when our ships briefly passed on Portobello Road. That's a frightening age to suddenly be designated a has-been. I didn't know it then but he was already well on his way to becoming one of the new decade's more prominent casualties. Free had recently broken up as a direct consequence of his drug problems. The group would be in mid-performance only to discover their guitarist had fallen asleep against his amplifier. Given his marching orders in late '71, Kossoff had quickly drowned his sorrows by moving into Ladbroke Grove's druggy nexus and drenching his senses in a haze of Class A narcotics and tranquillisers. As we edged around each other on the street that day, I locked eyes with him for a second and he shot me a quick mischievous little smile, the kind of look you'd get from a naughty schoolboy who'd just been suspended for getting caught smoking behind the bike sheds. If I'd known more about his ongoing situation, maybe I would have taken his presence before me as some grim portent, a warning of things to come, but those kind of reflections are only triggered by hindsight. I was too busy finding my own way in the world – or at the very least the elusive address I'd been given – to focus further on his sorry fate.

Finally, I found it – 305 Portobello Road. A hippie couple with strange black sores around their mouths were running a health-food shop on the ground floor and told me to ring the bell at the side door and then go up to the first floor, where *Frendz* had its office. This I did, only to find myself in a dimly lit room festooned with dilapidated furniture, sundry battered typewriters and filing cabinets and several beanbags masquerading as makeshift sofas. Hardly anyone was present apart from a young woman seated at a desk nearest the large window overlooking Portobello Road and typing away furiously. 'Are you by any chance Rosie Boycott?' I recall stammering out. She answered with a nod and smile that emboldened me to go straight into my pitch. I was a friend of Roger Hutchinson and he'd advised me to present myself here and offer my fledgling writerly services to your journal. I was interested in writing reviews and doing interviews with musicians rather than talking up the latest bomb-detonating activities of the odious Angry Brigade (some of whom had actually been part of *Frendz*'s editorial caucus in the not-so-distant past). Did she see an outlet for me here?

Amazingly, she replied 'Yes, of course' and urged me to write something at the earliest opportunity and bring it to the office for further perusal. I never encountered Ms Boycott again – though we briefly spoke on the phone in the early nineties just after she'd been made the editor of UK *Esquire*, the upmarket men's magazine – but have always held her in high esteem, mainly because her kindness and encouragement that day made me feel instantly accepted in this potentially daunting new world I was trying to break into. If she'd told me to piss off I would have probably junked all my career ambitions as a writer right there and then.

Drawing on my student grant I next purchased three records that had just been released that very week. One was a mediocre album by San Francisco's Quicksilver Messenger Service called simply *Quicksilver* and another was *Gonna Take a Miracle*, a soul-stirring collection of rhythm 'n' blues covers performed by the gifted Italian-American singer/songwriter Laura Nyro. I've forgotten what the third disc was. Burning the midnight oil in my student garret, I scribbled out in longhand my impressions of the music contained within until I'd fashioned three coherent reviews. The following day I returned to *Frendz* with my dogeared pages of handwritten text only to find that Rosie Boycott had promptly quit the paper for unexplained reasons. Her place at the main desk had been taken by a thin young man with impressively long Pre-Raphaelite hair called John May. I repeated my basic pitch and then handed him the sheets containing my prose. He read them and told me they were very good and that almost certainly they'd be published in the next issue. I was over the fucking moon.

For the next week or so, I shied away from the office and waited with baited, hash-stained breath for the publication of the next *Frendz* issue. Then one weekend I saw a fresh pile being sold in Compendium bookshop on the high street in Camden Town and approached with tingling trepidation. As I leafed furiously through the journal I couldn't find a trace of what I'd written but then on the last but one page there they all were – my three reviews and my name printed prominently underneath them.

It is always a magical empowering moment when a writer sees his or her considered words typeset and available for public consumption for the very first time, and I was certainly no exception. The writing itself wasn't particularly outstanding but the three efforts had an engagingly naive and energetic tone, which is just another way of saying they weren't very good but at least you could tell I was keen about what I was addressing. They worked like a charm anyway. When I returned to *Frendz*, I was greeted like a conquering hero and promptly offered the job of official music editor for the princely sum of £4 a month and all the freebies I could siphon out of the record companies. I felt like I'd just won the lottery. Suddenly I was a burgeoning force to be reckoned with in the freak-flag-flying enclaves of the London underground. Little did I know that its days were already sorely numbered. By the end of the year it would be virtually extinct.

By early 1972 London's various alternative press outlets were all struggling to survive in the face of ever-conflicting shifts in editorial direction and generally dwindling sales. *Oz* – the most notorious periodical of its ilk – had enjoyed a hearty sales boost in 1970 and briefly became a fully fledged cultural cause célèbre that same year when its three instigators were tried at the Old Bailey on charges of conspiring to pervert the morals of young children. But after being exonerated, Richard Neville, the magazine's key motivator, had left the enterprise to concentrate on writing books, as did their most interesting writer Germaine Greer, and *Oz* had quickly degenerated into an unattractive fusion of empty 'subversive' ranting and hard-core pornography. *International Times*, its sister publication, was struggling on, still baying for revolution, still trying to stick it to the man – but fewer and fewer hirsute young Brits were laying down their hard-come-by shillings and pence to hearken to the call.

The same was true of *Frendz*. It had begun life in 1969 as *Friends of Rolling Stone* – a London-based outgrowth of the seminal San Francisco fortnightly – but then Jann Wenner, *Rolling Stone*'s editor and owner, had quickly grown dissatisfied with their efforts and cut off all funding; finding new backers, the original editorial team persevered into the seventies, retitling their project *Frendz* and throwing open their doors to any drug-diminished dissident or street-dwelling nutcase who wished to contribute. As a result, the journal had a short turbulent history that's best evoked in the printed reminiscences of those who manned the staff, edited together in the final section of Jonathon Green's illuminating oral history of the sixties counter-culture *Days in the Life*. In the book there's an unforgettable description of a female acid casualty who haunted the office whilst dragging an old mattress behind her. She'd vanished by the time I turned up, I'm happy to say. I couldn't have handled her: there were already more than enough LSD-impaired individuals flocking around the premises for me to contend with. Syd Barrett even appeared one day – his last group Stars was possibly going to be managed by *Frendz*'s ersatz accountant, a fellow in a grimy white denim suit and satanic goatee called Dick – and stared like a lost dog at anyone attempting to communicate with him. He looked in a bad way – but frankly no worse than any of the other space-cases littering the room.

Frendz had one big trump card at this precise epoch: the unquestioning support and unstinting patronage of Hawkwind. The Ladbroke Grove-based self-styled space rockers had lately been promoted to the lofty position of resident Pied Pipers for the district's great unwashed. You'd see them everywhere – under the Westway on top of a mud-caked pick-up truck bashing out one of their endless space jams for free to a gaggle of saucer-eyed onlookers or striding around the streets purposefully in a swirl of hair, denim and cheap rococo jewellery. Most of all, I'd see them in the office of *Frendz* as they tended to use the premises for their own haphazard business purposes. Whenever they had a gig to play – which was practically every evening – they'd congregate there throughout the afternoon and the room would duly become transformed into an ongoing scene from a Cheech and

Chong movie with pot-smoke billowing from every corner and high-spirited badinage spouting forth from every pair of parched lips in the immediate vicinity.

As a musical collective, Hawkwind were closer in sound and spirit to a small army of psychedelic buskers than anything that you could conceivably refer to as 'virtuoso-driven'. In fact, several of the original members had actually started out as buskers or street entertainers and evidently hadn't felt the urge to improve on their instrumental techniques when they chose to go electric. This made them a somewhat unpredictable commodity. You never knew exactly what would happen when you booked the band for a show. I'd first seen them in a club in Crawley in mid-1971; only three members had turned up to perform. The audience that night were treated to Hawkwind's very own stripped-down version of 'Jazz Odyssey'. I'd love to have been a fly on the wall backstage when they tried to get their fee from the promoter afterwards. But by early 1972 they'd grown to twice that number and seemed to be adding new recruits by the month.

Dave Brock was their guitarist, tune-smith and – sort of – leader; he seemed somewhat older and grumpier than his colleagues and suffered from an acute haemorrhoid condition that the rest of the group never tired of lampooning – though never directly to his face. (Eventually he'd get his revenge by trade-marking the band's name and sacking everyone from the classic early-seventies incarnation, becoming Hawkwind's sole trustee.) Nik Turner – his second-in-command – was never going to cause Ornette Coleman any sleepless nights with his saxophone playing but he had a lot of natural style and even a hint of charisma and was also the only man I've ever witnessed who could convincingly sport eye make-up with a full beard and still not look

completely ridiculous. They'd recently brought on board a vocal-
ist/lyricist named Robert Calvert who was a real, bona fide nutcase. He had occasional flashes of illumination but suffered from
a particularly severe chemical imbalance in his cerebral faculties
that often compelled him to seek temporary solace in various
'rest homes' dotted around the British Isles. Also along for the
ride were two 'electronics experts' – Dikmik and Del Dettmar –
who were really just a couple of former pot dealers who'd fallen
into music-making by pure happenstance. The rhythm section
was actually the key ingredient to Hawkwind's growing appeal.
Drummer Simon King and bassist 'Lemmy' Kilmister – both
newly recruited – were able to create a solid rumbling groove for
the others to play over and it was this cohesive piledriving contribution – hard, primitive, metronome-like – that ultimately made
the group so prized around the country as purveyors of proto-
stoner rock.

Their gigs in London and out in the suburbs quickly became
homes away from home for the nation's young drug-dabblers,
not unlike 'raves' in the late eighties except with a bunch of hairy
biker types playing electrified instruments in place of an anorak-
sporting DJ gurning over the turntables. Every day was a new
adventure for Hawkwind and those who happened to find themselves in its giddy orbit. No one at this juncture was in it for the
money or nurturing any kind of fame-seeking agenda. If the
group were offered the choice of playing for free in a field somewhere or performing at a paying venue, they would almost always
go for the cash-free option. Hawkwind played numerous
impromptu benefit shows for *Frendz* and were ready to show up
for virtually any alternative community cause you could throw at
them. In this respect, they were more authentic ambassadors of

Ladbroke Grove's bohemian demographic than the Clash, who in the late seventies used the Westway as nothing more than a handy photo-op backdrop for their own further self-glorification.

If Hawkwind had one shortcoming at this time it resided in the undeniable fact that their music – live or on record – invariably didn't sound too good without the listener first partaking in some form of further chemical assistance. This was made further manifest when the group invited me and some other *Frendz* contributors to accompany them to a concert being held in one of London's college venues in early February. The act performing that evening were label-mates of Hawkwind's – both were signed to United Artists records – and based in Germany. That's how I got to see Can playing their debut show in England. *Tago Mago* had just been completed and would soon become available, so the group – a quintet with Japanese vocalist Damo Suzuki very much in the foreground – spent the set further exploring the themes and grooves they'd recently developed in the recording studio. From the moment they began playing, you could tell that these guys were in a different class as instrumentalists. Three of them were master musicians who'd studied in conservatories and who now wanted to liberate themselves from the constraints of academia by playing free-form fusion jams on electrified instruments to stoned hippies. The music had obvious druggy connotations but you didn't need to be 'on drugs' to appreciate it. The spell they cast together was bigger than that.

Over the next two years, I'd come to know the members of Can quite well and can tell you from first-hand experience that they were scholarly types who also liked nothing more than to indulge in magic rituals and take drugs. But there was clearly some method to their collective madness because whatever they were doing simply seeped into the music itself, to the point where it seemed to glisten before the listener like a snake hypnotising its prey as it coiled its way around the room. Miles Davis had been exploring similar other-worldly musical terrains of late on albums like *Bitches Brew* and *Live-Evil* but Miles's new music had quickly proven itself too radical and abrasive-sounding for the UK prog bands and jazz-rock-fusion combos still in vogue to attempt to copy; only the German 'underground rock' bands of the late sixties had been affected by it, and from out of their ranks only Can had been able to take the basic ingredients – a James Brown funk rhythm and plenty of spacey dissonance from the keyboards and electric guitar – and create something genuinely awe-inspiring. What they were doing back then was never going to trouble the mainstream, but thirty-five years later Can's musical influence on what passes today for contemporary rock is far easier to pinpoint than the paltry legacies left by Jethro Tull and Yes, that era's most popular platinum-selling 'cerebral rock' entities. In this respect, the Cologne-based outfit played a similar role in the early seventies to the one the Velvet Underground played in the late sixties. When they were both actually in existence, only a few people bought their records or saw them live, but those same few were sufficiently moved by what they'd heard and seen to start their own groups as a direct consequence.

Still, Can's arrival on the London live music scene was something of a well-kept secret, attended by only a small smattering of ticket-holders and freeloaders and garnering little press coverage. All eyes were fixed instead on another act then working the same circuit to riotous acclaim. David Bowie's Ziggy Stardust and the Spiders from Mars project was going through the roof. The record wasn't even out yet but the hype was everywhere in the

press and on billboards, and Bowie was causing havoc throughout the country with his new live show.

These days, when people talk about the end of the sixties they
like to say that the decade didn't actually die until 1974 or even
1976. They're wrong: the seventies came into full effect in January
of 1972 when David Bowie reinvented himself as Ziggy Stardust.
The role made him an instant megastar and gave him the
momentum to stamp his personality across the new decade in the
all-imposing way the Beatles had managed in the sixties. He'd
spent years marooned in the backwaters of the music industry
but now – royally abetted by a cigar-chomping mega-manager
named Tony Defries who modelled himself obsessively on Elvis
Presley's mentor Colonel Tom Parker and a pushy Yank wife
named Angie – Bowie suddenly held the keys to the super-
highway.

It had started in early January when he appeared with freshly
cropped red hair on the cover of *Melody Maker* trumpeting his
bisexuality and generally being outrageous. A few short days after
the paper's publication, Bowie had performed his London debut
concert as Ziggy Stardust, a show I managed to attend. As he and
the Spiders from Mars were about to play their first song, the
equipment malfunctioned and there was a sudden agonising
silence that was instantly felt throughout the hall. If Bowie hadn't
reacted promptly, he would most likely have been laughed off the
stage that night and Ziggy Stardust's fate would have been seriously compromised. But – being a born trouper – he'd risen to the
occasion by injecting just the right hint of self-mockery, pointing
to each flamboyant article of clothing he was adorned in and reciting the name of its designer in an exaggerated camp falsetto.

Then the power came back on and he and his co-workers –

guitarist Mick Ronson, bassist Trevor Bolder and drummer Woody Woodmansey – immediately went to work. What they unveiled that night was a more upmarket, cerebrally involving strain of glam rock than the fizzy pop/rock then being made by Marc Bolan's T.Rex or America's Alice Cooper. Bolan was mainly for the teeny-boppers anyway, whilst Cooper appealed specifically to shock-rock aficionados, but Bowie's new approach had unlimited commercial range. Teenagers struggling with their sexual identities were able to instantly relate, whilst bookish students and young adults could obsessively sift through the lyrics and unravel subtle references to Nietzschean philosophy. Suddenly he'd struck the mother lode, becoming the era's most adored teen idol, sex symbol, rock star and Dylanesque pop sage in one fell swoop.

I wanted Bowie to be my first in-depth interview for *Frendz* but his management and press officer were always erecting obstacles; 'I'm sorry – David's at the dentist's all this week' was one line they kept using on me. What they were really saying was that their client was already way too high and mighty to waste valuable time explaining himself to some small-circulation rag. But then a call came through to *Frendz* headquarters that the MC5 had freshly debarked from their native Michigan to take up residence in London and try their luck on British shores. Ronan O'Rahilly – an Irish-born would-be cultural provocateur who'd been a prime mover behind the UK pirate-radio boom of the mid-sixties – had bankrolled the move and was now busy contacting the underground press offering access to the group. I ended up doing my first-ever interview with them at their press officer's ground-floor Chelsea flat in early February.

The MC5 had been a big noise back in early 1969 when their debut album *Kick Out the Jams* – a rambunctious audio vérité capturing of a typical live performance – was released. A biker named J. C. Crawford opens proceedings with the most unforgettable blast of verbal rabble-rousing ever committed to audiotape. 'Brothers and sisters, you have five seconds to decide whether you are going to be the problem or the solution,' he intones mesmerisingly in a hellfire preacher's resonant baritone. Then the group hit their first chord and you can hear the room they're playing in being suddenly rent asunder by the sheer volume and intensity of their evolving performance.

The 5 were a truly phenomenal live act – the only white US band who could potentially upstage the Rolling Stones in a concert hall – but they also liked to cultivate a rough and ready image of themselves as 'anything goes' political revolutionaries that quickly backfired on them in the marketplace. Elektra, their record label, let them go shortly after *Kick Out the Jams*' release because their soulmates in Michigan's White Panther Party had alienated a leading record-selling outlet with a controversial advert campaign in the local Motor City media. Shortly after that, White Panther kingpin John Sinclair – also the group's manager – was jailed on drug charges and the 5 were suddenly cast adrift from their social circumstances. They signed to the Atlantic label and made a couple of studio albums but never seemed to find a solid supportive fan base outside the Midwest. It was at this point that heroin started finding its way into the less affluent areas of Michigan state and various group members began falling under its spell. Moving to England then was partly a way of distancing the group from bad acquaintances and the dangerous places they tended to frequent more and more whilst still resident in their old home stretch.

The group looked like they'd been dragged through a bush

backwards when I met them. They still talked a lot about starting a revolution but this time it was a less specific revolution of the mind, not one involving 'drugs, loud music and fucking in the streets' – their oft-quoted manifesto of yore. Their former evangelical, new-world-conquering ardour was now seriously tempered by an old-world, ever-increasing bitterness about not being more successful in the music business. Their luck had run dry and everyone was suddenly busy being reborn under a bad sign.

The general tone for the MC5's 1972 sojourn in the UK was set shortly after our meeting, when the group were billed to headline a small charity gig in the Ladbroke Grove area. They turned up late and had their set rudely curtailed after two numbers by an enforced power cut. From that point on, bad luck, calamity and public indifference called all the shots on their attempted progress. They were next scheduled to perform a week-long residency at a newly opened West End club called Bumpers. I turned up on the first night to find only two other punters standing around the dance floor in anticipation of the group's appearance. One was Viv Prince, the Pretty Things' legendary ex-drummer, generally regarded by those who knew him back in the day as the closest thing to Sid Vicious that the sixties ever managed to vomit forth. The other was a local Hells Angel crony of Prince's with his left leg wrapped in a cast and a large canine by his side. The MC5 that night quite literally played to three men and a dog. It would have been funny if it hadn't been so bloody tragic. England just didn't know what it was missing. The country's concert-goers were still hypnotised by the spectacle of musicians sporting mutton-chop side-whiskers and standing like trees in the wind as they noodled their way into the mists of mediocrity. The MC5's high-energy approach was simply too dynamic for sleepy

London town and its neighbouring precincts to comfortably relate to. It was a criminal oversight on their part because – despite the ongoing problems – the MC5 were still firing on all cylinders as a live combo. That Bumpers show – notwithstanding the complete absence of a paying audience – was one of the most thrilling and memorable live showcases I've ever witnessed. A masterclass in how to create rock 'n' roll as a living, breathing art form instead of some corny abstraction.

Being around the MC5 also brought me into contact with my future collaborator, the photographer Pennie Smith. We were introduced at one of their shows. John May had told me about her talents and so I approached her about taking photos to accompany my interviews. She looked at me a bit dubiously at first – but later in the evening she became friendlier and even tentatively agreed to bring her camera along to my next rock-star chinwag.

Getting in Pennie as my creative partner quickly became the smartest move I ever made as a fledgling journalist. Apart from being a brilliant and innovative capturer of photographic images, she filled every room she entered with an air of beauty and mystery, and musicians invariably found themselves irresistibly drawn to her, particularly the old-school late-sixties blues-rock breed who tended to regard me with extreme suspicion. You'd see it when they first clapped eyes on me. *Who is this skinny hermaphrodite and what on earth does he have to say about music to me?* Then they'd see Pennie hovering enigmatically in the background and their icy expressions would instantly thaw. *But at the same time he knows this deeply enchanting woman so he must be doing something right.* The dynamic between the two of us was strong and mutually beneficial, plus you couldn't ask for a better friend than Pennie, a genuine paragon of virtue in an all-too-imperfect world: calm, giving, insightful, non-judgemental, devoid of ego and tantrum-inciting. Never took drugs. Didn't sleep around. A lot of people thought we were having an affair but it was always strictly platonic love between me and her. For as long as I've known her, she's been happily married to the same man – Tony Veseley – another dear friend of mine.

Pennie was there at my side when I got to do my second actual interview. David Bowie was still playing hard to get but his place had been taken this time by an even more auspicious entity: Captain Beefheart right at the top of his deeply wacky game.

Beefheart – alias Don Van Vliet – had been a teenage bosom buddy of Frank Zappa's and had first come to prominence on the mid-sixties music scene of his native California by fronting a relatively conventional Rolling Stones-styled mop-haired rhythm 'n' blues combo. But something deeply life-altering had befallen him during this period. Van Vliet's cousin would later confide that 'Don was a pretty normal guy' until one evening he found himself trapped in a drive-in cinema watching *The Incredible Shrinking Man* on acid. After that, his perceptions were never the same. He started talking to trees and believing he possessed supernatural powers. In 1967 he released a potent debut album of psychedelic blues entitled *Safe as Milk* with a stunning guitarist – Ry Cooder, still a teenager – in his back-up ensemble, the first Magic Band. But Cooder quickly abandoned ship when Beefheart experienced an LSD-impacted meltdown during a live performance at the outset of the Summer of Love. No matter: Beefheart simply replaced him with someone almost as good and recorded a second album, *Strictly Personal*, that got released sometime in 1968. Both efforts were roundly ignored over in America but in England John Peel became bedazzled by them, playing tracks unceasingly on his Radio One *Top Gear* show every Sunday afternoon. Hearing Beefheart's demented lupine growl blaring out of your little transistor briefly became as common a sonic manifestation of the late-sixties quiet UK Sunday as pealing church bells.

But then in 1969 Beefheart went into a whole new orbit of otherness. He replaced his old band members with some teenaged acid casualties and brainwashed them Charles Manson-style into doing whatever he told them to. He bashed out some music on a piano – an instrument he couldn't play – and then browbeat his new charges into replicating every nuance of these 'compositions' on guitars, bass and drums. Amazingly, they succeeded – though it took more than six months and almost all their remaining sanity to do so. Beefheart next alerted Frank Zappa, who took them to his studio and engineered two sessions, one for the backing tracks, miraculously captured in a single three-hour session, and a later one for Beefheart's vocals. When it came time to do the latter, the singer made a point of not wearing headphones so he couldn't actually hear the music as he was vocalising over it.

By all standards of conventional logic, it should have sounded like caterwauling cacophony but the resulting album, *Trout Mask Replica*, was inspired cacophony at the very least and a completely unique musical statement to boot. Beefheart still did his Howlin' Wolf-abducted-by-aliens vocal routine but his band had somehow struck out on a whole new musical hybrid: Delta blues in a surreal head-on collision with free jazz. You'd listen to it with your mouth agape, trying to locate a conventional beat or groove, being accosted instead by a succession of fractured rhythms that seemed to have been designed for a ballroom full of one-legged patrons. It positively defied you to dance along to it. Nor was it something you'd want to throw on the turntable to set up a romantic mood – unless you were deeply disturbed in the head. I recall reading a Kurt Cobain interview once when he claimed he and wife Courtney Love had enjoyed 'great sex' whilst listening to *Trout Mask Replica*. I knew then that their relationship was doomed.

Beefheart and his new Magic Band had recorded and released two more albums by the time our paths crossed. They were still largely unknown quantities in the States but John Peel's unstinting patronage via the UK radio waves had provided them with a healthy cult following throughout England, and so they chose February and March of 1972 to undertake their first-ever tour of the country (Beefheart had actually played the same circuit once before but with a different Magic Band). Old Blighty would never know what hit it.

My father once told me a story about *Citizen Kane*'s illustrious director Orson Welles. Either he or a colleague had to follow Welles around some picturesque Irish village in the early sixties and record his every spontaneous utterance as he wove his way uncertainly from pub to pub. Welles's glory years were far behind him at this juncture and he'd become reduced to living off his legend by talking whimsical blarney for travelogue TV shows. Yet his reduced circumstances had no visible effect on his self-image. Everyone he encountered that day he'd regale with the same priceless piece of information: 'I'm a genius.' He said it countless times – to his long-suffering co-workers, to uncomprehending barmen and waitresses, in fact to anyone he came directly into contact with. I only mention this because Captain Beefheart was exactly the same, utterly smitten with himself.

The world at large might have been blissfully ignorant of his accomplishments to date but Captain Beefheart was still 110 per cent convinced of his own artistic pre-eminence. He told me he was a genius at least twice within the first five minutes of our interview. Another five minutes passed and he started telling me that he was so in advance of all other living artists – be they painters, sculptors, poets or composers – that 'I'm going to have to create a whole new art form just to express myself in for the future.' He believed in himself with the same nutcase totality that propelled him to believe that he could converse meaningfully with shrubbery and insects. Again like Welles, he was that infuriating combination: part authentic creative visionary, part outrageous bullshitter. Still, I couldn't help but find his self-besotted boasting deeply entertaining and, more important, he warmed to me – enough anyway to extend an invitation the following day to travel with him and his band on their rented tour bus up to Brighton, where they were booked to play a concert at the Dome.

I arrived in the early afternoon to find Beefheart and his co-workers already dressed up as if about to take the stage. They were all wearing such retina-scorching colours and fabrics it was hard to look at them seated before me on the bus without getting dizzy. As soon as the vehicle started moving, Beefheart sat down next to me and began talking virtually non-stop. Several subjects were clearly transfixed in his mind. One was Frank Zappa: he couldn't abide the man and called him a 'charlatan' and an arch-manipulator. This was a bit rich when you consider that Zappa had been the childhood friend of Van Vliet's who'd actually invented the whole Captain Beefheart moniker for his young pal and then bankrolled the creation of *Trout Mask Replica*. But Beefheart was unimpressed by this largesse. He was on the warpath against his old colleague because Zappa had dared to release an album by a mentally ill street singer called Wild Man Fischer on the same label – suitably named Bizarre – that he'd released *Trout Mask* on. Beefheart found this unpardonable: 'He was trying to market me as a goddamned freak! The gall of the man!' he kept repeating. At one point, his attack on Zappa became so vitriolic that his new bassist, a quiet Mexican named Roy Estrada who'd played with Zappa on all the Mothers of Invention's late-sixties albums, tried to intercede on his former boss's behalf. 'Aw – c'mon, Don,' he offered meekly, 'Frank's OK.' 'Frank's OK?!' Beefheart parroted back with a thunderstruck expression on his face. 'Frank's OK?! Listen to yourself, Estrada. He's got you brainwashed too.'

The other subject that got him all hot under the collar was drugs. He couldn't tolerate the perception that his music was – in any way – drug-related. 'Look around you – none of my band takes drugs. We don't make music high on LSD or anything else. That's all just vicious misinformation.' I looked around and immediately noticed the eerie thousand-yard stares beaming out of the eye sockets of his Magic Band accomplices. Collectively speaking, they made a singularly unconvincing advertisement for drug-free living. Years later I'd read a biography on Beefheart and discover that certain members had imported PCP – a mind-befuddling tranquilliser used to stun farm animals – into the country to smoke during their leisure time on this tour.

The bus they'd hired to transport us started malfunctioning as we approached Brighton itself and completely gave up the ghost just as we started coasting along the seafront. This meant that everyone had to suddenly disembark and walk the half-mile distance to the venue itself. I suddenly found myself in a brand-new role – that of Captain Beefheart and his Magic Band's resident shepherd. I felt like I'd been abducted into an episode of *The Twilight Zone*. Everywhere we walked, fellow pedestrians would stare at us open-mouthed as if we'd just landed from some faraway galaxy. Beefheart was dressed up like some Las Vegas nightclub conjurer complete with flowing cape. I kept expecting him to produce a couple of white doves from out of his sleeves at any given moment. And no one had even the remotest sense of earthly direction. I had to keep checking that one of the Magic Band hadn't strayed off and gotten himself hopelessly lost.

Finally, we reached the concert hall just as dusk was starting to settle in the sky. In due course, the ensemble walked out on stage and plugged in, whilst the drummer – whose real name was Art Tripp III – seated himself behind possibly the smallest kit ever commandeered for a live performance – a single bass and snare drum alongside one cymbal. Beefheart – in full evening dress – then entered to much acclaim from the audience and gruffly counted in the first song. As soon as the first notes were struck, time stood still. Music like this had never been heard before – or since. The group performed most of 'The Spotlight Kid' and a couple of selections from *Trout Mask Replica* but the studio recordings barely hinted at the mind-scrambling majesty of their live renditions. Like Thelonious Monk, Beefheart had a totally unique 'out-there' aesthetic sensibility and the scary strength of personality to project it directly onto not only his band but also his paying public. There was a genuinely superhuman power coming out of the PA system. People just sat there slack-jawed and pinched themselves to see whether they'd fallen asleep into some alternative dream dimension. None of us could believe we were hearing music this visceral and dementedly alive. You could practically see the electricity coursing through their instruments and taste the phlegm bubbling in Beefheart's larynx. He wasn't kidding when he called them the Magic Band.

Another 'magic' band from America's West Coast who'd adopted LSD as a means to break down existing musical barriers and create a more wide-open sonic sensibility were San Francisco's Grateful Dead. Ever since 1967 they'd been fondly recognised as psychedelic-rock pioneers and all-purpose community-minded righteous hippie dudes by John Peel's lank-haired listeners throughout the British Isles, but they'd only ever managed to play one concert in England to date, at a festival in Staffordshire in the early summer of 1970. In early '72, though, the group and their record company Warner Bros. bankrolled an extended gig-playing trek through Europe that included a short tour of England. In late March, they and their extremely large 'extended family' moved into a swanky Kensington hotel in anticipation of the shows and duly became my third interviewees.

In stark contrast to their reputation as championship-level LSD-gobblers, they seemed a pretty down-to-earth bunch when confronted one-on-one. They dressed like rodeo cowboys and talked like mature overseas students checking out foreign culture. The drugs had yet to bend their brains into some inexplicable agenda like Beefheart's bunch. Their music may have been further fuelled by a healthy desire to embrace utter weirdness but none of them was weird per se. Jerry Garcia in particular was totally exasperated by their image and reputation and the way it constantly impinged on his privacy. Every acid casualty in Christendom wanted to corral him into some 'deeply meaningful' conversation and he'd simply had enough of indulging all these damaged people. Hippies the world over looked up to him as though he were some deity or oracle but Garcia was really just an intelligent, well-read druggie with a deeply cynical streak who felt increasingly ill at ease with the role he'd been straitjacketed into by late-sixties bohemian culture. In time it would get so intolerable that he would withdraw from society in general by compulsively smoking high-grade Persian heroin. This in turn would prove fatal: after twenty years of addiction, the drug would end up hastening his death in 1995.

At the same time, he was one of the most singularly gifted musicians of the latter half of the twentieth century. The Grateful Dead were an odd bunch in that they were always being called a rock band but they couldn't play straight-ahead rock 'n' roll to save their lives. They'd started out instead as a jug band before branching out into folk and electric blues and playing long jazz-influenced jams whenever the mood struck. By the end of the sixties they'd even morphed into a credible country-and-western outfit. By 1972 they meandered between these various musical genres, performing sets that rarely ran for less than three hours in length; there were – inevitably – valleys and peaks. You'd sit there for what seemed like an eternity watching them noodle away on stage silently praying that they'd actually finish the song and put it out of its misery. But then – all of a sudden – the group would take off into the psychedelic stratosphere and Garcia would step forward to the lip of the stage and begin navigating his way to that enchanted region where the sagebrush meets the stars. Cosmic American music: Gram Parsons coined the phrase but it was the Grateful Dead who best embodied the concept even though – after 1972 – they began slipping into a long befuddling decline.

Both Beefheart and the Dead turned up to play at a three-day festival held in the Northern town of Bickershaw during the first weekend in May '72. The event's shady promoters had envisaged it as a grand unveiling of the whole West Coast live rock experience to the John Peel demographic but it soon degenerated into a sort of mud-caked psychedelic concentration camp filled with miserable-looking young people on dodgy hallucinogenics being lashed by torrential wind and rain and sold inedible food. Beefheart and the Dead performed splendidly, the former delivering a sudden earth-shaking a cappella version of Howlin' Wolf's 'Evil' that struck terror into the hearts and minds of several acid casualties at the lip of the stage who reacted as if suddenly struck by lightning – but there was no getting around the fact that the whole ugly debacle was destined to be acid rock's last hurrah here in the British Isles. A relentless downpouring of bad weather, bad facilities, bad drugs and (mostly) bad music: it had worked like a charm three years ago at Woodstock but it wasn't working any more.

Mind you, I had a great time. A bunch of *Frendz* collaborators had hired a large van we could all sleep in and had succeeded in getting VIP passes, so we were always close to the action and safe from the inclement storms raging over the bedraggled spectators. I remember on the first night standing at the side of the stage smoking a joint and watching some underwhelming folk singer braying into a microphone when a rotund, Afro-headed figure dressed head to foot in frayed blue denim suddenly approached me. 'Are you Nick Kent?' the figure enquired; he seemed to be on speed and was also suffering from one of the most pungent outbreaks of body odour my nose had ever encountered. When I replied in the affirmative, he added, 'Well, if you write any better than what I've read of yours lately, I'm going to seriously have to consider breaking your hands.' This was my first-ever conversation with Charles Shaar Murray, my soon-to-be collaborator at the *New Musical Express*.

But I'm getting slightly ahead of the actual flow of events in early 1972. Sometime in late February I'd managed to meet Iggy Pop, an encounter that had a cataclysmic effect on me personally. During one of my fruitless attempts to snag a David Bowie interview, an employer at his management firm Mainman had let slip that Iggy had lately become one of their clients too and had just moved from the States to take up temporary residence in a house in London's Maida Vale. He even gave me the address. At first I was too scared to make direct contact, having read all about the singer's unpredictable ways whilst fronting the early Stooges, but then I became friendly with a girl called Debbie Boushell, who'd recently left her native Michigan to immerse herself in swinging London. Back in the day she'd known both the MC5 and the Stooges personally, and when she heard that I knew Iggy's exact whereabouts in England she eagerly suggested we visit his premises together at the earliest opportunity.

One sunny afternoon we actually made the trek, walking for ages along streets rimmed with elegantly cropped hedgerows and exquisitely maintained gardens until we came to the Stooges' UK headquarters. I rang the bell, half-expecting a naked wild man to suddenly materialise and wrestle me to the ground. But instead the door was opened by a slender young person dressed in a woman's sleeveless smock and a pair of circulation-constrictingly tight silver leather trousers. I'd always imagined Iggy Pop to be a bull-in-a-china-shop kind of guy – a walking sea of turbulence – but the fellow facing me – for it was he – was the epitome of charm and well-mannered cordiality.

In point of fact, I didn't really meet Iggy Pop that day. I was treated to an encounter with his alter ego, Jim Osterberg, instead. This was most fortuitous: Jim can be a genuinely nice human being to spend time with, Iggy less so. He was attempting to lead a chemical-free existence at this precise moment and Iggy only came out to play back then when the drugs started kicking in. I couldn't get over how polite and intelligent he was. He had exquisite manners and spoke penetratingly about Gore Vidal's novels and avant-garde European cinema. He was trying to assimilate English culture and I remember we watched an episode of *Steptoe and Son* on his black-and-white television, me attempting to explain the rag-and-bone back-story behind its plot line. As per usual, Albert and Harold Steptoe were constantly at each other's throats over some petty infraction, shouting comic insults at each other across the scrapyard. Iggy turned to his guitarist James Williamson, who was sharing the Maida Vale digs with him. 'That'll be you and me in a couple of weeks' time.'

He and Williamson couldn't get over the fact that television in Great Britain during 1972 tended to cease broadcasting after 10.30 in the evening. Back in Michigan, the Stooges had bonded over after-midnight reruns of George Romero's *Night of the Living Dead* flickering in the old homestead. Now all they had to while away the witching hours was a test pattern. The pair were both acquainted with the Rolling Stones' song 'Street Fighting Man' and its refrain about sleepy London town, and now they were discovering for themselves the reality of its sentiments. London simply wasn't swinging any more. Everything closed down too early and the only places that stayed open after midnight seemed to be hosting a perpetual gloomy wake for the sixties.

At first Iggy tried to make sense of his new surroundings, to check out the English way at close quarters. I saw him a lot during the next few months. He could often be espied walking around the city alone, mapping out the London terrain street by street until he'd covered every postal district on foot. Like Napoleon, he was busy working up his own plan of attack on the metropolis. He'd sometimes turn up to a gig alone and lurk in the audience, scoping out the competition. He spoke highly of a T.Rex concert he'd witnessed at Wembley – the same show that was filmed by Ringo Starr for the *Born to Boogie* film. Iggy was quite a fan of Bolan's back in the day – he'd even managed to get hold of a pre-release white-label acetate of *The Slider* album and played it a lot at the Stooges' London headquarters. He seemed to hold Bolan in higher esteem than his new pal Bowie – at least on a musical level.

Iggy and Bowie may have been linked by management and general word of mouth but their individual agendas were poles apart. Bowie was a culture-vulture tourist, a magpie chameleon furiously ransacking all manner of cutting-edge influences in order to create a sophisticated multi-layered pop consciousness for himself and his audience to share in. Iggy meanwhile was a fervent purist intent on rechannelling the bedrock blues aesthetic – two or three chords and a hypnotic groove – through the whole white bohemian stream-of-consciousness mindset mixed in with some performance art. Put simply, Ziggy Stardust was 'show business' whilst the Stooges were 'soul business'. The first was deeply glamorous and alluring to behold, the latter less attractive but potentially more life-changing to be exposed to.

Some might now see it as the difference between art and artifice but that would be a wrong-headed claim to make. Bowie's Ziggy-era music was certainly artfully conceived and he had a far more sophisticated and varied approach to basic songcraft than Iggy. Bowie understood what was happening in the cultural Zeitgeist and was able to play on its various ongoing obsessions – the sci-fi-inspired future, Orwell's *Nineteen Eighty-Four* scenario, androgyny, *Clockwork Orange*, Warholesque superstardom – to his own inspired purposes. Iggy by contrast was a musical primitive not unlike John Lee Hooker and proud to be so. They could only enjoy a meaningful creative and personal relationship when Bowie finally elected to leave all his personality-transforming masks back in the closet, which he did in the mid-seventies when the pair moved to Berlin together. During the early seventies, though, they were often at cross-purposes. Bowie adored Iggy but was less enamoured by the Stooges' input, feeling the singer would be better served with a more conventionally proficient back-up ensemble. Iggy meanwhile had his own private reservations about Bowie's effetely theatrical live shows as well as the Bromley alien's unfortunate tendency to hire mime artists to share the stage with him. One was fated to levitate to the very toppermost of the global poppermost over the next two years, whilst the other was doomed to lay destitute in its outer margins during the same period of time. Partly this was due to their manager Tony Defries, who focused ruthlessly on Bowie's career throughout 1972, keeping Iggy and the Stooges out on the sidelines and unemployed, save for the recording of one album and a single live performance. But mostly it was due to the fact that the world was still not ready to accept what the Stooges had to offer it.

Their one and only European show took place on July 21st 1972 on a Saturday night at London's King's Cross Cinema (later known as the Scala), just across the road from the train station.

The night before, Lou Reed had made his UK live debut at the same venue and the fledgling glitterati *du jour* had all come out in force to feast their eyes and ears on the revered former Velvet Underground kingpin's latest musical venture. Members of a fascinating new English act known as Roxy Music were amongst the gauchely attired attendees seated up in the balcony. The Stooges were there too, scoping out the competition with their customary snake-eyed nonchalance. Backstage I caught a glimpse of Reed before he went on. Slumped in a corner of his makeshift dressing room, his whole body was shaking uncontrollably and his facial expression was that of a man awaiting his own execution. His performance that night quickly degenerated into a fiasco. The backing band he'd hired – and christened the Tots – managed only to transform his old Velvets repertoire from edgy art rock to fecklesssounding bubblegum pop. And Reed's stage fright was so palpable his voice kept cancelling out on him because his vocal cords and neck muscles had become rigid with fear. He was also seriously overweight, a condition not helped by his choice of apparel – a rhinestone-encrusted black velvet suit several sizes too small for his portly girth. After four songs, his trousers burst their seams, his zipper broke and the waistband began to slowly descend, billowing around his thighs. Iggy and James Williamson – standing at the front of the stage – found this spectacle particularly amusing and began pointing at the falling strides with suitably contemptuous facial expressions.

There were no such wardrobe malfunctions when the Stooges took the same stage just twenty-four hours later. But there was only a fraction of the audience that had turned out for Reed. No celebrity onlookers could be found in the building – no Roxy, Reed or Bowie, although the latter pair had been photographed arm in arm with Iggy that very afternoon during a joint press conference at a London hotel. No more than 200 people were present for the show and at least half of them were only there because it was a cheaply priced all-night event that provided warmth and shelter to cushion the hours before London's tube trains began operating again at 6 a.m. Many in the balcony were already fast asleep when the Stooges began playing at 2 in the morning. They didn't stay that way for long. From the opening notes, the big room was suddenly sucked into a world rife with menace and malevolence.

The songs the Stooges chose to perform that night had never been heard outside of the group's rehearsal studio – and they never would be again. Nothing was reprised from their previous two Elektra albums and nothing they played would be later immortalised on *Raw Power*. Instead, they performed a jolting succession of primitive works in progress. 'This next selection is entitled "Penetration",' Iggy would inform the genuinely terrified crowd. But the song they performed had absolutely nothing in common with the hypnotic track of the same name that would appear eight months later on the Stooges' third album. 'Thank you,' Iggy then announced. 'This next selection is called "Penetration" too.' And off they'd go again bashing out this scary, Neanderthal jungle music that no one present had ever heard the likes of before this night.

Iggy meanwhile gave one of the most superhuman physical displays ever seen in public. Every nuance of his performance is still engraved in my memory – his absolute fearlessness, his Nijinsky-like body language and the mind-boggling way he seemed able to defy even the laws of gravity. At one point he placed his mike stand right at the lip of the stage, bent backward until his head touched the ground and then threw his whole body forward onto it. As he and the stand descended into the audience pit, he managed to execute a full somersault on it whilst still in mid-air. Landing on the floor in a deft pirouette, he then proceeded to crawl around the crowd's feet on his chest like a reptile.

No one had ever witnessed anything like this in England before. The Who had been loud, anarchic-sounding and genuinely shocking as a live attraction once upon a time but they'd never physically confronted their audiences in such an alarming fashion. Four years hence, UK crowds would become totally entranced by just this sort of spectacle but in 1972 it was way too much way too soon. The audience at the Stooges show looked genuinely traumatised by the end. As soon as Iggy had leapt off the stage and into the crowd, people generally scattered backwards and stood close to the exit doors, peering nervously at the action and praying that the singer wouldn't come over and start tormenting them. At the same time, they couldn't keep their eyes off him so it made for an interesting dynamic in the room, to say the least. John Lydon has always claimed he was one of those present in the audience that night and that he was left unimpressed by the Stooges' performance, but that is quite frankly impossible to believe. For what Iggy and co. achieved that night was to provide the basic blueprint for what the Sex Pistols attempted three and a half years later: short sharp shock rock that mesmerised whilst at the same time scaring its audience witless. Take it from one who was actually there and saw the whole process slowly developing throughout the early seventies: Iggy and the Stooges invented punk just like James Brown and the Famous Flames created funk. They were the first and they were the best. Many self-styled punk experts have since come forward to chronicle the genre in lofty tomes but unless you were one of those 200 jittery punters watching the Stooges' only European show in the summer of '72, you weren't there at the real beginning and don't really know what you're talking about. End of sermon.

The performance had a profound effect on me, anyway. It offered me a definitive glimpse into the decade's real future – the new wild frontier of Western pop culture – as well as providing the catalyst for more gainful employment. A week or so later, I got an unexpected phone call from a gentleman I'd never spoken to before named Nick Logan, who claimed to be the assistant editor of the *New Musical Express*. He told me the paper was looking to run an article on Iggy and the Stooges but that they'd been unable to secure any kind of interview via their management. As I'd already encountered the group and had recently seen them perform, would I be at all interested in penning a short article on the subject for their next issue? He then spoke the magic words: fifteen quid would be paid for every thousand words I could come up with. I said 'yes' on the spot and agreed to visit the paper's offices in Long Acre in order to discuss further projects.

The *NME* and I already had one thing in common: the broadsheet publication first appeared in 1951, the year of my birth. Its premier issue featured my dad's pal Vera Lynn – the former 'forces' favourite' – as its cover star. But the weekly periodical's initial focus on fifties crooners and light-entertainment flavours of the month soon changed to embrace a younger demographic when Elvis Presley exploded over in America leading the way for home-grown imitators like Tommy Steele and Cliff Richard to beguile Britain's post-war youth.

By the early sixties the journal was on a circulation ascendant as the country's pre-eminent pop sheet. Beatles fans bought it religiously each week in order to find out all the latest info about their mop-haired saviours. Its golden era to date had been the so-called British invasion beat group years but it started to come seriously unstuck during the second half of the decade when rock went counter-cultural and pop was suddenly viewed as music for morons.

The *NME* at first simply couldn't grasp this new state of affairs and stumbled on cluelessly trying to incorporate the two conflicting strains – hairy 'underground sounds' and fly-by-night chartbusters – into their ink-stained pages whilst its rival publication *Melody Maker* – formerly a bastion for trad jazzers – quadrupled its own circulation figures by throwing its full editorial might behind the rising prog regime; by the outset of 1972, the latter was notching up weekly sales of close to 200,000 copies whilst the *NME*'s readership had fallen to less than 60,000. Their parent company IPC duly took note of the situation and in late spring told those responsible for the *NME* that it had only twelve issues left to turn around its dwindling demographic or cease existing. IPC would inject extra money into these issues and conjure up a nationwide publicity campaign to hopefully draw more attention to them, but they stressed the editors had to speedily come up with some kind of new direction in order to keep it from becoming extinct.

With little time to waste, the paper's two principals – Logan and first-in-command editor Alan Lewis – began frantically recruiting young music-driven writers from the London underground network. Charles Shaar Murray had been the first approached and the first to sign up as a staff member for the new enterprise. Ian MacDonald and I were headhunted shortly afterwards. MacDonald was a Cambridge graduate only two or three years older than me with long receding hair and a forehead so large you could have landed a plane on it. Behind that oft-furrowed mega-brow of his lurked a brain that was even larger – an all-devouring intellect that had few equals anywhere else in the world. By midsummer the three of us had formed our own subversive little nucleus within the journal. We weren't particularly thrilled to be there initially. The *NME*'s recent track record as a viable youth-based periodical had been utterly dismal, to put it kindly. But we were young and keen and arrogant enough to think we could make a decisive difference to its fortunes whilst simultaneously upgrading its actual contents.

The existing staff members could have reacted badly to our arrival but instead welcomed us into their midst with surprisingly good grace. The most approachable of the old-school breed was a bloke named Tony Tyler, a Liverpudlian Ichabod Crane lookalike who'd known the Beatles back in their Hamburg days and had roadied for Bob Dylan and the Hawks in 1966. The most instantly unforgettable was Roy Carr, a short, barrel-shaped Sancho Panza from the North of England with a strange hair-weave and porn-director goatee who sometimes turned up to the office dressed in an alarmingly flamboyant suede bolero jacket festooned with a fringe that extended to the floor. He told us all proudly this sartorial relic from Woodstock Nation was a personal gift from the singer of Blood, Sweat and Tears. Like Tyler, Carr had played in beat groups during the sixties and claimed to have been sexually propositioned by practically every female vocal talent of the era. Like Tyler, he adopted the role of benevolent uncle to us callow young scribes, and both gave us their collected insights on how to stay afloat in the murky waters of Tin Pan Alleydom.

Their advice was as follows: don't say nasty things about Elvis Presley in print because his fans were mostly psychopaths who thought nothing of personally stalking and then beating up anyone who knocked their hillbilly deity. And don't ever write anything uncomplimentary about any act managed by Don Arden. We saw the wisdom of their second suggestion early in the autumn of 1972 when Arden and two of his burly henchmen paid an impromptu visit to the *NME* offices with the firm intention of hanging an older staff member out of a third-storey window by his feet. The luckless journo had penned a live review of Arden's pet project the Electric Light Orchestra. It had been a mostly positive write-up and he'd only mentioned in passing that the drum solo had gone on a bit too long, but this was enough for the most feared man in Tin Pan Alley to turn seriously bloodthirsty and leap into attack mode.

Apart from those pearls of wisdom, we were left to our own devices. Lewis and Logan never tried to rein us in. We were given carte blanche to pretty much run wild through the early-seventies pop/rock spectrum and whatever we scribbled would be printed unedited. Sales suddenly improved dramatically; we were a winning team at this point and none of us failed to grasp the heady realisation that we were in exactly the right place at the right time.

A new decade was actually starting to define itself and anyone with even a hint of talent and personal magnetism stood a fighting chance of making their mark on it provided they had the right instincts. The *NME* became the ideal periodical to reflect what was about to transpire because it was fighting for its own future too and was prepared to go to unorthodox extremes in order to stay in circulation. Why else would they have even considered employing someone as potentially trouble-prone as me? I couldn't even type my own copy. I'd turn up literally three hours before a deadline was due, drink twenty-seven cups of coffee and then scribble furiously onto a series of sheets of paper, each one getting instantly shuffled over to some long-suffering secretary who then had to make sense of my haphazard longhand and turn it into coherent typewritten text. Unlike Murray and MacDonald, I'd chosen not to become an actual staff member. In all the years I worked for the paper, I was always employed as a freelancer. I never wanted to be chained to a desk or trapped within some dull office routine. I wanted to always be where the real action was.

Glam rock was at its popularity peak throughout these months and it was a trend I found easy to exploit, mainly because I looked like a lanky girl. My choice of clothing became more ostentatious and I began wearing clumsily applied black eyeliner. Thus the *NME* tended to assign me to doorstep the genre's leading practitioners. Alice Cooper was having a bumper year, with 'School's Out' blaring from every jukebox throughout the British Isles. He and his group were all staunch heterosexuals who'd nonetheless anticipated the whole androgynous cross-dressing fashion in rock in order to stand out in their local LA club scene at the end of the sixties. They'd started out making hard-on-the-ear art rock under the patronage of Frank Zappa but subsequent exposure to the Stooges' more anarchic allure and a lucky encounter with a savvy young Canadian producer named Bob Ezrin inspired them to record a spate of risqué but still reassuringly commercial-sounding hit singles starting in 1971 with the teen-alienation anthem 'I'm Eighteen'.

From that point on they became showbiz interlopers shifting units whilst crassly upsetting the sensibilities of the world's self-elected fuddy-duddy moral crusaders. Once the shock wore off, though, the game was up for them. By the middle of the decade, Alice Cooper had shrunk from a quintet to a solo act. The singer kept the name and has continued to prevail as a wizened rock icon over the decades that followed. This makes sense as he was the only real professional in the entire set-up and also the only genuinely nice guy.

The same couldn't be said of Lou Reed. He had dead Peter Lorre eyes and a cold inhospitable manner that evening in autumn when I first interviewed him over a meal at a Kensington restaurant. The London glitterati may have been ceaselessly singing his praises that year but it had evidently done little to bolster his brittle, sullen mood. He spent most of our conversation bitterly itemising all the rip-offs he – as composer and instigator of the Velvet Underground – had been the victim of over the years. The Beatles, Stones and Dylan had been amongst the culprits, so he claimed. It was all grumpy, petulant ego-babble. Behind his mask of mummified disdain, Reed seemed seriously adrift. He'd just finished recording a second solo album called *Transformer* that David Bowie had produced, but its self-consciously decadent lyrical agenda and dainty hi-gloss-production sound seemed jarringly shallow when played next to his Velvet Underground recordings. Old Velvets fans – all five of them – were aghast at the change in direction, but Reed's studio dalliance with Bowie that year would still manage to provide him with the only two major hit singles of his entire career – 'Walk on the Wild Side' and 'Perfect Day'.

Of all the glam acts, only Roxy Music seemed prepared to give

Bowie a real run for his money. I met them that summer for the first time in their managers' Chelsea office and they were already a pretty haughty and self-possessed bunch, a sort of ex-art-school Lord Snooty and his pals in lurex. This was just when 'Virginia Plain' – their first big hit single – was about to be released and Brian Eno was still very much in their midst. Indeed, the flaxen-haired synth boffin with the perfect cheekbones was the group's most image-friendly asset at this point in time, fulfilling a picturesque but musically limited role similar to Brian Jones in the Rolling Stones. His arch hermaphroditic presence blended well with singer Bryan Ferry's more conventional handsomeness in concert and helped UK youth become quickly enthralled with a music that – as their debut album still readily attests – was often far from commercially accessible.

Roxy Music in 1972 presented the world with a camp, Buck Rogers take on the prevailing middle-class art-rock aesthetic that was both shockingly idiosyncratic and deeply tongue-in-cheek. Their songwriter Bryan Ferry wrote madly sophisticated lyrics packed with hip cross-references to other avenues of then-contemporary art and then wedded them to music he'd clumsily bash out crab-handedly on a piano utilising only the black notes of the keyboard. He'd sing the results with a deliciously sleazy quaver to his voice, like a gigolo with a knife blade held to his throat. At first exposure you couldn't help wondering if he – and his co-workers – were actually a comedy act merrily taking the piss. But Ferry was anything but self-mocking about his work and self-image. A Geordie milkman's son who'd been transformed by higher education and who privately dreamed of becoming a real-life clone of Scott Fitzgerald's Great Gatsby, he took his career and growing renown very, very seriously indeed. Just how seriously was duly brought home to all onlookers some twelve months later when he sacked Eno from the line-up and started to subtly demote the rest of the band to backing-group status.

Talking of glam rock, the *NME* got me to interview one of the form's key spiritual forebears, Liberace, that autumn. He gurgled when he laughed out loud and was as reassuringly camp as the proverbial row of tents. A week later, they sent me out to talk to Johnny Cash, who spoke from deep in his boots and looked like he'd been carved out of granite. Never let it be said that the journal didn't introduce me to the full gamut of celebrity manliness.

But I knew I'd really hit the big time when the editors invited me to accompany Led Zeppelin – then the world's brashest-sounding and biggest-selling rock act – on selected dates of an end-of-the-year UK tour. Actually I really have B. P. Fallon to thank for the assignment. A peculiar but not charmless little man who looked like a glam-rock leprechaun and spoke like an effete Irish hobbit, he'd lately taken on the task of drumming up press coverage for the group after their drummer John Bonham had shredded the clothes of their previous publicist – a long-suffering Tin Pan Alley stalwart named Bill Harry – during a drunken altercation in a London pub earlier in the year. He told me in advance that the group held journalists in generally low esteem and that entering their world could be something of a 'Daniel in the lion's den' experience – at least at first – but that if I could brass it out and not say or do anything to truly warrant their wrath, then perhaps a mutually beneficial relationship could be struck up.

These words would prove prophetic the night we actually intersected. It happened on December 12th 1972 in Cardiff – my old stomping ground – when Zeppelin were booked to play the Capitol Cinema. I knew the venue well; I'd been temporarily deafened there six years before by Bob Dylan and the Hawks. I'd arrived by train from London in time to be whisked into the back of the house by Fallon just as the quartet were beginning their first number. What followed for almost two and a half hours was a musical masterclass in big rock dynamics, 'bottle' and bravado.

I'd seen them once before at the 1970 Bath Festival. At Bath, they'd quite simply blown every other act on the bill right off the stage – indeed, their manager Peter Grant had quite literally pushed one band called the Flock off the stage with his gargantuan girth when their set threatened to clash with his boys' designated time-slot.

But this was now two and a half years later and the quartet had become even more adept at weaving their singular 'tension and release'/'light and shade'-driven hard-rock magic act to transfix live audiences. Plus they had two more albums' worth of new songs to add to their repertoire, with four selections from Led Zep IV illuminating the set and five exclusive tracks from the as-yet-unreleased *Houses of the Holy* also being performed. As a result, the show that night sailed from one giddy climax to another. Robert Plant preened and screamed out blood-curdling notes that seemed capable of suddenly sending the venue's aged architecture crashing down around us all in a heap of rubble like Joshua's trumpet destroying the walls of Jericho. Jimmy Page danced around a lot – even attempting a sliding manoeuvre with his feet that James Brown had first perfected in the early sixties – whilst at the same time leaving his fingers free to conjure forth a truly devastating multiplicity of guitar riffs and lead solos. But equally impressive were John Paul Jones and John Bonham, who – whenever they locked in together on bass and drums – made the whole room shake ecstatically with the intensity of their playing. As a foursome, they were unbeatable: no other group in the world – not even the Who at their peak – could compete with them when they were fully focused and firing on all cylinders as was the case with this Cardiff show. At the end of the perform- ance they even stormed into a brief rendition of 'Louie Louie' that sounded like the four horsemen of the apocalypse inventing the concept of testosterone-driven punk rock.

Five minutes after they'd finished playing, Fallon – or 'Beep' as everyone called him – ushered Pennie and me through the stage door and led us into a cramped space directly behind the stage. Shortly afterwards, Jimmy Page – still perspiring from his onstage exertions – joined us. He seemed very paranoid and ill at ease and began demanding pointedly if and when I'd seen Zeppelin play live before. When I recalled the Bath Festival performance, he seemed to relax a little but then began a heated rant about 'the last bloody interviewer' he'd been confronted with, who – it turned out – had only seen the group via their one-song inclusion in the film *Supershow*. As he was speaking, Robert Plant, John Paul Jones and John Bonham all entered the room and sat down, nursing alcoholic beverages and mischievous expressions. They'd been out under the spotlight all evening providing entertainment for the people. Now it was their turn to be entertained and it didn't take me long to realise that it was going to be at my expense. They sniggered whenever I opened my mouth to phrase a sentence. At least once, I heard the word 'wanker' being aimed in my direction.

Meanwhile, my 'interview' with Page was growing increasingly confrontational. He seemed to be wilfully misinterpreting my questions – hearing implied criticisms where there were only innocent enquiries – and reacting as though I was the Spanish Inquisition. At one point, I mentioned innocently that no

American band had ever managed to convincingly duplicate the four-piece heavy-rock formula that English rock quartets from Zep to Free had been so successful at, but Page somehow interpreted this harmless comment as a criticism too and went off on a petulant put-down of the 'aimless jamming' of 'overrated American bands like the Grateful Dead'. His three band members' smirking asides reached a raucous crescendo at this juncture. It was then that I impulsively decided to retaliate by bringing up the thorny subject of all those Zep lyrics that were in reality straight lifts from old blues numbers. Big mistake. The four members promptly walked out with disgusted looks on their faces and the next sound I heard was that of Peter Grant screaming ear-lacerating obscenities at B. P. Fallon in an adjacent room for having brought me into their world in the first place.

In a tricky situation such as this, it's always a distinct advantage to have a workmate as charming and alluring as the divine Pennie Smith. The group may have been deeply unimpressed with me but they couldn't help but be attracted by the mysterious beauty of the now-legendary photographer. As a result, an hour later, we were both invited to a late-night impromptu get-together involving the four members, Grant, Fallon, Richard Cole, their notorious tour manager, and Phil Carson, the head of the UK branch of Atlantic Records.

Compared to what I'd heard and read about Zeppelin's parties whilst on tour, it was a pretty tame affair. There was a certain amount of cocaine-snorting – but nothing excessive. Alcohol was freely available but nobody was particularly drunk. At one point, someone – not a group member – half-heartedly proposed trying to hire some prostitutes but no one else in the room felt inclined to take him up on his offer. Instead, they just talked, swapping industry gossip and telling funny stories about their past exploits. Jimmy Page regaled everyone with his tales of a teenage Jeff Beck briefly playing guitar in the Tornados, the Joe Meek-directed instrumental ensemble who recorded 'Telstar'. He seemed a lot more relaxed and even apologised for the way he'd reacted earlier. I became embroiled in a lengthy discussion about music with Robert Plant which soon transformed itself into a heated debate on who was better – the Byrds or the Buffalo Springfield (I stuck by the Byrds; Plant favoured the Springfield). Peter Grant told a hilarious story about wrapping Little Richard in a carpet and bodily carrying him to a gig he was refusing to perform at. At just after 3 a.m., things started to wind down and everyone retired peacefully to their separate hotel rooms.

The next evening, we stuck around for the second show and then set off by car back to London at midnight. As we were pulling out of the backstage area, Peter Grant stalked over to our vehicle and – staring ominously in my direction – bade farewell whilst making it abundantly clear that he wouldn't be at all happy if anything negative appeared in my write-up.

The big man needn't have worried. The article I turned in – split into two parts and run in the last couple of *NME* issues printed that year – was effusive in its praise of their live stature whilst diplomatically playing down any of the discordant moments that had passed between us. They even ran a photo next to the headline of me with kohl-ringed eyes and hair – which I'd cut myself – that was short and prickly on top with long rat's-tail strands at the back that reached to my shoulders. Looking at it now, I get the uneasy feeling that I may have helped invent the mullet a full ten years before it became the de rigueur hairstyle of the sartorially challenged eighties. I can find no ready excuse for this gross lapse in haircare judgement. But then again, one isn't really necessary. It was the seventies after all, a time when 'good taste' upped sticks and went into an extended hibernation.

Bedford College chose to toss me out of their corridors of learning just as Led Zeppelin and I were first getting acquainted. I got the letter that December. It was bound to happen: I rarely attended lectures and hadn't even shown up for the end-of-term examinations. I'd already spent too much of my young life in dusty libraries poring over the thoughts and words of long-dead authors. Now John Milton and his ilk could all take a hike.

I only have two negative memories from 1972. The first involved a speed-addled Scottish psychopath who'd sometimes stalk the *Frendz* office, pushing me against the wall, breaking a broom handle in half and then threatening to force the splintered part into my rectal passage. The second occurred when a rotund Jamaican landlady forcibly ejected me from the room in a musty old All Saints Road building that I was renting from her. I'd let one of the area's walking wounded – an acid casualty named Smiling Mike – sleep there in my absence and he'd supposedly done something unspeakable on the premises. Smiling Mike died two months after this incident. He fell whilst clambering up a drainpipe trying to break into the third-storey apartment above *Frendz*'s HQ. Hawkwind dedicated their next studio album to his memory.

Having to deal with situations like these was what ultimately soured me to the whole underground ethos. At this time in my life I had little time to be indulgent with burn-outs. That would only come to pass some years later when I became one myself. There were some focused and vibrant people still on board the counter-culture night train, but most conscripts I encountered that year were incapable of summoning up any kind of genuine work ethic to bolster their actions and rhetoric. That absurd hippie-entitlement – everything should be free, man – was still in the air like the stale scent of patchouli oil. Only now it was festering into a communal sense of frustrated bitterness over the fact that the revolution hadn't transpired and wasn't ever going to. The world was turning and they were still up on the hill like Paul McCartney's fool or King Canute on his throne as the waves surged towards him. What did I learn from this? That dreaming is never enough. Action and interaction are what count if you really want to lead a life of surprises.

When Charlie Murray and I began working for the *NME*, we both had to withstand our share of catcalls from certain self-styled underground potentates who told us in no uncertain terms that we were selling out by working for 'the man'. Charlie may have been more affected than me by these taunts as his roots within that community ran deeper.

Personally speaking, I couldn't have cared less. If 'selling out' meant being read by 100,000 people – without editorial interference – instead of 10,000, then bring it on. I'd become a very cocky fellow indeed by the time last orders were being called on 1972. The bashful kid I'd once been was now nowhere to be seen. But I had some cause for self-congratulation for I was now strapped mind, body and soul to the whirling Zeitgeist of cutting-edge popular culture until I could feel the aftershocks puncturing my very bones. Why, David Bowie had even written one of the year's most memorable songs about me. Not me specifically – but people like me certainly, the new breed come to unshackle the new decade from its now dysfunctional predecessor. 'All the young dudes carry the news,' the chorus went. It was an inspirational shout-out to me and all the other freshly empowered human peacocks to keep on defiantly kicking up dust in the face of a deeply uncertain future.

And yet I had to be careful. Glam was starting to run out of steam and I didn't want to end up some 'flash in the pan flavour of the month' type of guy. That could easily happen unless I got really, really good at what I was doing really, really quickly. The more I thought it through, the more the answer to my looming dilemma seemed to lie over in America. Kerouac had traversed its boundaries and come up with a masterpiece as a result of his incessant journeying. Maybe the land of opportunity would have a similarly transformative effect on me. I had the money for a return ticket and a few addresses. What was holding me back?

1973

In the last dying days of 1972 I was stricken with a nasty flu virus that had been circulating around London and hastily retreated to the comfort of my parents' home in Horsham in order to recuperate for the new year's dawning. Bedridden for the best part of a week, I had ample time to soberly reflect upon my sudden change in circumstances and the way it had affected my life and personality. Two contrasting self-images of relatively recent vintage continually danced inside my head. Just eighteen months earlier, I'd been a gangly, girlish figure in a school blazer dreamily skulking through the clean, unthreatening streets of suburbia – just another middle-class grammar-school-going geek trapped in the provinces. Flash forward to just three weeks ago though, and I'd suddenly gotten all brash and extrovert, dressed up like a glam-rock Christmas tree and snorting cocaine with Led Zeppelin at 3 o'clock in the morning in some four-star hotel. Two very different people in two very, very different universes.

But I don't recall ever feeling in any way daunted by the new pastures that fate had lately leapfrogged me into. Leave all that self-questioning introspection – all that 'do I really belong here?' uncertainty – to Cat Stevens and his lank-haired pallies. When you're caught up in the tidal wave of a career surge that has already extended way beyond the realm of your wildest expectations, it's best to just hang on to basic survival instincts and take each moment as it comes. With this thought uppermost in mind, I rejoined Led Zeppelin's tour of Europe on the 12th of January, when they were scheduled to set the heather ablaze throughout Bonnie Scotland.

This time around the group were more tolerant and accommodating vis-à-vis my presence in their ranks. My Daniel in the lion's den experience with them a month earlier was not repeated. I'd passed their audition and could now wander freely in their midst without fear of Peter Grant suddenly reading the riot act to me in his creepy East London lisp and then hurling me out of some third-storey window with a flick of his meaty wrist. This more congenial atmosphere immediately opened up a greater window of opportunity to study them up close and learn more about the group's peculiar human chemistry.

In Scotland, the first thing that struck me was how small the operation actually was, particularly when it toured Europe. Jimmy Page had his own guitar roadie, John Bonham had a mate of his named Mick Hinton to set up his drum kit, there was a sound mixer, whilst two other guys were employed to make sure the amps were in place and fully functioning, all under the fierce supervision of tour manager Richard Cole. From what I could tell, these six people made up the entire travelling road crew of the world's most successful band in early 1973. There were no big limousines outside the hotels and no bodyguards to protect the four musicians. With both Cole and Grant on board, there was no need for extra muscle. Imagine the entire Russian Mafia melted down to just two human forms and you'll have a fair idea of the effect that this pair had on any room they entered. People in hotel bars would just scatter when Grant and Cole sidled in together. One evil look from either of them could provoke rank strangers to defecate on the spot.

Cocooned by this two-Goliath army, the four group members bonded easily over matters involving music but seemed otherwise ill-suited to each other's basic temperaments. Page was cautious and self-contained, whilst Plant was gregarious and outward-going. Jones was the epitome of utter detachment, whilst Bonham was fiercely emotional and cursed with a notoriously short fuse.

There were deep philosophical differences also. Zeppelin's singer was at heart a good hippie son of Albion who always felt compelled to inject a light, airy love-generation sensibility into his lyrics and onstage banter. Their guitarist by contrast liked to cultivate himself as an Aleister Crowley-fixated student of the dark side and loved nothing more than to invest his group's mighty in-concert clout with an added whiff of the demonic. Page actually owned Crowley's former Scottish lair and after each show would drive back to its apparently haunted premises instead of booking himself into the hotels where everyone else was staying. He liked to shroud himself in a kind of Byronic mystique but was too inherently well-mannered and gentlemanly to be a fully qualified emissary of the 'mad, bad and dangerous to know' brigade. Uninformed people back then talked about Page's occultist dabbling as though the guitarist spent his leisure hours with his head in a cowl ritually slaughtering various species of livestock and then drinking their blood like some corny apparition in a Dennis Wheatley satanic potboiler. This was pure fiction. He was just another seeker after esoteric knowledge, a collector of old dusty books and committed student of the 'magical' information that was supposedly contained within their yellowing pages. And his interests certainly weren't shared by his fellow players, who viewed their guitarist's preoccupations with guarded amusement rather than any sense of trepidation. The real darkness looming over Led Zeppelin sprang from another source entirely.

The bullish John Bonham – I duly discovered – was the group's resident loose cannon, its most unpredictable component and scariest asset. He was a nice bloke when he was sober, but he was rarely sober for long and would often undergo an alcohol-fuelled Jekyll-to-Hyde personality transformation whilst inebriating himself in a way that was more than a little unhealthy to be in the immediate vicinity of. The rest of the group had long tired of witnessing their drummer on his frequent drunken rampages; Page, Plant and Jones simply excused themselves and left the room whenever they saw Bonham after a show downing shots of hard liquor in swift succession, his eyes turning harder and narrower with each gulp. In their absence, Richard Cole happily took on the role of Bonham's drinking buddy, and you certainly wouldn't have wanted to bump into those two down some dark alley after midnight. Cole was the real barbarian in Led Zeppelin's court – most of the deeply lurid tales of wanton cruelty associated with them actually stem from incidents initiated by him. His menacing, piratical personality dovetailed effortlessly with Bonham's belligerent drunken side; together they were double trouble writ large.

Seven years down the road, of course, Bonham's out-of-control drinking would drive the decisive final nail into Led Zeppelin's career coffin, but there was little that the others could have done to temper his thirst. In the seventies no self-respecting musician believed in twelve-step rehab and 'interventions'. Booze and drugs were just part of the landscape, something to lose yourself in whilst out on the road or in a recording studio. And Led Zeppelin in the early seventies weren't that excessive on the drug front. Plant and Jones liked to smoke pot, and all four enjoyed the odd line of cocaine, but when touring in Europe their chemical consumption was relatively frugal, particularly in comparison to what the Rolling Stones were getting up to during the same time line. Mind you, that would all change when the group toured America again just four months in the future.

It was in the eighties that some perceptive soul finally coined the ultimate description of cocaine as 'God's way of telling you you're making too much money'. Joe Boyd – in his insightful autobiography *White Bicycles* – is even more critical of the drug and its debilitating hold over the musical culture of the seventies. 'I never knew cocaine to improve anything,' he wrote. 'When the white lines came out, it was time to call it a night: the music could only get worse. If I joined in, the next day's playback would provide clear evidence of the deterioration of both the performances and of my critical ability to judge them. I suspect that the surge in cocaine's popularity explains – at least in part – why so many great sixties artists made such bad records in the following decade.'

Nowadays I concur heartily with these views. But back in the day I was less wise and infinitely more impulsive. The very idea of the drug had me hypnotised like a lemming scrambling towards a clifftop. The hype surrounding cocaine was that it somehow opened up the gateway to thinking brilliant thoughts, but the reality was invariably more brutal: sudden jagged mood swings, dry mouth, scary heart palpitations. The first time I tried it – backstage at a Hawkwind concert in October '72 – I almost fell down a long flight of stairs when the brain rush actually kicked in. The second time I was with a group called the Flamin' Groovies a month later and we all got pulled over by the police outside the dealer's Earls Court house. If someone hadn't tossed the incriminating packet of powder into a nearby garden, we'd have all been facing criminal prosecution.

God was evidently trying to tell me something, but I steadfastly refused to listen up. By early 1973 I was wasting one or two nights of every week snorting the devil's dandruff in the company of other young London-based pleasure-seekers. By the time dawn broke through the gaps in the drawn curtains of their basement lairs, I'd be feeling very brittle and twitchy indeed. The simple fact of the matter was that the drug didn't agree with my central nervous system and made me plain jittery. But I was too much of a schmuck to walk away from its temptation and most of what I consumed was offered to me for free anyway. I duped myself into thinking it would be impolite to refuse and carried on numbing my sinuses whenever the opportunity arose.

At the same time I was getting ready to launch my personal invasion on the land of opportunity. By early February everything was in place: I'd drawn all my funds out of the bank, paid for an open-ended return airline ticket to Michigan and had a special US visa stamped into my passport. In the middle of the month I boarded my flight and some ten hours later was standing on US soil.

At first the customs authorities didn't want to let me in. 'Are you a homosexual?' one of them kept asking me. If I'd said yes, they'd have sent me straight back to Limey-land. But I simply told them the truth until they relented and grudgingly allowed me entry into the Motor City. Soon enough I'd hailed a taxi and was sizing up my new surroundings: a big motorway covered with humongous gas-guzzling automobiles and bordered by huge billboards and head-spinning changes of scenery. At one point we dipped through downtown Detroit and the streets there seemed as menacing as they were congested. But then another strip of highway would open up and the buildings would suddenly look cleaner and the sidewalks a lot less threatening. Continuing seventeen miles north-west of Detroit, we arrived in a well-appointed residential area on the outskirts of Birmingham, Michigan, where Debbie Boushell and her nouveau riche parents dwelt. This would be my home away from home for all of one evening. After that I was on my own.

I'd always envisaged the Motor City as a Mecca for tough-sounding high-quality music but by the time I arrived there, the home-grown musical culture was facing a steep recession. A local heroin epidemic had killed off the MC5 and forced the Stooges to relocate in Hollywood, thus depriving the state of its two most promising hard-rock bands. Others like Bob Seger and Ted Nugent would still have to wait several years before they could start creating any kind of impact for themselves outside of Michigan. The one exception was Grand Funk Railroad, a shallow, bombastic power trio from Flint, Michigan, who played populist stoner rock specifically aimed at a new and disturbingly prevalent US demographic – teenage barbiturate-gobblers. Their God-awful records always seemed to be shacked up in the highest echelons of the *Billboard* and *Cashbox* top ten best-seller listings or polluting the airwaves in the early seventies. Like herpes, you just couldn't get rid of their feckless racket.

But the most demoralising blow to Michigan's culture had lately been dealt by Tamla Motown supremo Berry Gordy, the area's most revered music entrepreneur. In the late sixties the wily, always ahead-of-the-game Gordy had migrated to Hollywood in order to better monitor the career transformation of his beloved princess Diana Ross from singer to movie actress. He'd assured his old Hitsville U.S.A. employees that he'd never shut down Motown's original Detroit premises, but by 1970 he'd set up a more spacious Los Angeles-based studio and was compelling his most prized recent discoveries – the Jackson 5 – to record only at this new location. After that, the writing was on the wall. By October of 1972 – the month that saw Marvin Gaye reluctantly vacate his Michigan mansion and join the exodus to California – the label's downtown office had been closed down, its fabled studio – nicknamed the Snakepit – had been stripped of all its functioning recording equipment and its auxiliary session players – known as the Funk Brothers – were suddenly unemployed and not a little bitter about the way they'd suddenly been shunted aside by the big boss.

At least they weren't alone in their desolation. The whole state grieved alongside them. Motown's joyful music throughout the sixties had been such a morale-boosting tonic to the huge multiracial community from which it sprang that when the company stole away to supposedly greener pastures, Michigan felt deeply betrayed by the departure, as though their personal beacon of hope had been suddenly savagely extinguished. Motown was no longer a matter of great civic pride, the clarion call for a brighter tomorrow; it was the sound of a dream deferred, a promise unfulfilled. Detroit radio stations still played Motown's latest LA-shaped waxings but spiritually speaking this new fare had little in common with the cavalcade of uplifting hits that had been concocted at the Snakepit. The Temptations' 'Papa Was a Rollin' Stone' was the label's unavoidable smash *du jour*, the track I recall hearing the most in cars and bars throughout my stay. It was a long gloomy song about betrayal – the singer berating an absent father for deserting his family – and it perfectly nailed the local mood of brooding discontent and abandonment.

My first night in the Motor City is now something of a foggy memory – and perhaps that's just as well. I recall Debbie and her boyfriend driving me in the evening to a bar where an atrocious live band played the top-40 hits of the day. I recall a biker offering me some PCP which I politely refused. I then recall a tall blonde girl giving me a Quaalude – American Mandrax – and suggesting we both repair to a nearby motel, book a cheaply priced room and partake in sexual congress together. I can even recall entering the motel room with her, surveying its tawdry interior and thinking that Sam Cooke met his end in similar circumstances. Everything after that is a blank. I was suddenly knocked unconscious by the impact of the Quaalude on my already jet-lagged metabolism.

When I awoke many hours later, daylight was streaming through the windows. I was alone in the bed and a bird-faced Hispanic cleaning lady was standing over me ranting in an incomprehensible form of pidgin English. Debbie arrived soon after that – and boy, was she pissed off! The girl I'd accompanied to this godforsaken fuck-pit turned out to be one of her sworn enemies. She'd stormed out soon after I'd passed out, mistaking a drug-induced coma for callous rejection. I'd been in Michigan less than twenty-four hours and already had two of its native daughters on the warpath after me. Time to activate plan B.

Birmingham, Michigan – unlike its plug-ugly namesake in the English Midlands – was an attractive middle-class suburb boasting good schools, high-end property, condos, classy boutiques

Apathy for the Devil

and chintzy antique stores. But sedition still lurked within its carefully manicured borders: the town had lately begun to play host to *Creem* magazine and its rowdy editorial staff. The ferociously irreverent monthly had recently upped its national sales to 150,000 per issue and celebrated by splashing out on new office space on the second floor of the Birmingham Theatre building. Publisher Barry Kramer also rented a nearby house – 416 Brown Street – for the magazine's key employees to share. That's where I'd be spending my second night in the United States of America and most of my subsequent days and nights in the Midwest.

It had been a dream of mine: to link up with Lester Bangs and learn at the feet of the master of new rock journalism. Now my dream was about to come true. Once again I owe Debbie Boushell a debt of gratitude for helping to make it happen. She was the one who actually phoned *Creem*'s headquarters and told them about my plight regarding immediate accommodation until they relented and offered me a room for the night. She even drove me to the location. Mind you, we arrived well after midnight and I was – oh dear – once again under the foolhardy influence of the dreaded Quaalude. I may have even consumed two earlier in the evening in order to calm my nerves. I suppose I was looking to attain chemically induced courageousness. What I arrived at instead was mush-mouthed slobbering stupidity.

I remember staggering into a dimly lit living room and being surrounded by three male figures. One was short and bespectacled and introduced himself as Dave Marsh. A second – taller, California-blond and more muscular – answered to the name of Ben Edmonds. And the third was Lester Bangs. I'd never even seen a photograph of him before this night, so it was the first opportunity I ever had to gaze upon the physical reality of the man behind the byline. My first impression: he looked like a rodeo clown without the make-up. Or an auto worker on a beer break. He was a big guy with tousled black hair that was neither long nor short and a full moustache plastered across his manic grinning face. You wouldn't have called him handsome but he wasn't ugly either. Right away his basic sweet nature became apparent to me. There was a soulfulness about the guy that was palpable in its outstretched humanity.

Consider the situation for a moment. A complete stranger turns up at your front door after midnight – dressed like a god-dam professional ice-skater and visibly fucked up on tranquillisers and God knows what else – in hope of finding shelter for the night. Would you let him into your humble abode, make him welcome and even attempt to converse with him at some length? Of course you wouldn't.

But Lester wasn't like most people. He empathised with fuck-ups because he was often one himself. He gamely sat down and talked with me uncondescendingly for over an hour. He even took me upstairs to his bear-pit of a room and played me his just-received white-label copy of *Raw Power*. I don't remember if it was during that hour or the morning after that I asked him to be my teacher. I explained my situation anyway: young university drop-out lucks out at the *NME* but still needs to find his own voice as a writer in order to make the most of his good fortune. I craved guidance I couldn't find back in merry old England. Could Lester show me – by example – how to reach my full writing potential? Would he even be interested? 'Sure – OK then' was his immediate unblinking reply.

Just thinking about his generosity of spirit still makes my eyes moist. I didn't know it then but other young would-be rock scribes had already personally contacted him for tips and career guidance. One of them, Cameron Crowe, of course would later go on to write and direct an Oscar-winning film in 2000 called *Almost Famous* that evocatively transposed his real-life teenaged tutelage at the feet of guru Bangs onto the big screen. But I was the first to have made the trip all the way across the Atlantic in order to seek his indulgence, so maybe that's partly what sealed the deal. That and the fact that we both liked to get wasted. But mostly it was down to him being such a big-hearted guy.

Two days after linking up with Lester and his *Creem* co-conspirators – bingo! – I had my first face-to-face encounter with David Bowie. I'd spent a goodly portion of the previous year trying to finagle a meeting with the man – all to no avail. But in Detroit it actually came to pass. Once again I need to thank B. P. Fallon for making it happen. The imp-like Led Zeppelin publicist happened to be passing through the area with a group he was promoting called Silverhead, a London-based glam-rock quintet whose lead singer Michael Des Barres was already a drug buddy of mine. When we met up in downtown Detroit, I happened to mention that Bowie and his Spiders from Mars were playing at the nearby Cobo Hall that very night. Fallon immediately got it into his head that we should go to Bowie's hotel and make our introductions. This was a mad scheme. Bowie at that stage in his career had purposefully made himself as unapproachable as Greta Garbo. And none of us had ever actually met him before. But 'Beep' had once been Marc Bolan's PR and felt that this prior connection would suffice as a calling card. He was right too. Bowie's huge black bodyguard stationed at the door of his boss's imperial suite was handed a written note by Fallon, took it to the singer inside and came out to inform us that 'David' would be delighted to make our acquaintance later after tonight's performance. He advised us to return just after midnight.

The show itself was another mind-boggler. Not for Bowie's performance per se, which found him boldly previewing his *Aladdin Sane* material some two months before the record's actual release. He was great – more self-assured, more self-possessed – but I'd seen him live so often throughout 1972 that I already knew what to expect. No, what left me thunderstruck was the audience.

Back in little old England, Bowie's concerts had been peppered with young people dressing and behaving outrageously but it was mostly self-conscious silliness, a mickey mouse pose. They wouldn't have known real decadence if it had come out and bitten them on their bum cheeks. But over in Detroit Bowie's followers were like something out of Fellini's *Satyricon*: full-tilt pleasure-seekers devoid of anything resembling shame, limits, caution and moral scruples. I distinctly remember a local lesbian bike gang riding their bikes into the foyer of the concert hall and revving them loudly just prior to Bowie's arrival onstage. This had not been pre-arranged between the girls and Bowie's management. These women just turned up unannounced and were so scary no one dared bar their entrance.

Meanwhile, the toilets were literally crammed with people either having sex or necking pills. The whole building was like some epic porno film brought to twitching life. Back in London's West End, the best-loved theatrical presentation of the hour was an asinine farce called *No Sex Please: We're British*, a title that pretty much summed up the United Kingdom's awkward embrace of its libidinous potential even during the so-called permissive age. Put that reticence down to a mixture of instilled

Catholic guilt, cold showers, single-sex schooling and 'steady on, old boy' stoicism. Our young American cousins, however, had no such inhibitions to curb their lust. And with no life-threatening diseases then in evidence to cause further pause for thought, they were up for any kind of carnal and pharmaceutical hanky-panky you could throw at them.

This was not lost on David Bowie, whose new *Aladdin Sane* songs were clearly part-inspired by their composer coming into direct contact with the Babylonian sexual frenzy of young America in the early seventies. Two hours after he'd left the stage in triumph and had been driven back to his hotel, we gingerly approached his suite in the hope that he was still up for a bit of socialising. His man-mountain bodyguard duly beckoned us into a large room where – seated on an elegant settee – the man himself was. He immediately stood up and daintily shook our hands, welcoming us to his temporary abode. He had pointy carrot-coloured hair, shaved eyebrows, a ton of make-up slapped across his extremely pretty face and a slender androgynous physique – swathed in a red chequered blouse and electric-blue Oxford bags – that moved with the studied poise of a movie starlet from some bygone era just prior to the advent of Technicolor.

At first it felt like he had no fixed sexual identity. His mannerisms were as outrageously camp as those of any self-respecting drag queen but there was a bold streak of jack-the-laddishness immediately apparent in his general demeanour. He'd also chosen to invite several teenage girls who'd been lurking in the hotel corridor into his lair and was eyeing them up and working his charm. By the time we left, he'd already seduced one of them – a black girl. This wouldn't have been especially noteworthy save for the fact that his wife Angie was also present in the room. But she didn't appear to mind: she had her own boyfriend – a Detroit-based singer named Scott Richardson – with her anyway. I hadn't realised it at the time but I'd met her once before at the Stooges' Barons Court house sometime in the early autumn of 1972. Whilst her husband was busy touring the world as Ziggy Stardust, she'd been occupying her time consorting with Ron Asheton. Clearly she had a serious yen for rough-hewn Midwestern dudes. And even more self-evidently, the Bowies were committed swingers who enjoyed the most open of open marriages.

I can still recall the first words he directed at me. 'So you're Nick Kent. Aren't you pretty! And here I was thinking that all English rock critics looked like Richard Williams.' (Williams – one of *Melody Maker*'s most prominent writers during the sixties – was a straight-arrow Welsh clergyman's son who had been fiercely dismissive of Bowie's glitzy allure.) He stared at me coquettishly but with a wary glint in his two differently coloured eyes. It was like he had X-ray vision when it came to sizing up strangers. He looked at you and through you at the same instant. On the surface he was all lightness and breezy charm – the host with the most – but that lightning-fast brain of his hiding under the signature dyed-red hair was always in full effect, never giving too much away. He was drinking tentatively from a glass of wine but he and his wife were both very anti-drugs at the time: a girl in the room who started rolling a joint was ejected by a bodyguard at their behest.

Still, he seemed to be having a good time chatting away with other music-industry Brit expats caught in the culture shock of discovering America. I remember he kept playing 'Virginia Plain' by Roxy Music on a portable record player he had set up at one end of his suite over and over again. He thought the group was absolutely wonderful, the only other glam-rock act to truly merit his respect. That's when I realised how smart he really was. Almost anyone else in his position would have felt threatened by the advent of Roxy Music – they were UK chart rivals after all – but Bowie was intelligent enough to embrace and study what they were doing and in time appropriate some of their elements into his own evolving œuvre. That's why his career has lasted so long. He wasn't closed-minded like so many of his peers. He was a big thinker and a true professional.

Things went so swimmingly that Bowie – after chatting for a couple of hours – invited us back the next night for an impromptu party following his second show at the Cobo Hall. He told us that he didn't normally do this kind of thing – that his manager liked to keep him sealed away from all human contact as often as possible – but that his manager wasn't present on this phase of the tour and he suddenly felt the urge to mingle with the natives. Detroit's wildest young things then caught wind of this invitation and turned up in hordes to the hotel, determined to party down with their new rock deity.

The previous night we'd only been seven or eight in his suite – an easily containable collective. But now the same space was throbbing with bodies and most of them were conspicuously on some chemical or other. Bowie looked distinctly ill at ease in the centre of it all. Detroit had a well-deserved reputation as the most hard-partying city in the whole USA and even he was clearly more than a little taken aback by his gatecrashing guests' zeal for self-annihilation.

Meanwhile, outside his quarters and unbeknownst to him, his Mainman-employed touring minions were trying to initiate a series of orgies in their respective rooms with the numerous kids lined up in the hotel corridors waiting to touch their hero. Bowie's American management enablers during his Ziggy era were some of the sleaziest, most repugnant people I've ever had the misfortune to shake hands with. They were all oversexed gossip-crazed fame-seekers who'd spent time in the lower rungs of Andy Warhol's Manhattan social circle and who carried themselves with a sense of lofty self-entitlement that made the conduct of the royal family seem humble by comparison. They were so caught up in their own lust for personal celebrity that they couldn't help but resent their employer for being such a rising star himself. Still, it didn't take long for Bowie to draw much the same conclusion. Twelve months hence, he'd sack them all and initiate legal proceedings to extricate himself from Mainman's parasitical clutches.

The party wound down somewhere in the early hours of the morning. The hotel's hallways as I left the establishment looked like a modern-day rendering of a scene from *Caligula*. Suddenly I was alone and walking the streets of downtown Detroit in a drugged daze just as dawn was breaking. This was pure insanity on my part as the zone was known to be rife with muggers, rapists, killers and other predatory forms of human debris.

After stumbling down two or three streets, I decided to take refuge in the only bar that was open in the area at this ungodly hour. Now take a picture of this: me decked out like Little Lord Fauntleroy entering a run-down juke joint populated exclusively by seriously pissed-off black blue-collar dudes nursing their drinks and thinking criminal-minded thoughts. Nervously I asked the barman if there was a payphone on the premises as I was lost and needed to phone a taxi. He jerked his thumb towards the rear-end of the establishment, wouldn't even look me in the eyes.

As I was searching my pockets for change to make the call, I suddenly found myself encircled by three Negroes with brick-shithouse physiques and eyes like sleepy snakes. I sensed that I was not long for this world – but then after a nerve-wracking minute of sullen, silent scrutiny, one of them spoke up. 'Hey, man, you're English, right? Are you by any chance the guitar player for Elton John?' 'The very same,' I blurted back in a high-pitched nervous lying wail. And they actually believed me, too. Their expressions immediately softened as they told me they were big fans of 'Elton's grooves'. They were full of praise for 'my' fretboard contribution to 'Crocodile Rock' too and one of them even got me to autograph a beer mat for his wife before my taxi arrived and whisked me back to *Creem*'s headquarters.

This preposterous, potentially life-threatening incident was just one of many that occurred to me during my two-month stay in America. But somehow I always managed to come through unscathed. I honestly believed at the time that I was leading a charmed life and that nothing really bad could befall me. Laughable as it may sound now, being English was the only good-luck charm you needed back then to be instantly accepted in America. Yanks – particularly the womenfolk – had fallen head-over-heels in love with little old Limey-land when the Beatles 'invaded' their shores in 1964, and the infatuation was still going strong almost a decade later. They couldn't get enough of our quaint, wacky accents, bad teeth and bizarre eating habits. You could even talk in the incomprehensible cadences of a Geordie docker and still travel the continent getting laid from coast to coast.

Not surprisingly, my all-American male cronies at *Creem* were often resentful of all this anglophile ardour running riot throughout their proud nation. 'You goddam Limey fops!' Lester Bangs would rail at me. 'What's so great about your fucked-up culture anyway? We produce great art like the Velvet Underground, the MC5 and the Stooges, and you retaliate with David fucking Bowie and his Spiders from Mars. Whoopee! You're just reselling us Herman's Hermits for homos.' I'd retaliate by tartly informing him that unlike him I'd been born in the cradle of civilisation and that we Brits were making timeless art when Americans were still learning how to ride a horse, steal cattle and shoot each other in whore-ridden bar-rooms. That would generally shut him up.

The rest of the time we got on famously. Lester drove everywhere in a garbage-strewn jalopy that was one of his few personal possessions, and I would be there next to him in the passenger seat taking in the landscape and making sure he didn't suddenly nod out at the wheel. This sometimes occurred late at night after he'd mixed the liquor and pills and was a matter of some consternation amongst his *Creem* cohorts, who'd all experienced the phenomenon and were genuinely concerned that he'd drive into a wall one night and spend the rest of his life in traction.

These fears had recently intensified because Lester had started dating a young girl named Dori who lived in the Canadian frontier town of Windsor, Ontario, over one hundred miles away from Birmingham. He loved the place: the beer they served was extra-potent and you could buy codeine tablets over the counter at the local pharmacists. As a result, he would make almost-nightly treks there and back throughout my stay, and I would usually accompany him. Those long journeys driving across the muddy Detroit river with him at dead of night were heady experiences for me. Just five years earlier my schoolboy imagination had been seriously enflamed by reading *On the Road* and now I was actually living the full-tilt Kerouac dream, careening through the nation's ripped backsides in the company of America's latest championship-level wild man and literary blowhard.

The conversations we had ranged as far and wide as the country spread outside our speeding vehicle. Being in motion – and under the influence of amphetamines – always opened Lester up and he'd talk for hours, often littering his diatribes with intimate recollections from his mostly troubled past. He spoke emotively about his drunkard father who perished in a fire when Lester – who'd actually been christened 'Leslie Bangs' – was only nine and about his infuriating, still-living Jehovah's Witness mother whom he harboured deeply conflicted feelings for. His mother's suffocatingly possessive presence throughout his young life had scarred him with regard to developing healthy loving relationships with the opposite sex as an adult. He kept falling madly in love but the female objects of his worshipful desire – after a brief period of courtship – would almost always be put off by his kamikaze drunken mood swings and his intense emotional neediness. This was heartbreaking to behold because under his rowdy exterior lurked the beating heart of an incurable misty-eyed romantic who so desperately craved to share his life with a soulmate that his ongoing loneliness – and the demons it ignited – ended up growing like a malignant cancer within him.

Lester was equally unlucky in his choice of personal role models. One time I walked into the *Creem* house kitchen and found him in tears. He'd just finished reading a *Rolling Stone* feature in which Neal Cassady's long-suffering widow Caroline had spoken candidly for the first time about her life with her sociopathic spouse – the Dean Moriarty character in *On the Road* – and Jack Kerouac himself. The portrait she painted in words of the latter – Bangs's most revered literary idol – was far from complimentary. She called attention to Kerouac's inability to establish a healthy loving relationship with any woman, his terminal alcoholism and his hopeless mother fixation. She implied that he was basically born doomed. It was this revelation that caused Lester to weep so openly. He saw far too much of his own predicament in Kerouac's death-driven depiction.

He didn't do himself any favours in his choice of living heroes either. It's no secret that he idolised Lou Reed to the point of obsession and saw the Velvet Underground songsmith as rock music's most visionary iconic entity. A week after the aforementioned Bowie shows, Reed was booked to play a concert in Detroit and Lester managed to set up his first actual interview with the man and invited me to accompany him to the affair to act as his cornerman. It turned out to be an ugly spectacle: two drunks railing at each other over the glass-strewn Formica table of a tacky hotel bar. Reed was – relatively – civil to me but stared at Bangs throughout their long over-inebriated conversation as though he was face to face with some mentally challenged country bumpkin who'd just escaped from the local nuthouse.

Lester later wrote up the encounter in a piece for *Creem* he entitled 'Deaf Mute in a Telephone Booth' that's since been reproduced in one of his two posthumous collections. It's a vibrant, one-sided account of what happened that day but it neglects to mention at least one pertinent detail. Driving back to the *Creem* house directly after the interview had concluded, Lester was so distraught he veered into a garage by mistake, smashed into a petrol pump and almost totalled his precious car. For three days afterwards he replayed what he could remember of their meeting of minds and fretted about the contemptuous way Reed had beheld him. I told him that trying to locate anything resembling human warmth, empathy and decency in Reed's personality was as futile an exercise as trying to get blood from a stone. Then I bid him and the rest of the *Creem* corps a temporary adieu and boarded a flight direct to Los Angeles. I'd been entranced by visions of the Wild West ever since I'd seen my first Western at age six. Now the time had come to kick up some dust of my own within its untamed borders.

The first thing that left an indelible impression on my mental faculties once I'd debarked in the golden state and headed straight to Hollywood was seeing the profusion of palm trees poking out of the pavement on all the sidewalks. The second occurred when I actually walked around Hollywood on my first full day there and quickly discovered just how small it actually was. I was expecting a sprawling metropolis but the reality was more like being in a relatively opulent, sun-baked little village intersected by big highways.

Promenading down the Sunset Strip was all you needed to do back then if you wanted a one-on-one encounter with the city's resident music- and movie-makers; within twenty-four hours of being there, I'd passed both Jackson Browne and David Crosby on the street. Two blocks away on Santa Monica Boulevard I found myself queuing one evening alongside four-fifths of the original Byrds outside the Troubadour folk club. Later on, whilst walking down the same street, I heard live music emanating from a shopfront. I peered in the window and saw Carl and Dennis Wilson with members of their current touring band rehearsing

songs for a local upcoming Beach Boys show. I must have stood
there for an hour staring goggle-eyed as they worked up an
arrangement for their latest single 'Sail On, Sailor', but that hour
was my very own Californian dream come true. As a teenager the
Beach Boys' music had held me spellbound and now I was present in their idyllic stomping ground being treated to a private
concert all of my own. Could it get any better than this?

Actually, yes. Four days later I attended the show they'd been
preparing for and that ended up being my all-time quintessential
golden-state souvenir. I think back to that night and instantly
recall being surrounded on all sides by three thousand of the
most perfect human specimens imaginable – a moveable Aryan
super-race with surfboards instead of swastikas. I seemed to be
the only audience member in the building without golden
streaming hair and a golden walnut tan. It was like standing in a
field of swaying human corn listening to the music of the
spheres.

But golden visions aside, there was something deeply rotten
putrefying up the state of California in 1973 and nowhere more so
than in Hollywood itself: most of the time for me it was like getting to hang out in some biblical place of damnation with people
getting stoned on drugs instead of getting stoned to death. The
first week, I stayed at the Continental Hyatt House hotel with my
Brit pals Silverhead, who were playing a residency at the famed
Whisky a Go Go. Both buildings are situated less than half a mile
away from each other on the Sunset Strip and most evenings I'd
take the fifteen-minute stroll to the venue. Virtually every step of
the way I'd be approached by extremely intense young people
trying to sell me their home-made jewellery or trying to indoctrinate me into some wacky religious cult.

I'd already been around my share of 'damaged hippie' types back in Ladbroke Grove but their American cousins on the West Coast were a far more harrowing bunch. They'd rant on and on about the looming apocalypse until they were literally foaming at the mouth. And their eyes wouldn't leave you alone, always staring as though they could simply hypnotise you into following their will. Charles Manson was safe behind bars but his many acid-crazed messianic wannabes were still pimping up the streets of Hollywood every evening. People living up in the Hollywood Hills all had fierce guard dogs posted at the front of their properties. They weren't going to let what happened to Sharon Tate four years earlier happen to them.

Sartorially speaking, young Hollywood men still tended to stick to their end-of-the-sixties Neil Young copycat look: frayed blue denim work-shirt, dilapidated blue jeans, some native Indian jewellery around their necks or wrists if they felt like being flashy. But most of the teenaged creatures in the region were all over the freshly imported glam bandwagon like a rash on a wild dog. There was even a new club in town exclusively devoted to catering to their tastes: the English Discotheque fronted by Rodney Bingenheimer, a sad-eyed West Coast Zelig with no discernible personality of his own but an abundant love of all things English and celebrity-driven. Night after night he'd bludgeon the tiny mirror-walled dance hall with the shiny-sounding glam racket of Sweet, Slade and Suzi Quatro compelling hordes of scantily clad, barely pubescent girls to cavort suggestively whilst trying to stay aloft in their preposterous stack-heeled platform shoes. For jailbait connoisseurs and recruiting local chicken hawks, the place must have been a glimpse of heaven on earth, but it was really more like watching film director Russ Meyer's hilariously sordid Hollywood pop spoof *Beyond the Valley of the Dolls* being re-enacted badly by a cast of pill-popping, conniving twelve-year-olds.

I got to know several of these girls during my stay – though not in the biblical sense, you understand. They'd start talking to you and never stop. By the time you got a word in edgeways, you'd been given their entire life history to date. It was always the same: rich divorced parents, no love at home, lecherous stepfather, trouble at school. And they were all blindly convinced they were bound for glory. 'I'm thirteen now but when I'm sixteen I'll be as famous as Marilyn Monroe' was their personal mantra. All they needed was for Andy Warhol to walk into the English Discotheque one night and see them in action and – shazam – they'd be all set for their journey into the stratosphere. They'd fallen hook, line and sinker for that 'everyone will be famous for fifteen minutes' crap of Warhol's to the point where it had become their ditzy, all-consuming religion. The sad reality: they were just lost, damaged little girls like the Jodie Foster character Iris in *Taxi Driver* – deluded broken blossoms who'd grown up too fast and had all the innocence and wholesomeness fucked out of them at too young an age.

I should point out here that though temptation often came a-knocking at my door whilst in Hollywood, I generally refrained from indulging in full sexual contact. It wasn't a matter of personal prudishness so much as simple bad luck. Back in Michigan I'd managed to contract a urinary infection and a spectacular case of the crabs just prior to hitting the golden state and didn't have the simple common sense to go to a nearby pharmacy and buy some lotion to make the two conditions disappear once I'd arrived. Finally I had my pubic hair shaved by a Japanese woman

called Flower who'd taken several tranquillisers just prior to groping for the razor: not an incident I'd ever care to repeat. She and
her girlfriend let me stay in their Sunset Strip apartment for a
couple of nights. They were strippers – serious hard-core girls but
kind-hearted nonetheless. Her room-mate was often teary-eyed.
Her beloved drug-dealing boyfriend had been offed by the Mafia
just two months earlier. Compared to the glam-rock Lolitas in the
region, they were generally more level-headed and pragmatic in
their dealings with the outside world, but even they had bought
into the ludicrous notion that fame would one day be theirs for
the taking. Everyone living in Hollywood back then seemed sad-
dled with the same sorry delusion. The poor things.

In the midst of this weird little fame-hungry, sex-crazed town
lurked Iggy and the Stooges, who'd moved into a communal
house overlooking the Hollywood Hills just three months ago
after bidding a not especially fond farewell to London's more
limited nightlife. The Doors had been LA's most acclaimed musical ambassadors of darkness and dread but now, following Jim
Morrison's untimely death in 1971, they were gone and Iggy had
duly decided that he and the Stooges should assume the same
creepy mantle. Hollywood really brought out the beast in him:
the restrained, thoughtful young man I'd encountered in
London throughout 1972 had been replaced by a snake-eyed,
cold-hearted, abrasively arrogant trouble magnet.

He'd transformed his look too, dyeing his hair surfer blond
and using his considerable leisure time to cultivate a luxuriously
bronzed suntan under the relentless California sun. At first
glimpse he seemed positively aglow with rude health but the tan
and hair dye were really there to mask a darker secret: he was back
on the smack. And though it had yet to diminish his physical

allure, his re-embrace of heroin had already tainted his personality, making him generally mean-spirited, self-centred and plain loopy. Iggy's Hollywood persona was captured for posterity in a televised interview he gave in early '73 to the venerable disc jockey and US TV host Dick Clark. Clark – clearly ill at ease with his subject – kept asking Iggy if he was truly 'decadent'. The singer grumpily retorted, 'Decadence is decomposition and I ain't decomposing. I'm still here.' But what about moral decadence?, Clark continued earnestly. 'Are you morally degenerate?' 'Oh, I don't have any morals,' Iggy chimed back cheerfully. He wasn't kidding either. Now that's not something a sane human being would normally want to share with the rest of the world. But Iggy in 1973 wasn't a sane person. In his mind he may have been voicing his private vision of himself as the American Zarathustra – beyond good and evil, free as a bird in mind, body and will. But the remark also bore the hollow ring of a junkie's empty brag. Either way, his new amoral approach to life ended up making him few friends in the golden state and elsewhere.

In mid-March the Stooges returned to Michigan in readiness for their first concert on US soil in two years, with Detroit's Cobo Hall booked for the 23rd of the month. It should have been a triumph – the hooligan Stooges, bloodied but unbowed, returning to the baying hordes who first supported them with a new album, a new label and new high-powered management. But it didn't quite pan out that way. Iggy pretty much set the tone for what would transpire when he turned up to a live interview for a prominent Midwestern radio outlet a few days prior to the show. He proceeded to perform an impromptu striptease on the air whilst dancing around the room to tracks from *Raw Power*. The sound of his penis slapping against his lower torso was inadvertently captured on one of the studio microphones and beamed out to radio sets the length and breadth of its waveband.

I flew back to Michigan from LA purely to witness the Stooges' homecoming show. I remember Bangs, Ben Edmonds and I visiting them at the downtown Detroit hotel they were holed up in the night before the gig for a pep-talk. Iggy's room was dark – drawn curtains, no lights on – and his mood was darker. Real success was potentially within his grasp once more and yet the prospect seemed to spook him more than stimulate him.

The show itself drew a full house and the crowd was raucous and welcoming. The Stooges played well – most of *Raw Power* plus two new compositions worked up whilst resident in Hollywood – and Iggy was in pretty good form but the set lasted not much longer than forty minutes. The group left the stage to wild acclaim and were planning to return for an encore but manager Tony Defries – who'd flown in especially for the concert – expressly forbade it. He felt that true stars should always leave their audiences craving more and that encores were beneath his clientele. This kind of thinking may have worked for Bowie but for the Stooges it proved a tragic miscalculation. The hall duly erupted in a cacophony of boos and catcalls when the group refused to return. Bangs nailed the whole scenario best. Shaking his head sadly, he muttered, 'Once again the Stooges have managed to pluck defeat from the jaws of victory.'

Someone threw a party for the group after the show in a swanky Detroit house that everyone gatecrashed. In the living room, many guests were glued to a large colour TV showing the Oscar ceremonies beamed in live from Hollywood. On screen, a woman no one recognised was dressed up like an Apache squaw and was talking earnestly about the plight of the Native American Indian.

Marlon Brando – we later discovered – had sent her in his place to accept a best actor award for his role in *The Godfather*.

One of those captivated by the spectacle was Tony Defries, who'd commandeered the most throne-like seat in the room and had just lit up yet another jumbo cigar. A guy smoking a joint nearby turned to him at one point and asked, 'So, Tony, do you think David Bowie will maybe be handing out an Oscar next year?' 'No,' Defries replied with a feigned indifference, 'David will be accepting an Oscar next year.'

But upstairs trouble was a-brewing. Iggy was stalking the premises with narcotics in his bloodstream and malice in his heart. At one point a drunken girl made the mistake of trying to hug him and he bitch-slapped her away so forcefully she came close to falling backwards down a long flight of stairs. The party wound down soon after that.

What on earth was going on in this guy's mind to make him behave in such a fashion? It was the drugs pure and simple: Iggy liked them but those same drugs rarely seemed to like him. Heroin curdled his personality and cocaine stimulated instant mental disturbance. Downers left him comatose and uppers sent his mind reeling towards insanity. But still he persevered, believing in his heart of hearts that personal substance abuse and the cerebral disorientation they promoted within him were the key to attaining full Iggyness.

Bangs shared much the same philosophy too: he was an ardent apostle of the school of thought that believed the more you pollute yourself, the closer you get to true artistic illumination. Plus Iggy had bought into the whole Antonin Artaud shtick of the performer only being able to achieve greatness by staging his own madness in the public arena. That's what he meant by the lines 'I am dying in a story / I'm only living to sing this song' that he sang on 'I Need Somebody', *Raw Power*'s penultimate selection. It was a prophecy just waiting to be fulfilled. He and the Stooges were about to be slowly ground into dust for the second time in their short career.

Finally I wound down my American odyssey by spending a week in Manhattan in early April. Like other feckless boho wannabes of the era, I stayed at the Chelsea Hotel – renowned for having played host to Dylan, Leonard Cohen and the beat poets back in the mystic sixties. Unfortunately its vaunted reputation masked a shabby reality: the place was a literal fleapit with cockroaches visible in all the carpeting and grimy sheets, busted mattresses and malfunctioning black-and-white TV sets in every room.

Little wonder then that I spent most of my time outside. The New York Dolls were playing a week-long residency at a local joint known as Kenny's Castaways. I'd lurk around there most nights. It was like a tiny pub with a stage and room for no more than a hundred bodies to congregate. The group – playing some of their first shows since the death of their original drummer Billy Murcia – really made sense in this kind of low-key close-to-home setting. Whenever I caught them live on bigger stages and outside of New York, they were always a big disappointment. The pressure, unfamiliar locale and lack of easy-to-contact drug dealers would invariably cause them to play like a hard-on-the-ear train wreck in full progress.

But in a nondescript Manhattan watering hole like Kenny's, their limp-wristed hooligan magic could be summoned to full effect. The guitarists still posed far better than they actually played but their new drummer Jerry Nolan had brought a much-needed dynamism to their formerly clunky grooves and their singer David Johansen was as smart as a whip. His between-songs repartee was always priceless and he sang in a deep lascivious croon like Big Joe Turner sporting nylon stockings and high-heeled slip-ons. He was the brightest, most professional and most ambitious of the bunch, the only one you could imagine going on to enjoy a long-term showbiz career, if not as an inspired Jagger clone then at least as a credible stand-up comic. The others, though, were too fenced in by their own musical limitations. One evening they invited me to be a fly on the wall at a local studio where they intended to demo a new song called 'Jet Boy', and it became increasingly apparent as the session progressed that certain players barely knew how to even tune their instruments correctly. This carefree indifference to basic musical convention coupled with a shared state of chemical befuddlement would ultimately prove their undoing in the months to come.

Unless they were otherwise engaged, the Dolls could always be found every midnight doing their usual human-peacock routines at Max's Kansas City, Manhattan's most exciting nightspot. On the ground floor was an excellent restaurant and bar, with a private room for the Warhol crowd and other self-styled celebrities. People came mostly to get loaded and socialise but the most enticing part of the establishment for me was the tiny upstairs room where they put on live concerts. In the days I was resident in Manhattan I saw Lowell George's Little Feat, Tim Buckley and Gram Parsons perform unforgettable shows in a space you'd have been hard-pressed to swing a cat in.

Buckley in particular was a revelation. I'd been a fan of his back when he was attempting a sort of angel-voiced jazz-folk synthesis, but he'd recently jettisoned that approach and hooked up with a straight rock band in order to sell more records. He had a brand-new album out called *Greetings from L.A.* which I didn't particularly like and so I attended the show with certain misgivings. As I'd suspected, his back-up unit were nothing to write home about but Buckley was so on fire that night that he didn't really need any support. I've never seen or heard another performer use his or her voice as bewitchingly as he managed to do before or since that performance. The guy was gifted with an extraordinary five-octave range and he could summon any sound from his larynx – from a blue yodel to a jazz trumpet to a police siren. Take it from one who saw both live: his son Jeff was great but Buckley senior was greater. Women were just wilting in front of the stage whenever he sang.

The same couldn't be said when Gram Parsons followed Buckley's brief residency some days later. He looked bad – a vision of toxic bloat in ill-fitting cowboy duds and a boozer's moustache – and his voice was distinctly frail. But inspired by his new partner Emmylou Harris's rich harmony counterpoint, he slowly rose to the occasion and the pair duetted emotively on a brace of shit-kicker country ballads that normally would have sounded distinctly out of place with the glitzy demi-monde frequenting Max's. But I looked around and the little room was littered with people who looked like they'd just stumbled out of a bad Lou Reed song, wiping actual tears from their eyes. That was Parsons's gift: he could still break anyone's heart with his music, no matter how fucked up he was or they were.

Finally in mid-April my money ran out and I flew back from New York's LaGuardia Airport to Heathrow. Once through customs, I went looking for a newsagent in order to buy the latest *NME*, a paper I'd seen little of in the past two months as it wasn't sold anywhere in America. Leafing through the issue I'd just purchased I came to the centre and found that a long article I'd scribbled and then posted from Michigan about my afore-mentioned encounters there with David Bowie was taking pride of place.

The first night we met, a young girl present in the room had taken a photo of Bowie and me, and when I bumped into her in a club a few nights later, she gave me the little colour snap she'd had developed. As a joke, I'd sent it along with the article to the paper, never thinking they'd actually be able to print the thing. But there it was – me and the Dame grinning and holding each other like a couple of New Orleans transsexuals during Mardi Gras – taking up a large portion of one whole page. My first reaction on seeing it was one of stark horror: after all, it wasn't exactly the most manly image to have projected out to the general public. But it certainly got me more noticed. Blokes at gigs would suddenly sidle up and offer me a joint with the inevitable damp cardboard filter. Women in London nightclubs would wink and flirt with a more promiscuous air. Old people would invite me to open their local garden fête and big dogs would nuzzle up and lick my hand whenever I promenaded down the streets. Actually, I'm lying on the last two counts – but still these were heady times and I was twenty-one, unattached and soaking up every second with unabashed glee.

One thing I learned though: 'Everybody loves a winner' is an often-quoted truism but it isn't – strictly – true. When someone attains success rapidly, former acquaintances often tend to experience pangs of excruciating envy that inevitably destabilise the ongoing relationship. You get your face in the papers often enough and rank strangers begin harbouring grudges against you for no clear reason. It's not all champagne and blow jobs in other words. Things can start to get nasty. You can quickly find yourself the victim of ugly, unfounded rumours. You'll be in some bar and some drunken oaf will get up in your face, nail you with his spittle and beery breath, call you a wanker and offer to beat you up in the car park. Fame is a double-edged sword in other words. It's great to wave around but you don't want to be falling on its blade.

In point of fact, fame and celebritydom have long been the proverbial kiss of death for creative writers. Truman Capote was destroyed by the success of *In Cold Blood* and his heedless embrace of the American talk-show circuit. Hunter S. Thompson never wrote anything great after *Fear and Loathing* made him an American stoner icon. More recently, both Salman Rushdie and Martin Amis have seen their talent decrease at the same alarming rate as their global notoriety has increased. It's elementary, really; writers by the very nature of their work need to stay lurking in the shadows in order to do the job properly. That's where you can stand back and get the big picture. The more invisible a writer is, the better placed he or she will be to fully penetrate the subject matter. If, however, you get enticed into stepping into the celebrity spotlight yourself, you're only going to make yourself feel self-conscious, and that self-consciousness will end up paralysing your creative perspective and leaving you bereft of insight.

My employers at the *NME* shared a different view, however, and missed no opportunity to push their writers further into the pop spotlight. I couldn't knock it as a form of instant ego-gratification but it always had its share of bad repercussions. Charles Shaar Murray and I started getting unhealthily competitive around this juncture. Back in '72, he, Ian MacDonald and I had briefly bonded in a Three Musketeers 'all for one and one for all' kind of way. I'd crashed at Charlie's Islington flat from time to time and we'd often shared each other's hopes and dreams like young men on the cusp of achieving full-blown adulthood are sometimes prone to do. But that open channel we shared soon got dismantled and I'm still not exactly sure why the breakdown and ensuing animosity occurred.

My memory tells me that once I'd returned from the USA our friendship speedily soured. Partly it was to do with his meddlesome girlfriend – who'd gone to the same university as me. I knew her to be trouble and had warned Charlie early in the relationship that she wasn't ideal 'wife' material. But he was too love-stung to see her shortcomings and my remarks may have been misinterpreted as unwarranted interference. That was the start, anyway. All I know is that from then on there was a chilly edge between us and our basic temperaments clashed so much that I sometimes found it hard to physically be in the same room as him. Looking back, I can see it now as a couple of juvenile hot-heads having a never-ending ego stand-off, but at the time I was still too immature, and none of the older, supposedly leveller heads at the paper chose to step in and talk real sense to us.

Maybe they liked the unfolding drama and thought that pitting Charlie against me would be a further sales boost. That was the problem, see: few amongst them – apart from Nick Logan – seemed to behave like real adults. There was an axis at the *NME* that was like still being stuck back in primary school. I'd sit and listen to them sometimes and close my eyes and it would feel like I was back in the playground again, watching someone get their sweeties stolen. These people were closing in on thirty and yet they were still talking like they were thirteen in the head. I couldn't fathom this at all because I'd not been long out of school myself and couldn't wait to catapult myself into the furthest recesses of hard-core X-rated young adulthood. The fucking playground was the last place on earth I wanted to return to.

One striking example of this infantilism that really got my goat was the way certain staff members took such unholy glee in deriding Roxy Music's Bryan Ferry. Tony Tyler – the ringleader – had previously worked at Roxy's EG management company as Emerson, Lake and Palmer's press officer and he remembered Ferry often haunting the premises prior to RM's actual formation. He even once auditioned unsuccessfully to become King Crimson's resident vocalist. According to Tyler, he'd been a humble, self-effacing Geordie lad back then but recent success had spun his head into another stratosphere and made him haughty and feverishly self-fixated. He may have been right too but his decision to needle Ferry ceaselessly by calling him a series of ever-increasingly silly names in print was a spectacularly wrong-headed way of venting his concern.

This was doubly short-sighted because Roxy were really taking off in the spring of '73. Their just-released second album *For Your Pleasure* was all the rage throughout most of Europe and – with Bowie spending most of his time breaking the States – they'd lately become Britain's best-loved thinking person's glam ambassadors. The *NME* needed them to keep expanding their weekly sales base, but Roxy needed the *NME* too in order to stay in the big media spotlight. That's where I came in: the group heartily detested my colleagues but were nonetheless amenable to inviting me on tours with them. I'd once dubbed them 'lounge lizards' in a review – it was a term my grandfather used to employ to describe the louche gigolo types he'd encountered in his youth – and they'd taken a shine to me from that point on.

On the road, we tended to enjoy each other's company. They were still snooty and arrogant, but by this time I'd become pretty snooty and arrogant myself, so we were a good fit in that respect. Roxy was still a group at this point but, unbeknownst to the rest of us, Bryan Ferry was getting ready to assert his dominion on the project. That summer he gave Brian Eno his marching orders against the wishes of other group members and installed a young prog-rock-schooled multi-instrumentalist named Eddie Jobson to take his place. It was a potentially suicidal decision on Ferry's part – Eno, in spite of his instrumental shortcomings, had always been a major asset to the group's image and personality – but he could no longer bear sharing the acclaim and spotlight with someone as wilfully ambitious as he.

It's funny for me to think back on it now but Brian Eno and I actually got quite close during that specific period. We'd hang out together a lot in London, visit cinemas and nightclubs and generally swan around, trying to impress the girls with our hermaphroditic allures and fledgling pop-star creds. He was good company then: extremely witty, extremely bright but not pretentious and full of himself like he later became. Still, our budding friendship was doomed to be short-lived as we differed so fundamentally as people. Brian didn't take drugs and was generally scornful of those who did. As you've already probably ascertained, this was not a view I happened to share.

But I had a much bigger problem relating to his concept of 'what art really is'. To me, art was a deep expression of the human soul, something you needed to struggle with in order to get fully expressed. To Eno, though, the creative process was simply about throwing different things at the wall and whatever ends up actually sticking to the wall – hey, that's art. I saw this approach executed at close quarters later that year when he recorded his first solo album *Here Come the Warm Jets* in a tiny recording studio situated somewhere in Clapham. Hawkwind's drummer and I contributed the anarchic piano part to one of its tracks, a number called 'Blank Frank', earning us the credit 'Nick Kool and the Kool-Aids' on the vinyl album sleeves as a consequence. But I didn't really like his music and possibly told him so or wrote something in the *NME* to that effect – I don't exactly remember – but from a certain point on we rarely socialised. Understandable, really. We were both on diametrically opposed career and lifestyle paths.

One evening in early summer he and I attended a Gary Glitter concert at the Finsbury Park Rainbow. Two girls approached us in the foyer as we were leaving and invited us to a party they were throwing a few days later. I thought nothing more of the invitation until one of them later phoned me at the *NME* office to repeat the offer. Having nothing better to do that evening, I went along.

The address was somewhere deep in the bowels of North London: a big house, as I recall. But nothing was really going on to constitute a genuine party atmosphere. The girls were glib and full of small talk and there were no drugs to be had anywhere on the premises. I was getting ready to make my excuses and leave when a tall skinny girl suddenly entered the living room, where everyone was awkwardly mingling. She was dressed from head to foot in blue denim and looked strangely agitated as she paced around. Then she opened her mouth, addressing no one in particular. Her accent was instantly recognisable to me: it sprang from the American Midwest. But it also had something of an unsettlingly whiney edge to it. 'Oh man,' she began, 'my life is just so shitty at the moment.' And then she proceeded to itemise all her recent personal setbacks in excruciating detail. At first I sat there watching her in a state of quiet alarm. I thought to myself, 'Who is this badly dressed harridan and why should I be even remotely interested in listening to her sorry lamentation?'

But then all of a sudden she terminated her list of woe by moaning, 'And the worst thing is, man – someone stole my Stooges albums. Now I've really got nothing to live for.' In that very instant, an invisible bond was forged between us. Stooges fans were so few and far between back then that whenever I met another like-minded apostle, I instantly made a point of getting better acquainted. I told her I actually knew Iggy, and that got her attention. 'So should I know who you are?' she asked. 'Not necessarily,' I replied. 'Well, I'm Chris,' she continued. 'Chris Hynde from Akron, Ohio.'

We started chatting away about how *Fun House* and *Raw Power* were the two greatest rock albums ever made, but then a drunk bloke – who I later discovered was the manager of a Scottish band called Nazareth – began sexually propositioning her in an extremely blunt fashion. She told the guy to go fuck himself and then invited me to share the fare of a taxi back to her one-room accommodation in Clapham South. I didn't find her that physically alluring but I could already tell she was intelligent and wanted to continue our conversation, so I tagged along.

When we got to her lodgings, the first thing that struck me was that one of the four walls was covered with photos cut from newspapers of Keith Richards and Iggy Pop. Right away, I could tell the woman was blessed with exquisite taste. Apart from that, the room was pretty bare: no record player, no portable telly, one chair and one single bed and not much else. So we sat down and talked late into the night, and it became quickly evident to both of us that we had much in common. We'd both been to university, she at Kent State, where four protesting students had been shot to death by riot police just three years earlier, an incident that Neil Young immortalised in his song 'Ohio'. We'd both lost our virginity at age nineteen and then followed it up with extended periods of sexual promiscuity. We both loved great rock music with an all-consuming passion. She'd been turned on to it at the same time I had – just when the Beatles were coming into vogue. She told me that when she first heard their records, it was so overwhelming she literally got down on her knees, placed her hands together and prayed to the radio whence they came.

It was a different story though when she talked about her current situation. She'd arrived in London three months ago and nothing had really worked out for her since. She'd briefly sung with a bar band back in Cleveland and wanted to pursue some kind of musical career here but had yet to find any kindred Limey spirits to share her dream with. In the meantime she'd gotten stuck in a nine-to-five job, making coffee and answering the phones in some architect's office; her life had lately become somewhat aimless – she readily admitted – and she was starting to feel so depressed she was seriously considering returning to Cleveland.

Then she said something that truly floored me: she said one of the key deciding factors in her coming to London was an article she'd read some months ago in a British music paper about her beloved Iggy Pop. I asked her to describe it further and realised the article in question was one of mine – my first-ever *NME* feature in point of fact.

A deep connection was starting to form between us but the hour was already late – 3 a.m.-ish – and it was time for counting sheep. She showed me to an adjacent room full of large sculpted gargoyles – the guy whose room it was created these hideous things to act as special effects in horror films – and I promptly fell asleep on the bed propped against one wall. Three hours later, I was rudely awoken. Light was pouring through a tear in the curtain and 'Chris' was standing before me in a blouse and knickers. For a split second, I thought that this was some kind of sexual come-on – but it most certainly wasn't. She was crying – tears running all down her face – and in obvious physical discomfort. She knelt down holding her stomach and started writhing on the bed next to me from the pain she was experiencing. I just lay there holding her and making soothing sounds telling her that it was going to be all right. What else could I do? I offered to take her to a hospital but she didn't want to go.

After more than an hour, the stabbing pain in her lower abdomen abated enough for her to return to her room. It was almost 8 a.m. and I had work to do, so I bade farewell to 'Chris' and strode to Clapham South tube station. I was due to interview Slade at Wembley Stadium in two hours and then had to write the encounter up in just twenty-four hours to make the Monday *NME* deadline. In other words, I had to focus on matters at hand and think of penetrating questions to ask Noddy Holder and his wacky brood of Black Country fashion victims.

Still, it was difficult to push the girl I'd just met to the back of my mind. I'd never met a young woman before who'd been so cranky and yet so intelligent, so tough-talking and yet so terribly vulnerable. It would be a further two weeks before I'd actually return to her Clapham bedsit and re-establish contact, but our first meeting certainly preyed on my thoughts throughout those fourteen days.

This is my version of how I met Chrissie Hynde. Chrissie's is different. She claims that after she invited me to her room, I returned the following day with all my worldly possessions in a removal van and simply moved into her room without even asking her in the first place. Her retrospective mind must be playing tricks on her. Her version is untrue and also manages to misrepresent the tenor of our early relationship. From the start, I felt protective towards her and treated her with nothing but tenderness and empathy. I wasn't trying to use her or exploit her in any way. It was the exact opposite, in fact: I wanted to help her find her place in London, to make her feel cared for and included. In strict point of fact, I didn't even move in with her until we'd known each other for at least two months and only after she'd openly invited me to do so.

You see, since returning from the States in April, I'd been essentially homeless. I had no bolt-hole in London to call my own and tended to float around, crashing on friends' sofas when not successfully importuning kind-hearted women for temporary accommodation. Then in either June or July I'd bumped into my pal Lemmy from Hawkwind at the Speakeasy Club. He and I shared much in common, specifically the same birthday and a committed taste for the wild things in life, and so when he mentioned that he'd just moved into a house somewhere between Gloucester Road and Earls Court and that there were other vacant rooms to rent there, I promptly decided to become a tenant too.

He then produced a spare front-door key from one of his many pockets and handed it to me. I thanked him and left him at the bar in order to inspect my new premises. Once I'd located the address and let myself in, it didn't take me long to work out that the place was in fact a squat. A worryingly thin young woman – the only person present in the house – took me upstairs right to the top floor and showed me the room I'd be inhabiting: it consisted of four walls, a small window and a mattress on the floor with a sheet spread over it. It was late so I disrobed and went to sleep on the mattress, using the sheet as covering. The next morning I awoke with a familiar feeling of deep irritation all around my scrotum. The crabs I'd recently left in Hollywood had come back to play havoc with my genitalia once more and this time I hadn't even had sex. They'd been lurking in the mattress. What was this godforsaken place that I had lately come to dwell in?

I got my answer as soon as I went downstairs. Lemmy was there with his eyes on fire surrounded by five or six German people who looked like they hadn't washed themselves since 1965. They were all hard-core speed freaks and they'd just scored some pure amphetamine sulphate powder, which they were furiously chopping into long lines and snorting, letting out wild whooping screams whenever the drug burned into their nasal membranes. Lemmy offered me a taste and I inhaled one tiny line. I didn't sleep after that for four whole days and nights. Fortunately, I didn't spend that time awake in Lemmy's house, otherwise I would probably have been netted in some police bust. I just left and never went back again.

It was after that experience – and a speedy visit to the chemists to once again eliminate body lice – that I mentioned my ongoing home-hunting dilemmas to Chrissie and she gamely suggested I

move in with her for the time being. So I did. My worldly possessions at the time amounted to about eighty vinyl albums, a cardboard box filled with well-leafed paperbacks, a record player, an
acoustic guitar and two large paper bags containing my flashy
clothes. They made the room less empty-looking and generally
more homely.

The first night I moved in, she reached out for my guitar and
attempted to perform one of her self-penned songs for me. Her
voice was strong and her phrasing as clear as a bell but her rendition kept breaking down because it took her a good half-minute
to regroup her fingers on the fretboard each time she had to
change chords. I could see she still had a lot of work ahead of her
if she wanted to become the confident professional musician she
dreamed of presenting herself as. But that was OK: she was a
human work in progress and so was I. More than that, I saw us as
kindred spirits whose fates were mystically intertwined. I was
starting to fall in love with the woman.

It was a somewhat gradual process, though, because – to be
frank – she wasn't the easiest person to show emotional warmth
to. There was an authentically wild and abrasive side to her personality – a trash-talking biker-girl mindset that she'd suddenly
assume whenever the mood would take her – that was often hard
to coexist with. She even boasted of having been initiated into
the local Cleveland chapter of the Hells Angels just prior to moving to London. She had a name for this loud shameless alter ego
of hers too – Bernice – which she had sown onto the back of her
regulation denim jacket.

She rarely drank liquor but on the odd occasions that she did,
'Bernice' would materialise and cause an almighty ruckus anywhere she happened to find herself. Sometimes I'd look at her

mouthing off and trying to start fights and ask myself, 'What in God's name are you doing chaperoning this shrill, charmless creature around? Can't you see she's a lost cause?' But then she'd lose the fake bravado and revert back to the more approachable personality that I'd first fallen in love with and that invisible bond we shared would once more reassert itself. I'd never experienced anything like this before in a relationship, but then again I'd never really been in love before – at least not in the adult sense of the word. I was about to find out, though. And so was she.

We kept getting closer until we were practically stuck together like glue. As the room we shared was a bit of a dump, we mostly floated around the night-time streets of London – sometimes going to gigs or taking in a late-night film but otherwise always on the move. The heels on our boots were always looking worn-down because of this restless trait. We seemed to share the same wacky belief that the more you walk around a place, the more it becomes your own personal fiefdom. It was sublime because at that point in time we were totally in sync with each other. It was like having a twin, only better because of the deep romantic attachment growing between us.

Meanwhile, the summer of '73 came and went without much pomp and circumstance. London was still the centre of the pop universe but there weren't many interesting new bands turning up on the local grass-roots club circuit. In retaliation, several London pubs began booking live rock acts in order to drum up more customers for their liquor and a new phenomenon was duly sired: pub rock.

Mostly it was the province of ugly blokes who dressed like roadies and played old Chuck Berry songs badly. But there was one band who stood out from the rest as a demented harbinger of things to come and they called themselves Kilburn and the High Roads. Throughout the autumn, Chrissie and I saw them on a succession of dilapidated pub stages, plying their trade to a tiny clique of admirers. The singer and drummer were both physically deformed, another member was a midget and the rest of the line-up looked as though they'd walked out of some fifties Ealing comedy about clueless East End spivs. Their music wasn't rock so much as a vaguely menacing *mélange* of cockney music hall and roots reggae, and it was far too wilfully eccentric to ever find favour with mainstream tastes of the hour, but I still wrote a glowing critique of their unique attributes in an *NME* article that autumn garlanded with the catchy headline 'Hardened Criminals Plan Big Break-Out'. Many years later and shortly before his death, Ian Dury – the Kilburns' crippled singer and key focal point – publicly thanked me for being the first to write about him in a feature about his early career that he wrote for *Mojo*.

He wasn't so courteous at the time, though. I remember him once approaching me drunkenly in a club in Camden Town and growling in my ears, 'I've got a gun in my pocket and I want to stick it right up your bum.' What do you say to something like that? I was glad when he found success with his Blockheads much later in the decade partly because he deserved it but mostly because if he'd stayed in the cultural margins much longer, he'd have become so twisted with rage he'd have probably ended up killing someone.

By early September, I was back in the big leagues. The Rolling Stones were touring Europe and the *NME* sent Pennie Smith and me out to cover their opening UK dates. I interviewed Keith Richards, Mick Jagger and Mick Taylor together in a pancake house adjoining their Manchester hotel one afternoon and got to ride with them to the show that evening in their bus. I couldn't stop flashing back in my mind to the time when I'd first met them ten years earlier.

I'd still been a child then and they'd seemed like a new hooligan-youth superpower. Now they were maturing men of wealth and taste who shared little in common apart from the music they still made. When the five members were together in the same space, the conversational repartee between them was usually so strained and hesitant it could have been scripted by Harold Pinter. The source of their group discomfort wasn't hard to locate: they were each at their personal wits' end about how to coexist harmoniously with Keith Richards, whose ongoing drug addiction continued to daily imperil their potential to work and make more money.

I coined a new phrase for him and his spooky girlfriend Anita Pallenberg, who'd lurked side-stage behind a pair of giant 'human bug' op-art sunglasses – 'wastedly elegant' – in the piece I submitted to the *NME*, and other journalists soon followed suit. The group must have been tickled by what I'd written about them because someone from their office phoned a few days later and offered me the chance to travel around with the Stones on the final leg of the tour and then write a book about the experience. The band would pay my travel and hotel expenses and also pony up for the text I'd be penning. This was like being offered a chance to attain nirvana for me, my wildest teenage dream becoming reality.

As fate would have it, the book – though duly completed – would never get published. As I've said before, this was no tragedy as the text I concocted rarely dared to go below the surface and confront what was really going on in the group's universe. Twenty years later, though, I wrote up a more substantial and honest account of that tour in a piece entitled 'Twilight in Babylon' that became a chapter in my first book, *The Dark Stuff*. I don't intend to repeat the basic information and character sketches contained within it here except to reiterate that the Stones were sinking more and more into the same dark vortex they'd unloosed at the dawning of the decade.

It made them an irresistible force for others to want to fasten on to. Bored European monarchs and their spoilt-rotten in-laws, leading international fashion designers and their self-fixated 'muses', sun-baked movie stars with a yen for cocaine and pussy, big-time gangsters turned out in expensively tailored suits to play down their Neanderthal physiques – all these and more flocked to ingratiate themselves within the group's touring entourage because they sensed the Stones were a musical mini-Mafia who possessed unique power, that they were in effect a law unto themselves.

Keith Richards kept getting busted every few months or so for possessing hard drugs and firearms but rarely even turned up to the law court where his misdemeanours were being judged, never mind facing any kind of jail time. Midway through the tour, the road convoy transporting the group's equipment was forced to pull over at a customs checkpoint and various officials dismantled the amplifiers only to discover that they contained sizeable quantities of various illegal Class A and B drugs hidden inside. Mick Jagger and tour manager Peter Rudge then got a high-ranking lawyer to tell the authorities that the Stones knew nothing about the drugs and that they'd simply been the innocent victims of 'international drug smugglers' who'd somehow infiltrated their equipment without their direct knowledge. Result:

the Stones were instantly exonerated of any wrongdoing and the case was conveniently closed. That's the kind of power they had at their disposal when the necessity arose.

But it evidently came at a steep karmic cost because the more their collective charisma and bargaining power increased on the world's stage, the less potent they sounded as a working musical unit. The Stones' best music is all about conjuring up just the right groove and then taking it somewhere interesting, but in 1973 they often found difficulty in locking together in live perform-ance because their prodigal-son guitar player – whose job it was to set the actual pace for each song – was on a completely differ-ent planet, chemically speaking, to most of his fellow players.

At the same time, he was also the coolest-looking dude in the known hemisphere. Back in the early sixties he'd looked less cool: big-eared, slightly bashful and distinctly human, someone who was best summed up in Andrew Loog Oldham's *Stoned* auto-biography when the ex-Stones manager recalled his own mother stating that Keith was the only truly decent human being in the group because he was kind to animals and always phoned his mum at least twice a week. But then he started pitching woo with Anita Pallenberg and daily testing his personal stamina with drugs and a most dramatic physical and spiritual transformation was set into motion. Lately it had reached the point where he'd begun to resemble a cross between a human blackened spoon and Count Dracula. This in turn provided him with a singularly intimidating demeanour to shield himself behind. It was so effec-tive that no one in the Stones organisation dared to initiate a frank exchange of views with him over the fact that his over-stimulated lifestyle was so sorely taxing the group's morale, music and money-making potential.

I broached this tender subject with Mick Jagger when we finally met for a lunch/interview in a gentleman's club he frequented near Piccadilly Circus more than a month after the tour had wound down. Jagger had actually been the one who'd chosen me for the book assignment – he told me so during our meal – but he and I had never actually spoken during all the time I'd travelled with them. Sometimes I'd seen him from the corner of my eye backstage checking me out, mentally sizing up whether I truly merited being in his group's exalted midst. He had his own way of intimidating people. But it was ultimately small beer compared to his soulmate Keith's championship-level scowling expertise.

'How do you deal with keeping the group afloat when your guitarist is so frequently in trouble?' I asked him. He turned reflective for several seconds and then said, 'Well, you've seen a bit of what he's like. He's not really someone who responds well to advice.' His famous mouth exploded into a broad grin. I tried to continue the line of questioning but he soon cut me off. 'Listen, I'm not going to judge Keith. I don't judge Keith – period. That's how our relationship works. That's how I am.'

These days Jagger habitually gets worse press – principally in his native England – than a convicted child molester and it's something that's always baffled me, particularly when his equally money-hungry peer Paul McCartney is fêted by the same media organs as an all-purpose paragon of virtue. It's obvious the guy isn't the most loveable and approachable human being to have ever drawn breath but he never wanted to be loved by the general public in the first place. Patronised and applauded – yes. But not 'loved' in the gooey showbiz sense of the word. He's always been smart enough to recognise that performers who actively look for love from their audiences often end up needy and burned-out like Judy Garland.

In order to understand Mick Jagger better, it's always instructive to recall the state he found himself in at the end of the sixties. On the one hand, he was the rebel prince of New Bohemia – someone millions of young people the world over idolised and aspired to be. On the other, he'd had to witness Brian Jones's pitiful meltdown and strange, sudden death as well as the descent into heroin addiction by the two people he was then closest to – Marianne Faithfull and Keith Richards.

Even more dramatically, he'd lately discovered that most of the money the Stones had made in the sixties had been pocketed by manager Allen Klein, along with all the rights to their recorded back catalogue. He had two basic choices: either join his soulmates in narcotic never-never land or assert himself and as a canny businessman steer the Rolling Stones' leaky ship towards more advantageous waters. The guy chose to survive and thrive. Without his relentless input, the group would have petered out after the recording of *Let It Bleed*. And yet somehow he always ends up the villain whenever the Stones saga gets recounted – the control freak, the cold fish, the cunning, heartless greed-head. It's become one big fairy story – the Rolling Stones as perceived by the world's media – with Jagger as the resident evil goblin.

So what's he really like then? Hard to say these days – I haven't been in direct contact with the man for over twenty years. But back in the seventies he was someone who always made it his business to be one step ahead of everyone else and who cultivated relationships mostly to achieve this aim. He was extremely shrewd too. He was amused by the clonish likes of the New York Dolls but recognised instantly that they were far too unprofessional and scatterbrained to ever cause his outfit any worried side glances. David Bowie on the other hand fascinated him. For Jagger, Bowie was the only white guy from the seventies who ever caused him to look anxiously over his shoulder. Mention the likes of Lou Reed and Marc Bolan to him though and he'd dissolve in laughter. He knew a thing or two about performers, did Mick Jagger. They had to be fearless, vain and deeply ambitious in order to cast their spell meaningfully night after night. Back in 1964 he'd gone toe to toe with James Brown on the T.A.M.I. show and he'd learned more about stagecraft from that one encounter than any of the new glam boys – apart from Bowie – could ever comprehend. 'It's hard work being me,' he once said in an unguarded moment, and that's what I most recall him being: a hard worker. Back then his life wasn't just about getting paid and getting laid.

And he could be really good company too when he was relaxed. But he was rarely relaxed in public situations. His problem was, whenever he'd walk into a room of strangers, people would invariably go stark staring mad. Women would suddenly lose all sense of decorum and men would start following him around like hypnotised puppy dogs. Jagger had to muster every atom of his considerable sense of self-possession in order to deal with the star-struck behaviour his very presence automatically tended to incite. That's why being Mick Jagger was ultimately such a hard gig. His ongoing retreat into the world of aristocracy and high society has been one way of distancing himself from such situations, I would imagine.

Perhaps this would be the ideal moment to end this chapter and draw a veil over 1973. I'd realised my most ardent teenage fantasy: acceptance and patronage within the Rolling Stones' inner sanctum. Plus I was crazy in love. It couldn't get any better than this. And it didn't, either.

I'm not complaining but too much had happened to me in too short a time and as exhilarating as they had been to live through, the previous two years had left me dizzy and disoriented. I needed an anchor in my life and that's what my relationship with Chrissie Hynde gave me – initially. For the first six months, it was bliss. But then 1974 dawned and our honeymoon period was over.

Something else deeply significant to my future standing in society happened right at the tail-end of 1973. I went over to Cologne in Germany to visit Can in their rehearsal studio there on assignment from the *NME*. Had a great time too. So great in fact that when someone in their entourage offered me a tiny line of heroin to snort, I did so without much forethought on the matter. I'd been offered the drug before on occasion but had always had the presence of mind to turn it down. This time, though, was different: my first time. I didn't know it then but in that one heedless moment I'd just opened the door to a world of hurt.

1974

1974 was the year when – glory be – I finally found my own voice as a writer. Before that, I'd been a wannabe, simply channelling whatever literary influences – Bangs, Capote, Wilde, Wolfe – I happened to be in temporary thrall to. But the apprenticeship I'd undertaken over the past two years had led me to adopt a very different perspective from my rock-lit peers on how to most effectively capture the sounds and sensations of pop life in prose form. Everyone else seemed to me to be writing about the 'idea' of rock as though it was some abstract concept. They liked to bracket the music's practitioners off into separate competing movements and spent far too much space and energy dissecting their lyrics as though they were all W. B. Yeats with an electric guitar. Their stilted prose and sheltered thoughts were typical of a particular mindset: that of the bookish bedroom hermit with a sociology degree who doesn't quite know what to do with the rest of his life. In other words, the kind of young adult I might have become had luck and the *NME* not sealed my fate.

My perspective was the polar opposite of theirs. I wasn't writing about rock as an idea: I was writing about it as a full-blown flesh-and-blood reality – surreal people living surreal, action-packed lives. From what I'd learned coming up, rock writing was fundamentally an action medium that best came to life when the writer was right in the thick of that action and yet removed enough to comprehend its possible consequences. The range of characters the medium offered was phenomenally rich. There was the lead singer with his monumental narcissistic personality disorders. The guitarists with their witchy girlfriends and ever-mounting drug-dependency issues. The managers feverishly working the money angle whilst secretly envying their wards' success and pulling power. The roadies building their own thuggish power base. The audience – like the children of Hamelin – hypnotised and bug-eyed with communal ecstasy. It's the convergence of human elements like these that made the form start to come alive for me. Some degree of windy theorising is always necessary – true – but only in small doses. Nothing longer than three or four incisive, well-worded sentences to establish a wider context and also pass judgement on the music actually being made. Then – back to the action.

The key trick, though, is to somehow create prose that flows with a distinct musicality all of its own. That's what I finally hit on in '74: the right tone and the right groove. Before that, there'd been something contrived about my writing as well as the literary persona I'd hastily adopted. But I'd toiled long and hard to find a style and approach that I was happy with. I took my evolving writerly skills very, very seriously during that whole period. I made a point of never taking any drugs just prior to and during the actual act of scribbling my texts out. I'd tried once or twice whilst on speed and it had screwed up my ability to focus and fuse together incidents to the best of my ability. And pot only befuddled my thinking whenever a deadline loomed. No, I really needed to be straight to do full justice to the talent growing within me.

That was one of the better aspects of my relationship with Chrissie Hynde: it wasn't a drug-driven liaison. We'd take drugs in social situations when they were being offered freely to us but didn't have any where we lived and rarely felt the urge to actually buy them. Chrissie was like me – she'd snort cocaine if she was given it but it invariably left her nervous and ill at ease. The best times we shared together were the ones when it was just the two of us, clear-headed and drunk simply on each other's company. You don't need drugs when you're truly in love and on the same wavelength as your intended.

But romantic love – as the poets have often pointed out – is a multifaceted condition of the heart that can end up deeply wounding those who fall under its spell. Some can ride its giddy momentum whilst others become destabilised and start to come apart from within. That's what was about to happen to me. The image I was trying to project out to the world was that of a self-assured, waspishly witty young sophisticate, but behind it I was emotionally still sixteen years old in the head: insecure and possessive – two qualities almost all self-respecting species of womankind have a built-in contempt of.

Meanwhile, weird scenes had been happening within the *NME*. Sales continued to increase throughout '73, but then in the year's final weeks the paper had been forced to cease production and go on strike. It was out of circulation for almost two months as I recall – a nerve-wracking time for its staff and contributors wondering if it would ever resurface. The strike coincided with our IPC paymasters taking umbrage at the *NME*'s new laissez-faire editorial policy regarding bad language. The word 'cunt' had lately cropped up in one feature and the higher-ups were mortified by this turn of events, threatening to shut the paper down if further obscenities were committed to print. A compromise was duly arrived at. We could use 'fuck' in moderation, as well as 'asshole' and 'bugger'. But any slang word for genitalia – male or female – was strictly out of bounds.

Mercifully, this petty-minded contretemps didn't put too deep a dent in ongoing office morale. Big changes were afoot in the *NME*'s Long Acre office space. Editor Alan Lewis chose this period to step down from his duties and hand the reins over to Nick Logan. This was a major step in the right direction. Lewis had been a canny opportunist, but Nick had the ideal mixture of sensibility and creative instinct to take us all to the next level, whatever and wherever that was. His first act as the journal's captain was most inspired: he persuaded Ian MacDonald to take over his previous post as assistant editor. Ian wasted no time in bringing all his daunting intellect, boundless intensity and unshakeable thirst for excellence to the role he'd been assigned.

The pair immediately green-lighted a visual make-over for the paper. The first post-strike issue to hit the shops in January '74 featured an arty full-length photo – of Bryan Ferry – taking up the entire cover. Before that, the paper had unimaginatively run their lead news story of the week in the same space. But now it looked classier, bolder and infinitely more pleasing to the eye. Pennie Smith was really coming into her own as a photographer, and Ian and Nick made sure her contributions were always laid out for maximum visual impact. Likewise, they knew how to get the best out of me and all the other writers on board. Thus began the *NME*'s true golden age. From that point on, we were truly a force to be reckoned with.

Of course, 'new journalistic directions' invariably require the constant hiring of new writers to keep the pot boiling. So it surprised no one when word came through that two fresh recruits would soon be joining up to bolster our ranks. The first to arrive was a Bert Jansch lookalike called Andrew Tyler – a fine writer and all-round good person. The second choice took me aback somewhat. It was Chrissie. Ian and Nick had socialised with her on several occasions when I'd brought her to the office and Ian in particular felt she had the perfect attitude to become an *NME* contributor. He basically told her so until he'd convinced her to actually sit down and churn out some text. They evidently liked what she submitted because the next thing I knew she was interviewing Brian Eno for a centre-page spread.

At first I was happy for her. She could dump her dead-end job at the architects' office and focus on matters that genuinely interested her for greater financial recompense. Suddenly she had her own profile on the London music scene apart from being my girlfriend. But her recruitment onto the *NME* masthead also left me distinctly wary. I felt the paper was pushing her into their big spotlight far too soon, that the editors should have allowed her to find her bearings as a music journalist before parading her in front of our readers.

One consequence of her being showcased so prominently so early in her career was that she always felt a terrible pressure whenever she had to turn out copy and found the whole process both taxing and deeply unenjoyable. That's unfortunate because she possessed some talent as a burgeoning writer. Over the first six months of 1974 she managed to complete and get published interviews/articles on acts as diverse as Brian Eno, Suzi Quatro, David Cassidy (a teen idol *du jour*) and Tim Buckley. The best thing she turned in to the *NME* was a touching write-up of an encounter with one of her heroes, the zen-cool veteran jazzer

Mose Allison that took place during a spring residency the piano-playing US singer/songwriter was undertaking at Ronnie Scott's Soho club. If she'd been given the chance to pen more low-key heartfelt pieces like that, maybe she would have continued longer in the profession than she did. After six months, however, she'd simply had enough and left the *NME* – and music journalism – to pursue other goals.

By that time, she'd found another avenue of employment for herself as a shop assistant at Malcolm McLaren's King's Road clothes store. Once again I'd first introduced her to McLaren and his clique, never thinking it would amount to much. I'd first noticed him in the spring of '72. His shop was called 'Let It Rock' then and it catered exclusively to a fifties retro crowd: brothel-creeping Teds from the London suburbs with nicknames like 'Biffo' and 'Crazy-Legged John'. He was a real fifties purist back then and I took a generally dim view of those who opt to live single-mindedly in the past.

But then the New York Dolls returned to London at the end of November '73 to perform a concert there and promote their critically acclaimed debut album. On a day off, they'd gone shopping and had trooped into Let It Rock together. The moment McLaren saw them, a major man-crush ensued. Suddenly the seventies came alive for him and he began obsessively following them around.

In December I flew to Paris to see the group play at the prestigious Olympia concert hall. The concert itself was a musical nightmare highlighted by guitarist Johnny Thunders abruptly leaving the stage in mid-performance at least twice to vomit behind the amplifiers. But afterwards there was a celebratory dinner at a ritzy restaurant and I found myself seated at a table with

David Johansen and McLaren. The latter was animatedly talking about a pet project of his: a filmed documentary of his hero, the gifted but physically frail UK former rock idol Billy Fury that he was struggling to find financial backing for.

I'd actually met Fury just a month earlier. Someone had convinced him to make a tentative comeback and so he'd duded himself up in a pink leather suit and Rod Stewart feather cut and started performing a greatest-hits repertoire in a Northern working men's club. His voice still sounded great, his face remained flawlessly beautiful and he was as thin as a whippet. But he was also far too sweet-natured and trusting, and lacked the gumption and physical stamina needed to sustain a career in the seventies. He also had a serious heart condition. I mentioned all this to McLaren and he was most impressed. It was the start of our very first conversation and it continued long into the night.

He revealed a lot about himself during that chat. He talked at length about his Jewish upbringing and his childhood living under the influence of a mad meddlesome grandmother who instilled in him the innate belief that he was so special he could achieve absolutely anything in life, no matter what obstacles were placed before him. He also mentioned his many years spent as a mature art-school student during the sixties. He hated that decade with a venom that would have been shocking had it not been so comical to hear about. He became apoplectic when he began railing against the Beatles, hippies and the whole peace and love movement of the time. The very idea of anything even vaguely spiritual and uplifting filtering into youth culture automatically filled him with nausea. At one point I got into a heated argument with him over who had been a more influential force in popular music – Bob Dylan (my choice) or Johnny Kidd and the Pirates (his). Kidd and his cohorts were an early-sixties English rock band of merit with one indisputably seminal recording to their credit – the original version of 'Shakin' All Over'. Dylan by contrast had over one hundred timeless songs under his belt and had been a far-reaching creative trailblazer whose name still inspired millions with awe. There really was no contest. But he still waffled on ardently about how Dylan was a talentless fake who'd influenced nothing and no one whilst Johnny Kidd – who'd been killed in a car crash back in 1965 – was someone who'd left a deep and lasting impression on the mindset of twentieth-century youth.

His own mindset was still hopelessly trapped in the late fifties as far as rock 'n' roll and pop culture in general were concerned. Gene Vincent – the sweet-voiced hillbilly psychopath – was his ultimate musical reference point, the figure that best summed up his vision of rock as something truly untamed and seditious. But then the New York Dolls walked into his life and he'd instinctively sensed that – behind their tacky transvestite outward appearance – something equally untamed and seditious lurked within them too. It turned out to be his very own 'road to Damascus' moment. For one thing, he got to hear that night for the very first time the fateful phrase he'd later claim he single-handedly invented – 'punk rock'. It either came from my lips or from one of the New York Dolls.

The upshot of this first encounter was that we stayed in touch back in London and he invited me out one evening in January. I took Chrissie along and she quickly bonded with McLaren's girlfriend, a feisty Northern lass called Vivienne Westwood. They shared several pointed character traits. They were both aggressively forthright in voicing their opinions in any given situation, used bad language liberally and liked nothing more than initiating confrontations with complete strangers when not driving their own boyfriends to distraction with their nagging ways. I liked Vivienne – she was a tough old bird who'd lived a tough old life prior to becoming McLaren's personal Eliza Doolittle – but I was also wary of her because I could detect something unhealthily malicious lurking behind her eyes. That's probably why McLaren and I grew close. We both shared the same sorry romantic predicament.

Still, what attracted me most was the guy's passion, intelligence and daring. He was always thinking outside of the box. Within the first six months of '74, he completely transformed his shop, changed the clothes he and Westwood were designing and even changed the name. In January it had still been 'Let It Rock', but by early summer it became 'Seditionaries' and began selling an exclusive range of leather and rubber fetishist clothing whilst all the other London fashion lairs were still stocking up on tacky satin jackets and bell-bottomed loon pants. He was quick-witted and audacious and – because he never took drugs – he also possessed the mental stamina and focus to will his mad ideas into fruition. Meanwhile, the rest of London was still stuck in the aimless pothead purgatory of the late sixties. You could say I was an early supporter of his work as a fashion designer. In the late spring of '74 I even interviewed him in the *NME* about his clothes-designing relationship with the New York Dolls and his thoughts on fashion and rock. It was one of his first-ever appearances in the media.

The most significant aspect of our relationship though was the way I took it upon myself to educate him on what had actually been happening in rock music over the past ten years. As soon as the Beatles arrived in 1963, McLaren had simply turned his back on rock music and buried his head in the ground like an ostrich. He didn't even know who Jimi Hendrix was until I forced him to attend a late-night screening of Joe Boyd's film documentary on the guitarist. He sat in that cinema utterly slack-jawed with wonderment. He told me he couldn't believe what he'd been missing out on.

I got him to watch *Gimme Shelter* too and he was deeply affected by its evocation of contemporary rock as a way to still incite blood-drenched mass pandemonium. He loved what he saw because it registered to him in no uncertain terms that rock's wild anarchic spirit hadn't died back when Elvis got co-opted into the army, that it was still obscenely alive and capable of raising a nuclear-sized ruckus in whatever social and cultural context you chose to set it loose in. It was great to be around him in those moments because you could see he was receiving major revelations from the screen. It didn't always work, though. One time I coerced him into sitting through the great D. A. Pennebaker Dylan doc *Don't Look Back* and he came out cursing the Bard of Beat with even greater vigour. And the Beatles were always a strictly no-go area. But he loved the Doors and the early Who. In many ways it was just like teaching a bloke who'd been living in a cave for ten years about what had transpired during his absence. But McLaren was a lightning-quick learner. You didn't have to draw him any maps. He'd just fixate on what became instantly fascinating to him like a magpie and then pilfer it into his own private agenda.

As my relationship with him intensified so my relationship with Chrissie began to unravel. Our first six months together had been heavenly. But the six months after that – from January 1st

1974 to early summer – became increasingly hellish for both of us. All love affairs have their honeymoon period when two hearts beat as one and joy is unconfined. But then reality descends and suddenly the lovers wake up and start having to grimly confront each other's shortcomings and personal eccentricities. Chrissie woke up first. I could see it in her eyes. You can always tell when a woman's truly in love simply by looking directly in her eyes. If she is, then there's an intangibly luminous glow to her gaze. It's a wondrous thing to behold. But when love starts to die, those same eyes will turn cold on you and you will see only irritation and unhappiness within them. I've seen it happen a number of times since but I learned it first from being with Chrissie.

The problem was, whilst she was waking up, I was still blissfully comatose inside love's young dream. Only a moment ago, we'd been giddily talking about getting married. Now she was suddenly pushing for us to live separately. With the aid of hindsight I can now see the merits of her suggestion: we were so glued together at first it was starting to become suffocating. But at the time I reacted to it as an act of colossal rejection on her part. That's what I mean about still being sixteen emotionally in the old noggin.

Plus the fact that she was suddenly doing the same job as me didn't help matters one jot or iota. Though neither of us was aware of it initially, working for the *NME* back then had a compulsory side effect. It put everyone involved in a position where they were automatically in competition with each other. It wasn't a soothing or nurturing environment to work in. There was an unhealthily divisive undercurrent to the way writers were pitted against each other. My relationship with Charles Shaar Murray had suffered because of this but at least I didn't have to live with

the guy. When Chrissie started adopting much the same confrontational attitude in our home, however, that's when major
indoor fireworks starting going off. I couldn't believe it at first. I
was still lost in love-land. But I felt the change soon enough. It
was like being on a plane when a sudden mid-air explosion
occurs. After the initial shock, I started looking around in earnest
for some kind of safety parachute to help break the free fall.

From what I'd observed, most examples of humankind facing
imminent heartache tended to pour themselves into a bottle and
let the liquor anaesthetise their woes. In fact, poor old John
Lennon was busy doing just that over in Hollywood, drinking his
way through a lost weekend that lasted through most of 1974
because he couldn't stand to be separated from Yoko Ono. But
immersing oneself in alcohol was never really an option for me.
Booze of any grain and potency tended to leave me dizzy and
red-faced. I was a died-in-the-wool drug snob anyway.

But which drug could truly comfort me in my time of sorrow?
Not cocaine – it just made me crazier and more fever-headed. Pot
couldn't quell the pain, either. Only one pharmaceutical really
possessed what I needed – the power to effect a complete shut-
down of all emotional feeling within me. It was called heroin and
it was becoming steadily more and more available throughout
parts of London – particularly in Chelsea, where many bored
young things with too much of daddy's money had fallen victim
to its lure.

As I've already mentioned, I tried it first in Germany at the end
of the previous year. But I don't think the powder I inhaled that
night actually was heroin. The effect was altogether too benign. A
month later Chrissie and I were at a photographer friend's Maida
Vale flat. We'd been snorting cocaine all night together and we

were both seriously wired. I asked the photographer if he had a Valium to counteract the tremors and he said no – but that we'd be less agitated if we both snorted a line of heroin. We were so desperate for any kind of calming antidote that we immediately took him up on his offer. This time it really was heroin. I have a dim recollection of us almost literally crawling our way back to Clapham South just as rush hour was commencing. Chrissie didn't take it after that for a long long time. I wasn't so cautious.

Actually it was my third encounter with the drug that was to prove the most fatal. I was spending a lot of my down time in Chelsea during '74. You'd often have found me lurking around McLaren's headquarters but I was also a regular presence at another World's End clothing emporium just a few doors down; Granny Takes a Trip had been fêted internationally as London's hippest and most exclusive haberdashers during London's psychedelic summer of 1967, the year it first opened. The Beatles, Stones and Syd Barrett had all their most flamboyant outfits made up on the premises that season.

The guy who actually set it all up was an enterprising young Englishman named Nigel Waymouth, but he soon tired of his creation and sold it to a couple of fashion-besotted young New Yorkers named Marty Breslau and Gene Krell at the end of the sixties. I first got to know these two when I began buying clothes from them in late '72. 'Granny's' was practically the only clothes shop in London at that time that still sold elegantly cut straight-legged trousers unencumbered by a flare and cool-looking boots without clumpy platform heels and soles, and I was always a stickler for both. Flared trousers should be worn only by those unfortunate people with one leg significantly shorter than the other. And only midgets need to even consider sporting platform heels. Anyone else who adopts their look is committing an abomination against both style and nature.

But I digress. I actually became friends with Gene and Marty during the Stones' European tour back in autumn. They'd turned up to several shows on the Continent as Keith Richards's personal guests. I didn't know it then but Marty was one of Keith's many heroin suppliers. He and Spanish Tony Sanchez – Richards's main drug courier and general enforcer who'd later co-write the scurrilous *Up and Down with the Rolling Stones* literary exposé – were thick as thieves. Marty was a handsome fellow – he looked like a stoned Warren Beatty with a girlish shag cut – and he'd evidently led something of a charmed life throughout his teens and twenties. But his luck changed dramatically when he met Keith Richards because he fell head-over-heels in love with the guy and – in order to remain in his presence – ended up destroying his career in the fashion world in order to become his drug dealer. It never got better for Marty after that and he ended up dying of an overdose in the early eighties. He wasn't what you'd call an especially nice guy – too vain, too tricky, too stupid – but I rather liked him all the same. Ditto Spanish Tony.

Anyway, one night in early spring I was over at their Chelsea Embankment luxury basement flat. Chrissie and I had just had a major spat back in Clapham South and I was seeking temporary refuge elsewhere. Marty and Tony laid out three lines of heroin and offered me one. And that's when it truly hit me – the drug, I mean. Suddenly I felt all my burdens melting from my shoulders, all that bad static in my brain – banished. And in their place – plugged into every atom of my being – utter serenity. Total palpable bliss.

Charlie Parker called it 'the cool world'. Once you've been

there it's hard to rid it from your thoughts. It's like discovering an enchanted island you can suddenly escape to where everything is safe and serene, where no pain can find you. Your conscious mind keeps telling you that you're stepping over a dangerous line here and messing with the forbidden but your subconscious keeps replaying the ecstasy of that moment when heroin first revealed its full power within you. You can already tell what was about to happen, can't you, dear reader? All the ingredients for impending disaster were stacking up around me.

And yet 1974 still managed to bring the best out of me to date as a writer. In March of that year I set out on a personal crusade I'd wanted to instigate since my mid-teens: to research and then write an article that would finally explain to the world what had actually happened to Syd Barrett. The Madcap now has apparently more than 30,000 fan websites devoted to his memory but back in '74 interest in the man was scant at best. Several *NME*ites were openly dismissive of the project at the outset. 'Barrett is a has-been and has-beens have no place in the pages of the *NME*' was one rationale I recall being confronted with. But I knew better. His old group had just had a worldwide no. 1 album, *The Dark Side of the Moon*, that was partly a concept album about madness. And Syd – from everything I'd been informed – had gone completely mad himself. It was high time his tale be fully told.

Here at last was a subject I could totally sink my teeth into. In 1967, the impish-eyed Barrett had been the world's most beautiful man – the golden boy of psychedelia. By 1974 he'd become a scary-eyed balding recluse whom former acquaintances couldn't even recognise any more. He lived alone in a flat in Chelsea Cloisters where he spent all his time watching a large colour television and eating meat he kept in a giant freezer in the kitchen. I thought about approaching him directly – I had the address – but was told he probably wouldn't answer the door. I spoke to at least two people who'd recently crossed paths with him and they claimed it was now impossible to have a coherent conversation with him. He rarely went out, never searched out old acquaintances and hadn't made music in two years. Everything was closing in around him and so it seemed more humane to just leave him alone and let others document what happened to him. In the end his absence worked to the piece's advantage because it further enhanced his mystique, made him even more distantly compelling as subject matter.

Almost everyone I interrogated about Syd openly bore the psychic scars of having witnessed his unforgettable deterioration. Several came close to tears as they recalled the way his wreckless use of LSD had fractured first his potential and then his every mental process. Others expressed the view that – as gifted as he was – he was too young and undisciplined, too over-indulged and too good-looking, and simply lacked the mental focus and spartan nervous system required to successfully sustain a career for himself as a rock star.

The Pink Floyd somehow got wind of what I was preparing and Dave Gilmour – whom I'd never met before – phoned me up out of the blue at home in Clapham South. He offered to do an interview on the subject of Syd because he wanted to put the record straight about his friend and hopefully counterbalance any misinformation I might have picked up along the way. I was scheduled to deliver the finished text – which eventually ran to over 6,000 words – to the *NME* on the Friday morning of the first week in April. But I couldn't start writing it until I'd finished my chinwag with Gilmour, which ended up taking place in a Long

Acre pub on Thursday evening. It was worth the added deadline stress because Gilmour gave me by far the most revealing account of Syd's rise and fall, and I'm eternally grateful that he saw fit to entrust me with his often intimate recollections. To him, his friend's breakdown wasn't simply triggered by drug abuse; the roots of it stretched back to Barrett's pampered childhood and his doting mother. His testimony proved to be the last crucial piece of the puzzle I had to conjure up in prose.

I left Gilmour at close to 10.00 p.m. and taxied back to Clapham South. When I'd interviewed Barrett's former co-manager Peter Jenner some weeks earlier at his office, he'd taken me down to the basement once my tape recorder had been turned off. The floor was damp and in one corner he located a large black plastic bag covered in grime and mildew. Inside were the blow-ups and contact sheets of practically every photograph ever taken of Barrett since the Pink Floyd's first formation. He then handed the package to me. 'You can keep them,' he said, 'I can't imagine anyone else being interested in them.'

It was these photographs that I placed all around the room just prior to putting pen to paper. The story I had to tell was all there in the eyes I saw staring back at me. In the early shots, Syd's eyes sparkled like sapphires but by late '67 those same eyes had turned full of foreboding. Then, in the photos taken to promote his later solo career, they looked hopelessly lost and uncomprehending. That was the trajectory I had to capture in the next twelve hours. I started scribbling away frantically and never stopped. No drugs, no coffee – just pure obsession. The story ended up telling itself, but by the time I'd finished, I knew I'd written something that was going to resonate. Logan and MacDonald gave me a hard time for handing it in three hours after the appointed deadline but then they read the thing and realised its potential.

Four days later, it appeared spread over the four middle pages of the *NME*'s April 13th issue, with an evocative wind-blown shot of Syd gracing the cover. It was the first time an English music weekly had ever run such a long piece. The response was immediate and deeply gratifying.

But there was also a serious downside. Suddenly I was inundated with correspondence and phone calls from every acid-damaged *NME* reader in the world. They only wanted to help Syd, they all informed me with scary self-assurance, and needed to be given his personal address immediately so that they could go down and comfort him. I thought I'd left these kinds of nutjobs behind when I'd absconded from the underground press. And Ladbroke Grove. No such luck. Everyone suddenly seemed to think I had some sort of personal access to the man, that I was a kind of intermediary between him and the outside world.

The Pink Floyd's reaction was more guarded. Gilmour let it be known that though he'd quite liked the piece, he also felt it occasionally dipped into the realm of 'sensationalism'. And Roger Waters apparently didn't like it at all. Still, it must have left an impact because – partly as a response – he wrote the song 'Shine On You Crazy Diamond' soon afterwards.

And Syd himself – how did it all register with him? Well, his mystique certainly benefited from the renewed exposure. He was suddenly a hot topic again. Peter Jenner called up to ask for the prompt return of all those photographs he'd 'given' me. And EMI, who'd recently deleted Barrett's two solo albums from their catalogue, promptly decided to re-release them as a special double package. Hoping to feature a new photograph of the man on the cover design, they'd then dispatched two former Cambridge pals of Barrett's, Storm Thorgerson and Aubrey Powell, down to Chelsea Cloisters armed with a camera. They told me later that they'd knocked on his door for several minutes without success. He wouldn't let them in. Still, they had a conversation – of sorts – through the letter box. At one point, one of them asked him, 'So, Syd – did you see that big piece on you in *NME*?' Barrett – with some hesitation – replied, 'Yes . . . No.' 'What did you think of it then?' asked Thorgerson. 'It was OK,' Barrett's voice came back drowsily, 'but I didn't read it.' That was Syd sure enough. Unfathomable to the end.

The only person to give me any serious grief about the Syd piece was Chrissie Hynde. 'Where do you get off thinking you have the right to invade the lives of mentally unstable people?' she once exploded at me. 'You're not a registered psychiatrist.' It was a moot point but the way she broached it smacked of professional jealousy. She even started giving me a hard time about working with the Rolling Stones. 'Those old guys are just trying to exploit you' became one of her oft-repeated scornful diatribes aimed at my ears only. In retrospect, this was pretty damn rich, particularly when you consider that thirty years later she and her group would be blithely supporting the senior-citizen Stones for negligible financial reward on one of their gargantuan money-siphoning American tours.

Things were just going from bad to worse between us. I should have moved out then but I was still too love-struck to make the break. I kept holding on blindly to the deluded notion that the bad period we were traversing would suddenly evaporate and we'd magically return to the idyllic times we'd shared back in the beginning. I was about to learn a very important lesson in life:

there's ultimately not that much difference between being a hopeless romantic and a feckless sap.

In May we agreed to a two-week trial separation and I used the opportunity to go off with a friend of mine, a New York-born, smart-alec photographer named Joe Stevens, to France on a much-needed holiday. We took the Paris night train down to St Tropez – what a sleazy, overpriced dump that turned out to be. I went there armed with the mad hope of somehow encountering Brigitte Bardot, a well-known resident of the tiny beach town, and ended up having to hide away from a fleet of drunken sailors who were overrunning the area and who took great exception to my pallid form and foppish attire.

Joe and I escaped to Cannes – only to discover that their annual film festival had ended just a week earlier and the streets were deserted apart from heaping piles of torn film posters. So we headed back to Paris. Springtime in Paris agreed with me. I felt suddenly light-headed again. But then temptation reared its sordid head – and with it came dire consequences. I started screwing around and, unbeknownst to me at the time, one of my conquests gave me a special going-away present: gonorrhoea.

Do you really need to know the rest? Yes, I suppose you do. June was hell on earth for Chrissie and me. We fought, we cursed. Then one night she got ill and experienced the same crippling stomach cramps that I'd seen her suffering from the first time I'd met her. I held her that night like I'd done the other time and tried to comfort her. It was the last truly tender moment we ever got to share. The next morning an ambulance came and took her to the hospital. She stayed there for three days. Meanwhile, I was starting to experience an unpleasant burning sensation whenever I took a piss. The doctors then told Chrissie that her gynaecological problems were caused by her having lately contracted a sexually transmissible disease. From that point on, she didn't really want to have anything more to do with me.

I moved out to a dingy two-room flat in Archway that I first had to have fumigated by the local pest-control. During my first evening there, I got an unexpected call from Chrissie. Her voice sounded less icy than of late, gentler and more forgiving. She told me she still loved me and that our living apart would only make our relationship stronger. She asked me to meet her the next day at McLaren's shop near closing time. We'd go out together. It would be a new beginning.

This was music to my ears. For the next twenty hours I was back floating on air. But then I turned up at the appointed time and walked into yet another nightmare scenario. Chrissie was not happy to see me. Her eyes were like poison darts. 'Go fuck yourself!' was her opening greeting. I reminded her about what she'd said the night before. 'Well, I've changed my mind,' she countered coldly. 'I met this guy and I'm going out with him now.'

That's when I saw red. I attacked her right there in the shop. McLaren was also present and he was so scared he ran off and hid under a table. I was about to hit her with my belt when a strange bloke who just happened to be on the premises – one of McLaren's mad brood – stepped forward and punched me in the face so hard my whole body almost flew through the shop window onto the pavement outside. Exit Chrissie. Meanwhile, I'm splayed out on the floor, pathetic and bleeding profusely from the mouth. That was the final scene in our great love affair. Everything changed from that moment on. Farewell charmed life – hello cruel fate. A bad moon was presently rising over Chelsea Embankment and now it had turned its ruinous glow on me too.

Where did our love go? That's what I wanted to know. All my life I'd been told that love was the answer, that it was what made the world go round, that it conquered all adversity and soothed the savage within. But the love I'd just lived through had been neither soothing nor strengthening and it had left me with more questions than answers. It had also left me with a dull, aching pain and a vastly diminished sense of personal self-esteem.

For a while there I became a very gloomy fellow indeed. I'd still socialise but my acquaintances soon became weary of my glum discourses on the treacherous lie that is romantic infatuation and told me so in no uncertain terms. Some offered a solution to my woes: a comforting line of heroin. At that point in time I saw little difference in being a lovesick fool and full-blown drug addict so I continually accepted their offer. At first I only indulged one evening a month. Then it quickly grew to once a week. Then it was every three days. By the end of the year it had become a daily habit.

I'd abandoned myself. It was partly due to my raging self-disgust. However much I tried to believe otherwise, it was me who'd been the weak link in our love-chain. I'd been too arrogant, too stifling, too immature. And yet I couldn't get around the lurking suspicion that I'd been used by her, that she'd glommed on to me to further her profile in London and then basically taken my initial kindness for cuntishness and dropped me like a bad debt once she'd established herself as someone of consequence in the city's music circles.

'The Love I Saw in You Was Just a Mirage' – the great Smokey Robinson and the Miracles heartbreaker – was on constant rotation in my lonely Archway pad that year. It spoke to my inner condition, my ongoing dilemma. All this time I'd been like a needy child craving the love of the loveless. But everyone just used everybody else in this world – that was the name of the game when it came to fundamental human interaction. Musicians were using me for their publicity whilst I was using them as subject matter and source material. The *NME* was using me to sell more copies and I was using them to extend my writing abilities and personal profile. And where was the love in all of this? Nowhere. It seemed to me there was no love. It didn't really exist. So – bring on the darkness. At least – as Spinal Tap once so eloquently put it – you know where you stand in a hellhole. The dark world tends to get a bad rap but it has much to recommend it – particularly if you're one of the broken-hearted. Faster women. Harder drugs. Drunker wine. When you're twenty-two years old, you don't think about the consequences. You just swan-dive in.

And what became of Chrissie? Well, McLaren sacked her shortly after our violent parting of the ways in his shop and she stuck around London for another month or two before decamping to Paris. She first shared a flat there with a transsexual guy who ran a local cabaret act. Then she started living with the junkie bass player for a local glam-rock act called the Frenchies. In due course, she became their singer. But the line-up splintered apart in early '75, and she returned to her native Akron.

I tried twice during that time to persuade her to return to me. Even flew to Paris once just to plead my case. Not a chance. I was just a bad memory to her. She wanted to move on. She returned to her new social circle and I went back to my drug buddies. I only realised it recently but our love affair turned out to be the very first proven casualty of the *NME* in the seventies. There would be others.

But enough of my dreary, milksop blatherings – at least for now. What was transpiring in the ongoing pop-culture Zeitgeist as summer turned to autumn and autumn turned to winter? I still had a ringside seat and continued to monitor the situation for my *NME* paymasters with due dedication. David Bowie – now an American resident – had lately gone disco, a move that utterly bewildered his UK fan base when they first read about it. Bryan Ferry meanwhile had stolen his thunder in England: Roxy Music were unstoppable even without Brian Eno. Wherever I went that year – to clubs or people's apartments – someone would always be playing a Steely Dan record. Or Al Green. Whenever I hear 'Let's Stay Together' or 'Do It Again' these days, the essence of 1974 is instantly re-evoked in my mind. I'm lurking around some dimly lit smoky club in a state of stoned semi-consciousness, scoping out the dead-eyed fellow revellers as though we've all just been shanghaied onto the set of a bad Peter Sellers movie.

The London pubs meanwhile had pub rock to keep their customers entertained whilst hoisting pints. The genre had lately been greatly boosted by the arrival of the one group that would actually go on to enjoy mainstream success in the coming months: a rough-and-ready R & B quartet from Canvey Island called Dr. Feelgood. The group didn't make it on looks alone. In point of fact, they were the seediest-looking bunch that ever stood on a stage in the seventies.

The singer had all the physical grace of a homicidal plumber, the guitarist with the pudding-bowl haircut was a bizarre black-suited blur, darting around the stage ceaselessly as though his legs had just been set alight, and the rhythm section resembled a couple of small-time penny-arcade pimps. They played strictly retro rock – mostly old R & B material with a few originals written in the same spirit – but virtually everyone who saw them live that year came away excited by what they'd seen and heard. Their music hasn't really lasted the test of time but they were still important because they heralded an important sea change in UK rock. Before them, the fops had ruled the roost. But the Feelgoods' ascension marked the pivotal moment when the spivs started creeping back into the big picture. Malcolm McLaren could often be espied side-stage at their shows taking mental notes.

The big event as summer turned to autumn was a Wembley Stadium show headlined by the recently reformed hippie dreamers Crosby, Stills, Nash and Young. They played for almost three hours, their voices audibly hollowed out by ongoing cocaine abuse. Half the band appeared to be struggling with recurrent nose-bleeding. It was a sorry spectacle all told – only Neil Young managed to fleetingly impress.

At the party afterwards at a West End watering hole called Quaglino's a wild-eyed, chemically impacted Young and an obnoxiously drunk-as-a-skunk Stills booed the ropey pick-up band hired to perform at their festivities off the makeshift stage and then climbed up and took over their instruments. Young immediately took control of the repertoire and started performing several sluggish-tempoed compositions from his just-released album *On the Beach*. Stills tried to play the drums but fell backwards off the stool after a couple of minutes. He then decided to approach the microphone and address the many illustrious English rock musicians who'd turned up to the event as invited guests. In a nutshell, he dared them to come up and match their playing skills with his. It was just a pissed-up brag but both

Jimmy Page and John Bonham volunteered and played a memorable ten-minute jam with Young still firmly at the helm. Robbie Robertson of the Band also stepped up and he and Young got into a lively guitar duel that would have involuntarily curled the whiskers of any bearded man present in the room.

Young was a force of nature that night. No one could intimidate him or outplay him. You could tell he was having an excessively good time. Even Stills's bullish presence didn't faze him. Why should it have? After all, Young was on a major creative roll that showed no signs of slowing to a halt in the immediate future. His 1975 masterpiece *Tonight's the Night* was already done and dusted. After that came *Zuma* and a slew of brilliant records, culminating in 1979's *Rust Never Sleeps*. By then, many were concluding that Neil Young had been the most consistently inspired male troubadour of the seventies. I wouldn't argue the point. No one else – apart from Bowie – had the same insatiable need to push ahead and keep challenging an audience's expectations and no one else had anywhere near the same mixture of self-discipline, creative gumption and sheer bloody-mindedness.

As Young was holding forth from the Quaglino's stage, his Canadian soulmate Joni Mitchell was sat in one of the more exclusive corners of the restaurant area surveying the human clutter around her with a fierce 'do not approach' look in her eyes and a haughty sneer creasing her lips. Bianca Jagger was seated beside her and together they made for a daunting double act in championship-level seventies snobbishness.

At least Mitchell had something to back up her lofty demeanour. Like her fellow countryman Young, she was right at the top of her music-making game at that point in time. She'd started out as a folkie singer/songwriter in the late sixties and musically and lyrically she quickly proved herself to be head and shoulders above the rest of her introspective, acoustic-guitar-picking peers. But of late her voice had grown deeper and more worldly-sounding and she'd begun letting jazz musicians tamper with her songs on stage and in the studio. This bold stylistic detour would ultimately cost her a large section of her audience but it was also the best move she ever made. The next two albums, *The Hissing of Summer Lawns* and *Hejira*, were both masterpieces, a major artist entering maturity at the very peak of her powers and focused unblinkingly on two big issues of the era: the spiritual bankruptcy inherent in aimless hedonism and status-seeking and the inevitable trials and tribulations of searching for love in a vanity-driven universe. She'd always been a spectacular talent but the songs on those two records somehow cast a spell that seemed to penetrate deep inside the listener's skin, clear through to his or her DNA. I continue to have boundless respect for Ms Mitchell but I'm also glad I never got to actually meet her.

In late September I was back living the high life with my boys the Rolling Stones. They had a new album poised for imminent release entitled *It's Only Rock 'n' Roll* that contained nothing particularly earth-shattering but which still managed to garner mostly enthusiastic reviews at the time. I did an interview with Mick Taylor which turned out to be his last as a Stones member. Unbeknownst to everyone else, he'd lately been encouraged by the engineer Andy Johns to start a group with the fiery-tempered Scottish bass player Jack Bruce. He was fed up with the Stones anyway. Jagger and Richards were way too intimidating for him to ever feel like he truly belonged in their midst. They criticised his playing and generally refused to give him a songwriter credit when he contributed to their tunes. He was starting to get strung out on heroin too. His brusque departure two months later was partly an attempt on Taylor's part to seek out a healthier avenue for his professional music-making expertise. As it turned out, it became more a case of 'out of the frying pan into the fire'. Too bad. He was a sweet guy and a massively gifted guitar player.

After seeing Taylor, I was invited to follow Keith Richards around London for what turned out to be something in the region of forty non-stop hours. He'd flown in from Switzerland without his family and was at something of a loose end. His new best pal Ronnie Wood was somewhere in Europe playing with the Faces and he was on his own looking for any like-minded druggie to share his time with. I'd always wanted to see up close what his life was really like – and then nail it in print. But his moment-to-moment existence back then was so mind-bogglingly X-rated and fraught with libellous content that I'd have to wait twenty years to do the story justice. The mid-section of 'Twilight in Babylon' from my first book *The Dark Stuff* is a detailed account of the first twenty hours of our encounter. It starts with us taking humongous amounts of drugs in central London, rises to a crescendo with the guitarist falling into a coma in Ronnie Wood's Richmond guest house and ends with me vomiting all over his welcome mat. But I've never documented the second half – the twenty hours spent after my unfortunate Technicolor yawn incident. Until now.

One thing about Keith during his junkie years – he was a remarkably non-judgemental host. Vomit on his premises and he wouldn't throw you out. He was definitely a live-and-let-live kind of guy in that respect. Instead he offered me more drugs, or 'the real breakfast of champions' as he called them. He laid out a six-inch line of heroin and cocaine mixed together, snorted it, laid out another and handed me a rolled-up pound note with a conspiratorial nudge. It was still 7 a.m. and a bit early in the day for me but nonetheless I honked the whole thing back without further thought. Hey, when in Rome . . .

The next few hours were understandably somewhat hazy but around midday Keith proposed we drive into London because he fancied something to eat. Whilst clambering into the passenger seat of his Dino Ferrari sports car, I offered up a silent prayer to the god of all London-bound motor-vehicle occupants that the man to my right would be more safety-code-conscious in daylight hours than I'd seen him be once night came a-falling. No such luck, of course. The open highway was just one big racetrack for him to burn rubber down. As far as he was concerned, heeding caution was strictly for sissies. Keith drove like a man transfixed. There was no conversation when he was in transit at the wheel. He just fixed the landscape in his windscreen with a withering glare and ramrodded into the bugger at full wheel-screeching velocity. He drove with the single-minded intensity of a tattooed man wading into a bar-room fight. It was a way of relieving some of his considerable inner aggression and frustrations.

We were only two streets away from our destination – a swanky restaurant nestling on the borderline between Chelsea and Earls Court – when Keith noticed an old man in a shed on the adjacent pavement selling copies of the *Evening Standard*. The cover of the paper featured a photo of the leader of T.Rex and alongside it the headline read 'Marc Bolan says "I am still the greatest"'. The headline had then been copied onto a makeshift poster that stood in a grille next to the man's shed. Keith saw the thing and instantly brought his car to a juddering standstill. He leapt out onto the pavement and started kicking the sign with intimidating gusto. The old bloke peered out of his shed and started remonstrating with Richards for damaging his property. Keith stood his ground and started jabbing a warning finger in his wizened direction. 'Listen, old man – you should be ashamed of yourself selling bullshit like that. Marc Bolan never has been the fuckin' greatest. He's just a mouthy little poof whose fifteen minutes of fame are all used up. You're misleading the public.' Then he got back in the car and drove off in a silent fury.

Keith – it has to be said – was not a fan of early-seventies rock. He couldn't abide glam rock. Couldn't stomach David Bowie's music and was extremely sniffy about Bowie's whole transsexual shtick. One time in a London club I saw Gary Glitter tentatively approach Keith. Before he could introduce himself, Richards had fixed him with such a disapproving scowl that poor old Gary practically wet himself on the spot. Like the Fall's Mark E. Smith, Keith maintained a zero-tolerance policy when it came to 'soft lads' trying to make their bones in the medium of rock 'n' roll. But Marc Bolan was by far and away the softest lad of them all from his exalted vantage point. Keith had a major bee in his bonnet and cursed him out at every opportunity.

Five minutes later, he'd parked his car and we located the restaurant. There's a great scene in John Ford's classic Western *The Man Who Shot Liberty Valance* when the hellion gunslinger Valance – played to perfection by Lee Marvin – abruptly enters a saloon bar with his faithful giggling accomplice at his side and all the action in the room suddenly grinds to an ominous halt. The roulette wheel stops spinning. The piano goes silent. All conversation ceases. Everyone stares at the intruders in stark terror. That's what it was like when Keith sauntered into the dining room. The place was packed with lunching yuppies – only they weren't called that then – who looked like they'd just dropped a gallstone when they saw him arriving. Suddenly the noisy environment was stilled to an eerie silence. The only sound to be heard was that of cutlery dropping to the floor in shock. Every eye there was warily fixed on him as though Vlad the Impaler had just stepped into the big room.

Not that the reaction he was eliciting fazed the guitarist in the slightest. I doubt if he even noticed. He just nonchalantly strode to a corner table, sat down and proceeded to disappear behind a fog of billowing cigarette smoke. I suppose he'd long grown accustomed to the supernatural effect he automatically set into motion whenever he chose to step out in public. Both he and Jagger shared a lucid grasp of the charisma they could radiate. That's why they'd lately started calling themselves the 'Glimmer Twins': 'glimmer' was the word they used to define their personal auras. 'A glimmer is more addictive than heroin,' Keith once told a journalist. He vividly understood the power he possessed.

After lunch, we moved on to the Rolling Stones' central London office, where Keith immediately espied yet another newspaper trumpeting a Marc Bolan interview inside its pages. This prompted a further avalanche of unprintable invective against the Boppin' Elf and his faltering career that lasted clear through the afternoon. Then – just as daylight was dimming out in the streets – Keith bumped into a drug buddy acquaintance called Rick Grech who'd been the bass player in Family and Blind Faith and who'd also co-produced Gram Parsons's first solo album. Grech returned to Ronnie Wood's guest house with us and then at midnight Keith took us both with him to a recording studio, where he was set to preside over a remix of the Stones' version of the Temptations' classic 'Ain't Too Proud to Beg' for future single release.

Sometime the next morning Ronnie Wood – fresh off the plane from Europe – joined Keith's little clan, followed by Jimmy Page later in the day. That night they returned to Wood's and wrote and recorded a song together in the same studio called 'Scarlet' – 'a folk ballad with reggae guitars' (according to Page) that remains unissued to date. I wish I'd been there to tell you more about it but I flaked out during the earlier mixing session and had crawled back to my dingy Archway shack for some much-needed rest and recuperation. Richards and I had been more or less awake for the same length of time – about forty hours – and I was dead on my legs whilst he was still wide awake and readying himself for three more days and nights of full-on wakefulness. Truly the man was a walking miracle of wayward stamina. Don't ever find yourself in a drug stand-off with him. No one throughout history has taken more drugs with more pleasurable consequences than Keith Richards. It's like going into combat with something out of Greek mythology. The grave-yards of the world are littered with the corpses of those who tried and failed. I'm profoundly lucky that I came out of it with some good stories and just an upset stomach.

Whilst on the subject of upset stomachs, I need to put the proverbial kibosh on a scurrilous piece of gossip that has been printed and reprinted about me and Keith Richards in magazines and books and which persists to this day. This story claims that one night the guitarist accidentally threw up on me and that I was so besotted with the guy that I continued to wear his vomit stains on my jacket for days afterwards as a badge of pride. Utter slan-derous poppycock! It's just pure fantasy and misinformation.

First, it's insulting to the guitarist who's rarely – if ever – thrown up in his entire life. The man was born with a stomach – as well as a will – of purest iron. And it's deeply belittling to me also. Indeed, this bald-faced lie was the beginning of a cruel perception that dogged me more and more as the decade progressed: that I was nothing more than just another Stones hanger-on/casualty. The *NME* have played up this bullshit angle too. In 2004 the BBC ran a documentary on the paper and one of the editors interviewed was droning on about me 'living the Keith Richards dream'. They don't know what they're talking about.

I didn't get into hard drugs – specifically heroin – so that I could be more like Keith Richards. I took the narcotic partly as a misguided way of temporarily gluing back together a broken heart but mostly because I liked the world it plunged me into, that instant all-embracing comfort zone. I would have become a user and addict whether or not I'd ever encountered Chrissie Hynde or heard a note of the Rolling Stones' music.

Neither was I ever – technically speaking – a Stones hanger-on. In practically all the time I spent with them, our roles were always pre-fixed. I was a writer on assignment and they were the subject matter. I never wanted to become a regular fixture in their entourage because I recognised early on that the only way to do that was to become a resident court jester for them, and I didn't need the condescension or fancy wearing the cap and bells.

As for being one of the group's many 'casualties' – well, once again I beg to differ. If you want to read a book about a real Stones casualty, then dig out a tome on Gram Parsons. Or read the last chapters of *Wired*, Bob Woodward's account of doomed comedian John Belushi's life and ugly death. Or check out the part in legendary US promoter Bill Graham's autobiography where he describes undergoing a complete mental breakdown as a result of being passed over by the Stones when they toured the States in 1989.

Probably all big rock acts have a personal trail of destruction stacking up behind them but the one shadowing the Rolling Stones is the biggest of them all, with corpses and broken spirits strewn far and wide across the universe mostly because the victims let their imaginations get too enflamed by what they heard and saw whilst in the group's orbit. But I was never one of them. On the contrary, I was one of the lucky few who stared into their dark vortex at close quarters and lived to tell the tale(s) with all my powers of recall still intact. I've always looked at our association as a boon not a curse.

When I wasn't busy consorting with the stars of the mid-seventies rock galaxy, the final months of 1974 would often find me lurking forlornly in my crummy bedsit cultivating a world-weary melancholy mood. I remember spending drugged-up hours alone listening intensely to Frank Sinatra's great Capitol albums – *Only the Lonely*, *No One Cares* and *Wee Small Hours*, the ones he made after being jilted by Ava Gardner. The pain in his voice spoke to me across the ages; Frank knew exactly how I was feeling.

But let's not get too down and dreary here. After all, I'd lately acquired new friends to help draw me out of the clutches of gloomy introspection. I even had a new girlfriend – of sorts. Her name was Hermine Demoriane and she was a performance artist. Her 'performance' speciality involved walking a tightrope stretched across a lake, thus giving the impression that she was actually walking on water. Imagine a younger Juliette Gréco with Yoko Ono's mind – that's how I saw her anyway. She was a lot older than I was, French, a real looker and eccentric as all hell. But that was OK with me. Consorting with the nuttiest broads in town was fast becoming my destiny as a young adult: like attracting like and all that. As a teenager I'd sat enraptured in front of TV sets and film screens taking in the French *nouvelle vague* films of François Truffaut and Louis Malle and I always carried a torch in my heart for the young actresses these great directors would employ – women like Jeanne Moreau, Stéphane Audran, Bulle Ogier and Bernadette Lafont. The characters they portrayed were invariably free spirits who couldn't be tamed by any one man and as such they heralded the first true wave of post-war feminism in Europe. Hermine was just like these women.

She was actually married to a poet with whom she still lived. They had a child as well – a daughter about to enter her teens. Theirs was an open marriage, though, with both parties free to explore other relationships. She approached me at a London club one night and told me she'd fallen in love with my writing and wanted to get to know me better. I was flattered but initially leery of her 'married mother' status – I didn't need to add the role of 'home-wrecker' to my list of dubious accomplishments in 1974. But when my relationship with Chrissie Hynde went into free fall, Hermine was there to console me. She just kept coming around and I kept letting her in. There was a peaceful aura about her that I appreciated. Most women I've been close to could talk the hind legs off a donkey but Hermine was the opposite – given to long, enigmatic silences. At first I didn't have particularly deep feelings for her as my heart still belonged to another, but as time passed we sought out each other's company more and more. Hermine actually cared for me a lot more than Chrissie ever did. As the decade progressed, she would become my personal guardian angel. Without her watching over me, I would surely have died. If there is a heroine to be found in the story I'm telling you throughout this book, then she is it.

Another daunting European female I found myself socialising with in the autumn-to-winter months of '74 was Nico, the German-born former chanteuse for the Velvet Underground who'd lately signed a solo recording deal with Island records' UK A&R branch. Whilst recording her fourth album *The End* in London, with John Cale once again producing, she'd met up with my pal Gene Krell from Granny Takes a Trip and they'd become romantically entwined for a brief period. The Chelsea apartment Gene shared with Marty Breslau became a home away from home for both Nico and me during those months because heroin was so freely available there.

I liked her a lot – and we developed a friendship. She was a fascinating individual and a quintessential bohemian free spirit. Part of her was like a child – naive and incredulous – but the other part – the part that kept her surviving – was ruthless and self-possessed. She saw herself quite rightly as a genuine artist. No man was ever going to make her his dutiful spouse. Poor old Gene tried and got his heart broken into a million pieces just like I did with Chrissie Hynde. He asked for her hand in marriage and she turned him down and ended their affair. 'You just don't amuse me any more,' she told him. I felt sorry for the guy but I still told him he was emotionally way out of his depth. You don't fall in love with women like Nico: it's like trying to bottle a lightning bolt.

Meanwhile, a much younger generation was vying for my attention in 1974. A few of them I cemented budding relationships with, others I let escape through my net. The most significant example of the latter breed was a precocious Mancunian youth called Steven Morrissey who wrote letters to me practically every week during that year. I wish I could tell you that these missives contained glimpses of the poetic audacity that he brought to his lyric-writing when he became the lead singer of the Smiths a decade later – but suffice to say this was not the case. How could it have been otherwise? He was only fourteen years old at the time. Instead he wrote ardently and single-mindedly about his fierce devotion for the New York Dolls. His teenage dream was to escape dreary Manchester and reinvent himself as one of the Dolls' glitzy entourage in downtown Manhattan. That's why I never wrote him back. I didn't want to inadvertently encourage an underage youth into embarking on a life of wilful self-destruction. I told him as much ten years later when I actually got to meet him. But I don't think he ever fully forgave me for ignoring him during his adolescent wallflower years.

Two teenagers I did become reasonably close to during that time were a pair of eighteen-year-old likely-lad law-breakers called Steve Jones and Paul Cook who hailed from the White City precinct of London. They approached me early in the year at McLaren's emporium. They had a group called the Swankers that they'd started with one of the shop's assistants, an art student called Glen Matlock. Matlock was a middle-class youth with better opportunities and a more responsible head on his shoulders whilst Jones and Cook were so working-class they could have been Arthur Mullard's two illegitimate sons.

Those two were always up to some kind of mischief. McLaren had initially caught them stealing from his shop but still let them frequent the place because he quickly became fascinated by their criminal-minded lifestyles. He saw Jones in particular as a seventies update of the Artful Dodger from Charles Dickens's *Oliver Twist* and in time would start fantasising that he could invent a role for himself as their very own Fagin. But that was all in the immediate future. In '74, Jones and Cook were out and about, ducking and diving, thieving and looting pretty much wherever they went.

Jones was the motivating force in all of this. He had major skills as a cat burglar – most specifically, the power to make himself virtually invisible whenever he entered an establishment intent on pulling off a heist. He'd recently succeeded in half-inching no less than thirteen expensive electric guitars one by one from various instrument shops situated on central London's Denmark Street. He even sold me one of his pilfered acquisitions – a beautiful black Fender Telecaster Deluxe. They were always up to no good. I remember their impromptu arrival that summer at a concert in a Kilburn cinema that Ronnie Wood and Keith Richards were putting on in order to promote Wood's first solo album. Jones, Cook and Matlock got in by literally dismantling and then climbing through a trapdoor on the building's extremely high roof.

Like McLaren, I could tell instantly that these oiks were going to go on to big things in the future – unless Jones and Cook got sent to jail first. At that point they could barely play at all but that didn't prevent them from projecting an aura of championship-level cockiness at all times. As I reported earlier, Dr. Feelgood were the hot up-and-coming band on the London club and pub scene that year, the one act everyone had high praise for. And yet Jones and co. were unimpressed. 'We could do better than those Southend cunts,' they blurted out more than once within my earshot. They even went so far as to refer to the

Feelgoods' large-domed guitarist Wilko Johnson as 'Fuckin' brick-head' one night to his face. They weren't what you'd call diplomatic or deep thinkers but I liked being in their company because they never took anything seriously and I found their continual tomfoolery an entertaining tonic to counterbalance my usual bedsit blues.

But the individual I became closest to during the second half of '74 was another rock journalist who'd climbed aboard the *NME* masthead that summer as the paper's newest staff writer. His name was Pete Erskine and he and I had already become fast friends when we were on an assignment together in New York at the beginning of the year. Pete was thin, pale and feminine-featured like me and we shared the same dark sense of humour so we just naturally gravitated towards each other. He was two or three years older than me, married with a young son and I think he was drawn to my company partly because my lifestyle at the time was less restrictive and fenced-in than his was.

That turned out to be our eventual undoing, however. Through being around me he first came into contact with heroin and succumbed to his temptation with little or no pre-thought. By the end of the year, we were both hooked on the stuff. Our brief honeymoon period with the drug was tapering off and trouble was getting ready to engulf us both. In Pete's case, he was never able to fully extricate himself from the jaws of addiction. He died nine years later. The official cause was a fatal asthma attack but that attack wouldn't have occurred if he'd been clean and healthy. It's always been my greatest regret in life that I couldn't help him redeem his circumstances and that I in effect contributed to his long decline by introducing him to the drug in the first place. But I also believe that he would have eventually fallen under its grip whether he'd ever known me or not.

Bad times were a-coming but in the dying weeks of 1974 I still maintained an upright 'cock of the walk' status within the music industry. The media bedazzled still lined up around the block to kiss my ass. And promiscuous women in London nightspots still dangled themselves before my gaze like overdressed car keys. But I'd long grown weary of their attentions. And I was becoming wary of the whole idea of thoughtless, passionless sex. With all the diseases I'd managed to pick up over the past two years, sleeping around had become indistinguishable in my mind from playing Russian roulette with my genitalia.

Meanwhile, music wasn't exciting me as much as it once had – at least not the new music I was hearing. There were suddenly far too many white guys trying to play funk and failing miserably. The glam thing was now dead on its legs. And the one new trend on the horizon – disco – sounded shallow and inconsequential when I'd hear it played alongside the great black rhythm 'n' blues music of the sixties. I knew what I was becoming – jaded – and I found the condition unsettling. I was still only twenty-two for God's sake.

Every now and then though something would transpire to temporarily rekindle my wavering interest in the whole pop process and the personalities contained within. Two close encounters during the final two weeks of the year still play vividly in my mind to this day. The first took place a week before Christmas. I went to visit a cocaine dealer friend of mine who lived off Edgware Road. Once inside his dimly lit apartment, I realised we were not alone. Two inebriated people were reclining on some cushions laid out across the living-room floor. One was a vivacious young black woman who spoke with a pronounced

American drawl – her name was Gloria Jones. The other figure – her boyfriend – was a short baby-faced man swathed in a floor-length Edwardian popinjay coat. It took me a full minute to actually identify him. It was Marc Bolan.

He looked a lot bulkier than the elfin figure he'd cut back in his glam messiah days. His once flawless features were now effectively rubberised by a bad case of toxic bloat and his body under that ludicrous coat of his seemed flabby and shapeless. What a turn-up for the books: the prettiest boy in the seventies pop stratosphere had prematurely gone to fat. At first I couldn't understand why. After all, he was snorting cocaine all the time and that usually acts as an appetite suppressant. But then I noticed how much alcohol he was putting away and realised that his added girth was all booze-related. He'd been doing the tax-exile boogie over in some bland Euro-trash hidey-hole like Monaco and had gotten so bored he'd just let himself go until he'd developed a nasty case of full-blown alcoholism. His physical deterioration also coincided with a marked dip in his personal popularity here in the UK. His records weren't setting the charts on fire any more. Most of his old fans had shifted their allegiance over to his arch-enemy David Bowie. In short, he was free-falling from grace at the speed of light and was unsure of how to rectify the situation. The musical formulae he'd still felt compelled to feed the media with were sounding more and more hollow and self-deluded.

At least he didn't launch into one of his 'I am still the greatest' diatribes that had so vexed Keith Richards just two months earlier. I ended up talking to him for a couple of hours – two Limey fop dudes on coke babbling away – and found him pleasant enough. On the surface he was woozy and effete but at heart he was a canny little hustler who knew how to turn on the charm whenever it might involve furthering his all-consuming fame-seeking agenda. But he also had a lively sense of humour and good taste in heroes. Syd Barrett was an obsession of his and he'd read my piece on the guy earlier in the year so he was particularly interested in learning anything about Barrett's current where-abouts and state of health. I told him that Syd had lately gotten fat too. He winced tenderly at the news: clearly he could relate.

Then we went off into a long debate about Bob Dylan, and Bolan told me a funny, oddly self-deprecating story about Dylan being his ultimate idol and how he'd finally met him in Los Angeles that year at the house of a mutual friend, songwriter Harry Nilsson. After listening to Bolan's effusive praise for several minutes without interrupting, Dylan had looked at him quizzically and asked, 'Say, man – are you one of those guys from the Incredible String Band?' The Bopping Elf was temporarily crushed – Bob didn't know him from Adam – but thinking about it afterwards – he told me – it only made Dylan seem more untouchable in his estimation. I told him that I'd heard a pre-release copy of *Blood on the Tracks* and that it was the first record Dylan had released in eight years that you could justifiably call a masterpiece. Bolan – who'd yet to hear the record – looked delighted. Complete artistic rehabilitation – that must have been his dream too. It's sad he didn't live long enough to truly achieve it. During the taxi ride home afterwards, I thought of Bolan and a line from the final track of *Blood on the Tracks* began replaying itself in my head over and over again. 'I've seen pretty people disappear like smoke.' Me too, Bob. Me too.

A week later, the *NME* sent me off to follow Rod Stewart around for a couple of days. As I've mentioned in an earlier chapter, Bolan and Stewart were the two golden boys of the fledgling seventies pop/rock mainstream, its two adored kingpins. But once they'd made it to the top of the charts in Britain, their career trajectories started to veer off in radically different directions. Stewart scored chart-topping records in America and quickly became a superstar attraction over there. Bolan didn't: he was simply too ethereal and too aloof for their earthy tastes. Stewart wasn't as pretty but he was a far better singer and projected a more fun-loving and altogether more approachable image out to the masses. Result: unwavering global megastardom was his to command throughout the entire decade. When we met, the critics still loved him and the fans still kept growing in numbers. He was the first to admit it: the guy was one lucky son of a bitch.

Stewart's career was about to find itself at a major crossroads. His group the Faces still hadn't gotten over losing their original bassist Ronnie Lane eighteen months earlier and were starting to stagnate as a musical unit. More problematic still, his faithful second lieutenant Ronnie Wood was spending more and more time in the Rolling Stones' druggy world. A couple of weeks earlier, Mick Taylor had quit the group and now everyone was expecting to see Wood take over his post. It was a foregone conclusion really. Jagger and Richards both wanted him and he was simply too besotted with the band to even think of turning them down. Stewart spoke long and candidly to me about his own views on the unfurling situation. Woody wouldn't leave him – he reckoned. He had too much of a good thing going with the Faces. Why would he willingly demote himself to hired-hand status for the Rolling Stones when he could stay an equal partner with his own lucrative outfit? It just didn't make sense to Rod. It would have been fair to say that he wasn't best pleased by the predicament. But Rod wasn't what you'd call a born worrier. Career issues would need to be addressed sooner or later but they weren't ever going to interfere too much with his constant pursuit of fun.

No one I've ever hung out with ever eked a better time out of being rich and famous than old Rod the Mod. It was like he'd been born into the condition. He took to the celebrity playboy lifestyle like the proverbial duck to water. The Faces played a series of pre-Christmas shows in Kilburn and on the last night Stewart invited me to join him on a visit to a central London members-only nightclub known as Tramp. The place reeked of new money, predatory women and European gangsters soaked in overpriced aftershave.

When Stewart walked through the door, the whole room stood up and applauded him like he was Father Christmas. One by one, wealthy dudes would stop by our table and kneel down as though they were about to kiss his ring. Women would suddenly materialise in pairs and offer to give him a blow job under the table – offers he cheerfully declined. At one point, he suggested I follow him to the toilets. Once through the door we were besieged by at least three adoring drug dealers determined to offer us free lines of cocaine. Back in the dining room he ate and drank like a Viking lord after being told by the maître d' that everything his table consumed was strictly on the house.

Stewart just took all the generosity being extended towards him in cheerful stride and drank it all in. He didn't have the kind of addictive personality that most musicians seem to struggle with so he could booze and snort without things getting seriously out of hand. He was suave, laconic and drop-dead funny as well – the closest thing to Dean Martin that England has ever produced. You couldn't have dreamed of better company. By the end of the night he'd lined up several of the most attractive women in the club and was instructing his chauffeur to ferry them all back to his country pile for further hanky-panky. He even invited me along to share in the festivities. I would have gone too like a shot from a gun but Hermine had turned up to the club in the interim and I didn't want to just abandon her there. Still, maximum respect and gratitude to Mr Stewart for extending the invitation in the first place. Shortly after our encounter, all his best musical instincts started to desert him and he began releasing bland codswallop like 'Sailing' and 'Da Ya Think I'm Sexy?' but I always kept a soft spot in my heart for the singer. To me, he'll always remain a prince amongst men.

I thought a lot about Rod in the final week of 1974. I mean, here was a guy who instinctively knew how to live the high life without getting needlessly bogged down in self-absorbed neurosis. I wasn't that lucky. Why couldn't I be that flippant?

Because I couldn't reconcile myself to what I'd lately become – a bad person. I didn't like myself any more. And I didn't like the smoky nightclub world and tawdry Tin Pan Alley sideshow that I'd abandoned myself to either. My dad had been right all along: the entertainment industry is a tainted, corrupting universe. And as the seventies hit their midway stretch I realised that I'd become corrupted too. Like the New York Dolls, I'd experienced too much too soon and part of me now felt like I'd been ground through a lemon squeezer. That's where the heroin came in: at first it glued me back together and gave me the get-up-and-go to continue to play out my role as the *NME*'s resident hit man.

What other options were there? The idea of stepping back into anonymity was unthinkable. I'd set out on this journey and couldn't back out now that the landscape had suddenly turned all bleak. Rock stars in the seventies were facing much the same dilemma. Neil Young wilfully ostracised his mainstream fan base by 'heading for the ditch. It was a rougher ride but I met more interesting people there.' And Sly Stone once stated that 'sometimes a man has to lose everything he's built up just in order to check himself out'. In other words, practically all the people worth a damn in music were headed for the low side of the road too.

The abyss was yawning – and so was I. I could have slept for a thousand years. My drug-drenched dreams now seemed more real to me than the moment-to-moment reality I was drifting through. And that's when the real darkness came seeping in. Real darkness and catastrophic bad luck. I'd entered the decade with a golden touch. Now – exactly halfway through its ten-year duration – it was about to be snatched from me and replaced by the mark of Cain.

1975

It was in early January of 1975 that I experienced my first significant bout of drug withdrawals. I shouldn't have been that surprised. My daily use of heroin – and cocaine, it balanced things
out – had become so pervasive of late I was now spending practically all my wages on the stuff. I was even writing to deadline
under the influence of the two drugs. If you ever download any
articles of mine from that specific era, you'll notice how the sentences get longer and more convoluted as the text progresses.
Now you know the reason why.

Then one day my Chelsea Embankment source ran dry for several days and my whole metabolism turned against me. The chills
and rapid changes in body temperature weren't unbearable but
the ferocious depression I felt eating away at my very soul for
some forty-eight uninterrupted hours wasn't something I wished
to visit upon myself again any time soon. This led to the last jolt
of common sense I managed to rouse within myself for the rest
of the decade. I decided I needed to distance myself from all the
druggy tristesse of the past six months. It would mean abandoning London and all its temptations and relocating to some more
exotic climate. But it also had to be a place where I could still
find work. There was only one option, really: America, more
specifically Los Angeles. I would get myself a golden suntan and

prowl Hollywood anew in search of wild tales to tell the folks back home. It seemed like a good idea at the time. But I'd neglected to factor in an important detail: Hollywood in 1975 was fast becoming the West Coast's very own re-enactment of Sodom and Gomorrah. Finding any kind of personal redemption there was a futile folly.

In the few weeks prior to my February departure, I became deeply embroiled in the music and short life of Nick Drake. Drake had died only a few months earlier – apparently it had been self-administered – but no obituary had appeared in any of the four music weeklies to mourn his loss. I'd been so taken up with my own sack of woe that at the time I doubt his passing even registered with me. But by year's end I was becoming increasingly aware that his untimely death was something that needed to be addressed just like the three albums of music he made in his lifetime needed to be celebrated – albeit belatedly. I'd always been an admirer of his, ever since I first heard 'River Man' waft spine-tinglingly across the airwaves via a John Peel-helmed radio broadcast. In the autumn of '71, just as I was installing myself into life at London University, I bought a second-hand copy of *Bryter Layter* and it quickly became the soundtrack for my brief middle-class student-drifter existence. I'd listen to the record and what Drake was singing about – the melancholy feeling of leaving England's green and pleasant land to chance your arm in London's gritty, isolating metropolis – spoke penetratingly to my inner condition. His was bedroom-hermit music taken to the level of high art, and the more I'd hear it, the more I became convinced that we had just lost one of the greatest English-born musical talents of the second half of the twentieth century. Ian MacDonald – who'd known Drake briefly when they were both students at Cambridge University – also subscribed to this viewpoint and was therefore enthusiastic when I told him I was planning a lengthy piece on the guy for the *NME*. It wasn't an easy assignment. Drake had always been an intensely guarded and private individual. Certainly none of the friends and co-workers of his that I spoke to were able to decipher the inner workings of his mind or explain his enigmatic aloofness. But most of them openly questioned the verdict of suicide that had been handed down after the inquest into his death and I could see their point. Only three tablets of an antidepressant known as Tryptizol were found in his stomach – hardly an amount to guarantee eternal oblivion. I wrote that Drake didn't wilfully take his own life and I've not read, seen or heard anything since to cause me to modify that opinion. The way I see it, both Drake and later Ian Curtis were the hapless victims of incompetent doctors who used them both as unwitting guinea pigs for pharmaceutical companies to test their most controversial new products on. The seventies was the decade of the nefarious pill-form antidepressant. Suddenly NHS quacks were doling them out to their patients like food to the famished. By decade's end thousands and thousands of middle-aged English housewives had turned into panic-stricken zombies as a result of being force-fed Valium in this insidious fashion. Nick Drake's tragic end can also be seen as a forewarning of their treacherous fate – the condition known as 'prescription death'.

My own Drake investigation was completed at January's end and printed in February. It's not one of my best efforts but it gave its subject's musical legacy much-needed acclaim and exposure and helped instigate a mystique around his name that has only grown with the passing of time. My next assignment was a sudden lurch from the sublime to the ridiculous. *NME* had found a patron to pay for my round-trip airfare to LA and a week's worth of hotel bills – after which I was to be left to my own devices. There was one snag, however: the patron was Jethro Tull.

In Christopher Headington's lofty tome *A History of Western Music*, Claude Debussy is quoted as having once claimed that he favoured featuring the flute in the foreground of many of his compositions because he felt the slender wind instrument possessed the mystical power 'of a melancholy Puck (the mischievous sprite in Shakespeare's *A Midsummer Night's Dream*) questioning the hidden meaning of things'. But Jethro Tull leader Ian Anderson showcased it in his own repertoire for less poetic reasons. He tootled away on it because it added a suitably mellifluous 'age of Aquarius' tonality to his group's otherwise generic late-sixties blues-rock bleatings and because it was also a useful prop for his incessant human-scarecrow posturing whenever he found himself in front of a paying audience.

The Tull had started out as trailblazing 'crusties' but soon jettisoned their initial 'playing the blues for greatcoat-sporting students who rarely wash themselves' game plan to climb aboard the good ship 'prog rock' and seek their fortune through playing electrified madrigals in 7/4 time with lyrics about high-born lusty temptresses beating stable-boys' naked buttocks with a riding crop. Against all conventional logic, their new direction paid off like a one-armed bandit choking up its entire contents of coinage to some dumb-lucky gambler. By 1975 they were one of the world's biggest-selling musical attractions. In America they could sell out all the mega-barns any promoter could throw at them. In Los Angeles alone, they'd been booked for four consecutive nights at the prestigious 20,000-seater-capacity Felt Forum. That's what I'd essentially been flown in to trumpet back to the home front. They seemed to think I'd happily adapt to the role of becoming their token media shill but as usual I had other more personal agendas to pursue.

Their US press officer – a shrill, hyperactive Bobbi Flekman lookalike with a voice like paint-stripper – met me at the airport and then drove me straight to the first of the Felt Forum shows previewed for that evening. I was already in a bad way from the jet lag – as well as probable drug withdrawal – and considered my imminent fate much like a prisoner about to face the gallows. Marshalling a half-hearted stiff upper lip, I staggered into the huge auditorium only to find myself in a scene to rank with Dante's inferno: 20,000 double-ugly Americans going completely gaga over a musical spectacle so bizarre that it beggared description and which none of them could have even remotely comprehended. If they had, they wouldn't have been there in the first place. Each song the Tull performed was as long and windy as a discourse on agrarian reform in the nineteenth century, and to top it all they'd incorporate old Monty Python sketches into their routines and pretend to their Yankee rube fan base – who'd yet to see Python on the telly in their country – that they were doing something audaciously original. I couldn't believe my eyes and ears. Where was the appeal? Why all the bums on seats? I asked Anderson these very questions later and even he was at a loss to explain his group's popularity. But I already knew – it was bad taste, pure and simple. They say good taste is timeless. But bad taste has been around just as long and is invariably more lucrative.

Anyway, after half an hour of this musical torture, I was starting to sag and wilt like an untended bloom. The press officer –

noting my haggard expression – passed me a Quaalude to aid my further discomfort. It was a decent thing to do, all things considered – but also deeply misguided. Five minutes later, I was out cold in my seat. Apparently I had to be carried out of the venue, placed in a car and then driven back to the hotel. I just remember waking up early the next morning fully-dressed in my hotel room with a dust bowl for a mouth and aches in all my joints.

Fortunately Iggy Pop arrived shortly afterwards. He lived virtually next door to my hotel on the Sunset Strip and had come over to renew old acquaintances and possibly scam a free breakfast on my room-service chit. I told him of my current dilemma: jet lag, drug withdrawals and, most of all, the prospect of having to witness yet another Jethro Tull show. 'Man, I wouldn't wish that combination on my worst enemy,' he winced sympathetically before suggesting he contact a friend to help me self-medicate throughout the whole ordeal. An hour and one phone call later, there was a knock at my door. Iggy opened it and in walked a tall, thin, clearly gay young black man dressed like a member of Little Richard's backing ensemble. His name was Johnny and he dealt heroin when not dipping his toes into other backwaters of small-time LA-based criminality with the aid of his equally overattired black boyfriend, who was known as Levi. He didn't say much. Just dropped a small packet on the night-stand and then stared at me as if to say 'So where's the money, sucker?' It was then that I had the sudden realisation that I possessed only English traveller's cheques as a form of viable currency. I showed them to him but to no avail. 'What the fuck is this shit?' I recall him saying. 'It's just worthless paper to me.' Fortunately, a compromise was reached. The hotel had a gift shop and Johnny needed a hairdryer so I basically paid for it on room service, as well as for a couple of chintzy items he also took a shine to whilst perusing the merchandise. This meant in effect that the Tull and/or their record company were footing the bills for our drugs. Looking back now, I can't say I'm proud of the incident. You could dress it up and play it back as an early punk gesture of defiance – me and the Ig literally ripping off the stadium-rock behemoths – but in reality it was just seedy junkie behaviour. Still, it got the job done – so to speak. That night, I sat through two full hours of Jethro Tull in concert and felt no pain.

Once I'd dispensed with all Tull-related duties I began scoping out the Hollywood terrain in search of fun, adventure and good music, only to promptly discover that all three were in woefully limited supply. Ben Edmonds, my old *Creem* pal, had recently moved there and I remember us going to Rodney Bingenheimer's English Disco only to discover the gnome-like Bingenheimer cueing up old glam records on the house turntable to an audience of just three pilled-up punters dreamily occupying the dance floor like extras from *Night of the Living Dead*. We stuck around for half an hour – just to be polite – and then made our excuses and ran for the exit door. As we were stepping outside, we noticed a disturbance on the pavement before us. Two of the three patrons we'd just been rubbing shoulders with were splayed out on the cold concrete like wounded birds. Just a few feet away, a young long-haired man in an expensive-looking fur anorak was staring at the human wreckage with undisguised glee in his cocaine-rimmed eyes. Ben recognised the guy: it was Glenn Frey from the Eagles.

We both understood the subtext. Two years earlier, glam had been the big noise in town but now it was dead on its legs and the rugged and rigidly heterosexual Eagles had lately risen up victorious as the new messiahs of West Coast rock. It wasn't hard to fathom out why. Their music was as comfortable and reassuring to mainstream America as slipping on a pair of old slippers. It didn't challenge its audience on any level or promote alternative lifestyles. It just blended together contemporary hippie mysticism with fanciful cowboy folklore and then served the combo up like a musical box of chocolates wrapped up in a ribbon-bow of mock-prairie harmonising. Their records were like those washed-denim jeans that were so in vogue at the time: bland, inauthentic but impossible to escape. More than any other home-grown act, they had their collective finger on the pulse of what America really wanted to hear in the mid-seventies.

Frey and the rest of his cocaine cowboy musical fraternity had their own upmarket Hollywood watering hole to frequent when they weren't cooking up new mellow tunes in the studio for further domination of the airwaves. It was called the Roxy and was situated on the Sunset Strip only a few doors away from the now-ailing Whisky a Go Go. There was a room to drink in, a room to eat in and a room to watch live entertainment in, as well as a dance floor, but most of the human interaction inevitably went on around the bar area. Every second-division rock musician in the region seemed to have a tab there and could be found draped over a bar stool on any given night trying to drown their professional and personal woes with copious shots of tequila. You rarely saw a smile on any of their faces. Hedonism had lately become a singularly joyless pursuit on the West Coast.

Meanwhile, out on the sidewalk the damaged and terminally drug-diminished were only growing in number. Wherever unsuspecting pedestrians went, they'd be approached by some intense young person attempting to indoctrinate them into one dubious cult or another. All these broken spirits had the same basic rap: the end is nigh, the devil has won, give up your ego and all worldly possessions and join us as we sink into blind submission to some crackpot deity.

Hollywood's moneyed elite – the town's real movers and shakers – had long since learned to avoid rubbing shoulders with its walking wounded. It was all too elementary. If you didn't care to be hassled by scary 'street' people, then you simply didn't go out in the streets. Employing this logic to its fullest degree, the area's superstars tended to lock themselves away at home in Malibu or Bel Air, only venturing out to record or visit their dealers. Every now and then there'd be some ugly public brouhaha: some liquor-looped English drummer and his troglodyte roadies smashing up a local bistro, or Sly Stone and his hoodlum cronies pulling guns on a receptionist at the Record Plant in a seriously misguided attempt to retrieve several master tapes Sly had recorded there without ever paying for the sessions. But most of the real madness of the time was played out behind the locked doors and gated driveways of remotely located luxury mansions once owned by movie stars from the silent-picture age that no one seemed to remember the names of.

Such an arrangement was ideal for at least one foreign body who'd lately beamed himself down into the community. David Bowie had moved to the City of Angels around the same time I had – sometime in February – but was clearly in no mood to celebrate his arrival with the locals. He was conspicuously absent from all the clubs and social functions during that month and the ones that followed. He'd first found fame as a flamboyant 'look at me' kind of fellow but now he seemed to be invaded by a Howard Hughes-sized craving for self-seclusion. It made sense.

He'd been going through many ch-ch-changes of late and, like a snake, had been shedding a lot of dead skin. Musically speaking, he'd daringly jettisoned glam only to plausibly reinvent himself as a white soul boy fronting an upmarket disco revue. His physical appearance had undergone a startling transformation too. Where once he'd resembled an alien transsexual from the planet Outrageous, he now affected the dress code of an emaciated hophead straight out of a Damon Runyon novel set in the McCarthyite fifties. Every time Bowie appeared in public that year, he looked like he'd just stepped out of an audition for *Guys and Dolls*.

Bowie was in LA partly to further distance himself from Tony Defries's ruinously extravagant New York-based management empire Mainman, which the singer had lately forged a legal separation from. On discovering that their meal ticket had left them in the lurch and flown westward, the fame-seekers who made up the organisation began a frenzied smear campaign of public gossiping that was heard loud and clear throughout the industry. Bowie – his jilted employees maintained – had lately become mentally unhinged, had a raging cocaine problem and needed to be institutionalised before he drove himself terminally crazy or – worse – killed himself. In the weeks and months that followed his exodus to LA, phone lines across America were throbbing with rumours of Bowie cavorting with white witches, pentagrams, exorcisms and Nazi theology. Hearing this stuff, it became obvious why he no longer felt the urge to embrace the madness of the Hollywood streets. From the sound of things, it was already all going on in his overstimulated mind.

Bowie also had a new album set for imminent release, his first full-tilt foray into contemporary soul music, which he'd recorded both in Philadelphia and Manhattan throughout the previous year. He'd briefly toyed with the idea of calling it *Shilling the Rubes* – Jewish slang for 'ripping off the peasants' – but had later relented, titling it instead *Young Americans*. A song of the same name was the opening track and RCA, Bowie's record label, had earmarked it as the project's first single as well. One sultry day in mid-February, I was in a Sunset Strip coffee shop with Iggy Pop when the radio playing over the loudspeaker system suddenly announced they were about to unveil an exclusive preview of David Bowie's latest musical caper. The song came and went, leaving me underwhelmed. True, Bowie once again had hit upon a brand-new musical hybrid – Johnnie Ray meets gospel – but the blend sounded as forced as a shotgun wedding. Iggy liked it, though. He genuinely admired Bowie's sense of creative ambition and thought he was a 'damned fine singer to boot. It's a good piece of work.' He kept repeating, 'He's still a white-hot talent.' Neither of us knew it then but in less than a month Bowie would start focusing that white-hot talent of his on heating up Iggy's own career. It wouldn't come a moment too soon.

Bowie and Iggy's personal circumstances at that point in time couldn't have been more different. The former had supposedly been stripped of a large chunk of his financial net worth in his recent legal battles with Mainman but was still a wealthy young dude with power, prestige and a doting entourage to cater to his every nutty whim. He could make a bizarre public spectacle of himself – as he did that same month when he'd turned up on US television screens to give Aretha Franklin a special Grammy Award, only to deliver a drug-addled eulogy to Lady Soul sounding like Peter O'Toole on PCP – and no one thought any the worse of him. He might have lately become a raving coke fiend like the gossips were claiming but it hadn't yet robbed him of his golden touch in the industry, and that was all that really mattered.

Iggy – by contrast – was poverty-stricken and semi-homeless, crashing in the spare room of his former Stooges guitarist James Williamson's modest Sunset Strip apartment and living an existence that can be best described as 'hand to mouth'. He was no longer – technically speaking – a drug addict, mainly because he simply didn't have the financial resources to sustain such a lifestyle. In February you could even see him early in the morning jogging the length and breadth of the Sunset Strip. But he was also bored and deeply gloomy about the state of inactivity his musical career had stalled into during the past twelve months, and these factors often compelled him to still get fucked up. He and Williamson were trying to put something together – a new band – with two local brothers, Hunt and Tony Sales, tentatively pencilled in as the rhythm section and a guy called Scott Thurston – whom Iggy always referred to as 'Doll-face' – who'd already worked with the Stooges on keyboards. But there was little local interest and no record-label patronage forthcoming. The Stooges had splintered apart with no record royalties or performance income to tide their members over and only bad memories and bad karma as a continued reminder of their very existence. Iggy was doing the only thing he knew how to do – just soldiering on – but he often felt he was beating his head against a brick wall. Worse still, the rest of Hollywood had seen him in some truly pitiful conditions out in public over the past two years and had reached the conclusion that he was just another lost cause.

In a town where fame and money are worshipped above all things, there is little pity and zero tolerance for those with the potential to achieve both who nonetheless end up broke, unemployable and out on the streets. On at least one occasion when Iggy and I were together in local clubs some 'industry insider' would take me aside and lecture me about the supposedly dire consequences of 'being seen with that loser'. 'Listen,' I'd fire back, 'Iggy Pop is not a loser. He's already made three records that one sweet day will come to redefine the very sound and vision of rock 'n' roll. The women are all still in love with him and most men still want to be him. This man you call a loser – really, he's the king of the world.'

Which was precisely how I saw him back then: bloodied but unbowed, still a worthy target for veneration despite his self-destructive skittishness and catastrophic run of bad luck. Over the next two months I spent a lot of time in his company, buying him meals, following him around from place to place in search of free drugs and generally listening to him philosophise at length about life, art and his tumultuous career to date. The guy presented me with such irresistible subject matter to write about later on. But mainly I was drawn to him like a young disciple seeking out his personal guru.

I didn't see his poor-boy status as demeaning and contemptible – I even found it oddly inspiring. Iggy – from my perspective – had lately turned floating through life like a cool breeze into a kind of zen art. It helped of course that practically every woman in the region nursed a raging crush on the guy and was only too happy to invite him into their homes, even if it meant only to share their drug stashes. There were a couple of lesbians living in the same apartment building as James and Iggy and even they were aflame with mad love for the man. Everywhere he went, females stalked him like bounty hunters. At first I thought it was just down to his personal charisma. But then late one night in early March we found ourselves both standing outside the Roxy surrounded by a bevy of equally intoxicated revellers. I was staring up at the stars in the sky above when I heard a sound like running water below me. I looked down to my left and saw Iggy holding what at first appeared to be a fire hose from which a flood of liquid was pouring onto the sidewalk. I looked again. It wasn't a fire hose, it was his penis urinating all over the club's courtyard. Everyone stopped their idle banter and stared at his wedding tackle in mid-gush. It was uncommonly big. Then he shook the last drops off, stuck it back in his jeans and walked off into the night as if nothing had happened.

Iggy Pop's penis is actually a bit of a thorny topic with me. I wish he'd keep it under wraps when it comes time to step out in the public arena. Seeing it or hearing him describe it in song is just too much information. David Bowie is apparently of the same opinion. 'I wish Jim wouldn't keep exposing himself,' he informed a French newspaper back in the nineties. Put our reactions down to an Englishman's natural sense of reserve. Back in the old country people called them 'private parts' for a reason.

Maybe he had the same problem when they later shared an apartment in West Berlin that I encountered from time to time in 1975 when I happened to pass out on the sofa at James Williamson's place and ended up spending the night there. The next morning I'd awaken with a fierce hangover only to see Iggy parading around stark naked before my ill-focused eyes. There was inevitably something slightly intimidating about the ease with which he let himself be witnessed au naturel. And it only got worse when I later joined him for an impromptu swim at a nearby hotel pool. My own more modestly proportioned sexual apparatus was duly stricken by some serious shrinkage just as soon as I'd jumped into the cold water. Iggy, as you might imagine, didn't seem to suffer from this kind of humiliation. See, that's the problem whenever you hang out with a fellow who just happens to possess unfeasibly large genitalia. He's got a huge penis, you don't, and the contrast inevitably begins eating away at your personal sense of manly self-esteem. But I never let the matter sully our relationship because I was always more interested in what was going on in the man's soul. And I sense that David Bowie felt the same way.

In all the biographies and articles written about Bowie and/or Iggy, it's claimed that the pair stepped into a studio to write and record together for the first time ever sometime in May 1975. But the session actually occurred some two months earlier, in mid-March by my recollection because Iggy told me about it the day after. Bowie had phoned him up clear out of the blue and invited him to collaborate on some new material he was set to demo in a local Hollywood recording facility. Iggy turned up at the appointed time to find a rail-thin Bowie alone in the studio apart from an engineer and an oval-faced teenager who turned out to be the journalist Cameron Crowe on assignment for both *Rolling Stone* and *Playboy* magazines. After snorting cocaine together, Bowie and Iggy set about composing and then recording three impromptu songs – 'Turn Blue', 'Speak to Me' and 'Sell Your Love' – with the latter supplying both lyrics and vocals and the former playing and overdubbing all the instruments himself. There were scattered moments of open conflict. At one point Bowie admonished Iggy for sounding 'too much like Mick [Jagger]'. 'I don't sound like fuckin' Mick,' the Mighty Pop snapped back sniffily. But this experiment in creative human bonding turned out to be a successful one for both parties. Iggy was elated to be back in a studio and working with such a quick-thinking and prestigious presence. And the prestigious presence was thrilled too – if Cameron Crowe's account of the session later printed in *Rolling Stone* is any indication. 'Bowie clutches his heart and beams like a proud father watching his kid in the school play . . . "They just don't appreciate Iggy," he is saying. "He's Lenny fucking Bruce and James Dean. When that adlib flow starts, there's nobody like him. It's verbal jazz, man!"'

It was Iggy's talent for 'verbal jazz' that ultimately attracted the newly christened Thin White Duke to work with him – rather than a desire for some *Velvet Goldmine*-like sexual trysting. David Jones had devoured Jack Kerouac's *On the Road* as a teenager. Now, in his twenties, he'd found the ultimate wild American friend – his very own Neal Cassady – to share his life with.

History now indicates that Bowie and Iggy did indeed become travelling companions, globetrotting the world – and elsewhere – together. But these journeys only began taking place the following year. After the session, Iggy didn't hear from him for months. The Thin White Duke had other more pressing matters to regulate. There was a film being shot in Mexico that summer entitled *The Man Who Fell to Earth* that he'd agreed to play the starring role in. There was a new manager and new business advisers to select and monitor. But, most urgently, he needed to be put in touch with a reputable exorcist. In her autobiography *Backstage Passes* his then-wife Angie recalls receiving a barely coherent phone call from her husband that must have taken place shortly after the Iggy session: 'He was in a house somewhere in LA and three people – a Warlock and two witches – were holding him for some terrible Satan-related reason. He wanted to get away . . . but the witches wouldn't let him leave.' Flying over from London to help calm her spouse's paranoid fantasies, she ended up consulting a white witch herself about the best way to exorcise demonic spirits from their temporary LA homestead. The real problem, she strongly implied in her text, was that these spirits were nothing more than hallucinations visited upon Bowie due to his grave overdependence on cocaine and a general lack of food and sleep.

Iggy too had hellhounds dogging his trail. His demons were real though: poverty, public indifference, a stalled career, boredom, frustration and flat-out despair. He still had his patrons. A gay youth named Raymond who'd somehow managed to con his way into receiving ATD – financial aid for the totally disabled – even though he was quite able-bodied would turn up every month to share his drugs and government cheque with his downtrodden hero. A teenaged girl whose father was a rich Mafia lawyer would raid her parents' jewellery stash, pawn the stolen items and then give the money to Iggy to tide him over financially for a couple of weeks at a time. He'd mastered how to survive in the margins alongside the rest of the dispossessed and how to gainfully court the kindness of strangers. But he was also going stir-crazy because he'd been born with a hyperactive nature and couldn't stand being made temporarily redundant as a performer and musician. He always needed some work-related pursuit to keep him halfway anchored or else he'd be off somewhere running wild, spinning like a spinning top in a hurricane. Drugs were still a problem for him because he still intuitively believed he needed to be intoxicated in order to summon forth the essential all-defiant Iggyness that lurked within his otherwise somewhat guarded and inward-looking personality. But the drugs weren't working any more because his nervous system couldn't take the continued abuse. Back in the not-so-distant past, chemicals had helped ease the pain and beat the odds but now they were only pushing him further and further into the black hole of despair.

Another outstanding LA-based music-maker struggling to hang on to his sanity in the mid-seventies was Brian Wilson, the Beach Boys' former guiding light. Iggy had encountered him once at a mansion in the Hollywood Hills. Alice Cooper had also been on the premises. Wilson – overweight, sweating profusely and dressed only in pyjamas and a dressing gown – had tried to get the two singers to harmonise on a version of 'Shortnin' Bread' that he'd improvised on a nearby piano. I asked Iggy how Wilson had seemed that night. 'Like a total, certifiable lunatic,' came the reply.

Everyone in Hollywood had their own 'crazy Brian' anecdote to share. Iggy and James Williamson's next-door neighbour was a woman who'd recently become the personal astrologer of Wilson's wife Marilyn and she'd often recount with saucer-eyed incredulity the dysfunctional vibe of her new employer's Hollywood home. A guy living just down the hall had once stumbled upon Wilson passed out on someone's lawn. It often made for painful listening: people invariably invoked the term 'some kind of permanent brain damage' when attempting to define his mindset.

I was staying in the spare room of Ben Edmonds's rented house at this point and most mornings I'd awaken to the gentle pitter-patter of early morning rain just as dawn was lighting up the sky. By 7 a.m. the sun would be gleaming and I'd fleetingly feel that healing California glow I'd come in search of. To keep that good feeling flowing, I'd play Beach Boys records through-out the morning way into the afternoon – early stuff like *Summer*

Days (and Summer Nights!!) and the incomparable *Today!*. I needed to rid myself of all the jadedness I'd lately become engulfed by, and the Beach Boys' vintage music proved a bracing tonic in that regard. It still thrilled me the way it had when I'd first been exposed to it as a dreamy-headed pre-pubescent sprog. There was hope yet. And the more I listened, the more obsessed I became with trying to fathom out what had really happened to Wilson in his rise and fall from grace. Without at first realising it, I'd found my next project for the *NME*.

When the penny dropped, I went into full 'investigative journalist' mode, tearing around the region in search of clues and Beach Boys acquaintances who could still remember what had transpired in the LA music community over the past fifteen years. His evolving story soon started to feel like a potent metaphor for La-La Land itself. It had once been the closest thing in the Western world to a Garden of Eden. But disruptive forces had taken dominion over the terrain and turned it into a sun-baked snake pit. Many of the carefree golden boys and girls who'd roamed the beaches with surfboards back in the sixties were now crazy-eyed human wreckage. No wonder Brian Wilson had retreated deep inside his bedroom and become scarily obese and creatively inactive. He just wasn't made for these times.

With the promised land's native spawn starting to turn distinctly frayed and crispy around the edges, it was down to the bulldog-breed expat rockers who'd lately installed themselves in this balmier clime to bring the requisite star-power and sparkle back to Tinseltown. Like David Bowie, they'd come to luxuriate in the American dream after having spent far too long cocooning in England's dreary landscape only to find the drinks more toxic, the lines growing fatter and the laughs getting thinner. No fewer than two ex-Beatles, Paul McCartney and Ringo Starr, were holed up there now, though they generally made a point of never seeking out each other's company. The still boyish-looking McCartney – in town to mix Wings' *Venus and Mars* album – had lately sullied his usual squeaky-clean image by getting busted driving around Santa Monica with reefer in the car. Wife Linda saved him from possible extradition by taking the rap. Starr meanwhile had fallen into the role of Hollywood's most illustrious town drunk, with local lesser lights like Harry Nilsson and ex-Monkee Micky Dolenz providing a raucous and ever-willing entourage at watering holes dotted throughout the region. But lately he was facing stiff competition: Keith Moon had moved into the area too and was bent on drinking the town dry. Everyone remembers Moon nowadays as this mischievous imp who caused mayhem and merriment wherever he went but the man I saw night after night out in the clubs rarely corresponded to this image. He'd be sitting in a corner with a look of utter misery on his face, pouring booze down his neck to drown his sorrows and still his inner demons. Where had all the good times gone for these guys? Those crazy days and crazy nights, those high-spirited Pied Piper sixties? One minute they and their peers were high and happy and on the brink of some shared state of enlightenment, the next they were nursing dour faces and stiff drinks and practising the dark art of self-obliteration. The spell had been broken – that was it. The good magic just wasn't happening any more and everyone who'd lived in the cloud-cuckoo-land of Utopia now had to face the painful descent back to planet Earth and the harsh realities of broken marriages and aimless hedonism.

And how was I personally bearing up in this godforsaken sun-blistered environment? As well as could be expected. I'd take half a Quaalude most evenings: it made life more fuzzy and Felliniesque. I even started drinking furtively for the first and only time in my adult life. The Rainbow served this formidable concoction called a Velvet Hammer which contained vodka but tasted exactly like a chocolate milkshake. Just one shot would send me reeling.

Those two months I spent in Hollywood were also the last time I did any serious womanising. The girls there were very pretty and sexually up for anything. But they often weren't that bright. So I got myself a girlfriend instead. Her name was Sable Shields and she briefly became my very own California sweetheart. I'd actually first met her two years earlier when she was a local legend, trading under the name of Sable Starr, LA's wildest wild child and most brazen groupie. She was only fourteen years old back then but had packed so much worldly experience into her short life that she scared me at first. Now she was sixteen and – after ill-starred romances with both Iggy Pop and Johnny Thunders – was once more living with her parents, attending school and generally trying to keep out of trouble. We ran into each other at the Whisky a Go Go one night and a mutual attraction sparked between us. I started taking her out on dates – to concerts, movies and the like. Considering our lurid pasts, it was a relatively chaste relationship to begin with. But then of course the inevitable occurred: we soon ditched the lovey-dovey stuff and concentrated more on getting high together and making out. It was the seventies we were living in after all – not some dorky episode of *Happy Days* – and it just made more sense to kick back and go with the carnal and chemical flow. It was fun too – at least up until the night I nearly died of a heroin overdose whilst in her company.

That unfortunate incident still looms large in my memory, as do the events throughout the week leading up to it. Rod Stewart and the Faces had arrived in town to play a series of sold-out shows at a nearby enormodome and the stars came out in force to welcome them. Backstage on the first night I was standing around jawing with Stewart when a deeply tanned, well-heeled middle-aged couple stepped in to greet the singer. It was the actress Joan Collins, accompanied by her obscenely wealthy husband of the hour. Rod was his usual charming self and Collins wasted no time in then introducing him to a friend of hers whom she'd also brought to the concert. The face, form and flowing blonde hair looked distinctly familiar. "Ere Nick – say hello to Britt Ekland,' he shouted at me. 'Rod 'n' Britt' soon went on to get designated as the ersatz Burton and Taylor celebrity couple of the rocktastic seventies but this was the moment they first actually met. I don't recall the Rodster being much impressed by Miss Ekland's charms at first glance. 'She's all right,' he told me after she and Collins had exited the dressing room. 'But I'm really waiting for Wednesday. Julie Christie's supposed to be coming down to the show that night.'

After the first-night performance, Cher threw an impromptu party for the group at her well-appointed Hollywood eyrie. It was meant to be a celebrities-only bash but Ronnie Wood very kindly invited me along to mingle in the glamour, and it was just too good an opportunity to refuse. Fortunately no one bothered to inform the hostess of my profession or else I'd have probably been turfed out without further ado. The sultry songstress was getting a rough old time from the international press at this precise juncture because of her peculiar love life. On the one hand, she was bona fide well-respected Hollywood royalty with a hit

TV show still high in the ratings. But ever since she'd broken up with husband/Svengali Sonny Bono, she'd been making distinctly catastrophic choices when it came to finding new suitors and the tabloids were hauling her over the coals for her oddball trysting. She'd recently been linked romantically with feared entertainment-industry power broker David Geffen. Unfortunately he turned out to be gay. Now she'd turned her amorous gaze on Gregg Allman. Allman was the vocalist and gaunt blond-haired figurehead of the Allman Brothers Band, arguably the most popular and successful home-grown US rock act of the early seventies. The Southern rockers were loved nationwide for their often turgid blues-rock improvisations but they were feared too, particularly by industry insiders who'd already seen their barbaric side at close quarters. Their roadies were supposed to have been homicidal thugs. One of them had even done jail time for stabbing a Mafia-affiliated promoter to death in his own club. But the definitive legend surrounding the group involved their guitarist, one Dickey Betts. Apparently he'd been out riding his Harley one day when he became peckish. Seeing a bull grazing in a field, he'd stopped his bike, ambled over to the animal, beat it to death with his bare hands and then cooked it and ate it before casually returning to his vehicle and speeding off again. Clearly, these were fellows it didn't pay to trifle with.

It was providential indeed then that Gregg Allman was the only 'bro.' present at Cher's little soirée and that he was so utterly cabbaged that night he'd have been hard-pressed to punch his way through a sheet of Kleenex. They say that love is blindness and in Cher's case this was all too evidently true. It had taken her ages to divine the homoerotic sexual leanings of her previous boyfriend and now she – an ardent anti-druggie – had somehow managed to become smitten with the most notorious celebrity junkie in mid-seventies America. At one point, Allman staggered over to a white piano and attempted to perform a slow blues for his girlfriend's guests. Whatever drugs he was embalming himself in, they certainly weren't doing his musical chops any favours. Only Ronnie Wood was impressed by the impromptu recital. Seated next to me, he looked awestruck and mumbled words to the effect that we were both privileged to be in the presence of such a gifted entity. That's when I came to the realisation that Ronnie Wood wasn't exactly the brightest light bulb in the great fuse box of life.

But then again, no one ever required the cerebral acumen of a rocket scientist in order to become a successful rock guitarist. He might not have made an ideal contestant for Bamber Gascoigne to browbeat on *University Challenge* but the happy-go-lucky fellow with the jackdaw face and pineapple hair was still nimble-fingered and personable enough to be sought after by the musical crème de la crème *du jour*. On the second night of the Faces' LA festivities, Mick Jagger turned up backstage seemingly out of the blue. There was a tense moment early on when he found himself face to face with the actor Ryan O'Neal, who'd recently been accused in the tabloids of having had a fling with his wife Bianca; Jagger came perilously close to bitch-slapping the grovelling thesp. But his mood lifted once he found the tune-up room, where Wood was strumming away surrounded by several cocaine dealers who were all offering up their merchandise for free.

After the show, we all returned to Wood's hotel suite. Jagger started talking about a one-day festival show he wanted to set up somewhere in the States that would involve a bill featuring just three acts – the Faces, Led Zeppelin and the Stones. 'Who'd be the headliner though?' asked Wood. 'We can work that out later,' sniffed Jagger. 'The thing is – I'm still not sure where we could actually stage it.' 'How about Death Valley?' I offered. No one thought that was very funny. Jagger stayed glued to Wood that night. Back in England Keith Richards had been jamming with an American guitarist called Wayne Perkins and was grooming him as Mick Taylor's replacement in the Stones. But Jagger was unconvinced and still hankered for 'Woody' to fill the role. That's what this visitation was all about for him, a way to fathom out how the land actually lay for the Faces and whether their guitarist could be easily uprooted from it. In fact, I'll wager that it was on this very night that Ron Wood first tentatively committed to life as a Rolling Stone. Mick Jagger just wouldn't let him off the hook.

An even more momentous rock icon left his lush Malibu hidey-hole just to mingle with Woody and his scampish bandmates on their last night in the city of fallen angels: Bob Dylan. The wiry little troubadour with the sagebrush facial hair and the deeply sardonic eyes was still in his Garboesque reclusive phase despite being the comeback king of the season with *Blood on the Tracks* nestling at the top of the US album charts, but to everyone else's astonishment made a point of coming out to party down with the Faces. I later wrote in the *NME* that I'd actually gotten to shake his hand that night but I don't think I was telling the truth. I hope so anyway because I was 'in a very bad place' that evening. Just prior to attending the event, I'd driven over to Danny Sugerman's house with Iggy and Sable. Johnny the black gay dude I've already introduced you to was there with some Mexican heroin he wanted to offload. Mexican heroin was very different from the Chinese rocks I was accustomed to back in

London. The latter was ideal for crushing down and snorting but this Mexican stuff was like black chocolate, practically impossible to reduce to powder form. Injecting it directly into a vein was the only way to feel its power. So I persuaded someone present to do just that – to shoot me up for the first time. Oh boy! I just remember the needle piercing my arm, the tiny spool of blood it left when it was removed and then – a rushing sound in my head like migrating birds furiously flying out of my skull. After that – nothing. The next image I recall was Iggy standing over me, shouting and slapping my face. Danny Sugerman was behind him, screaming obscenities and demanding that the singer remove my prone cadaver from his bathroom floor, get the fuck out and never darken his towels again. So Iggy and Sable propped me on their shoulders and dragged me out into the driveway. I couldn't understand what the fuss was all about: I wanted to fall back into the coma I'd just been rescued from. But Iggy kept getting in my face, shaking me and making sure I was still semi-conscious. We drove around for what felt like hours with the windows down and the breeze from the highway rushing into my face. At one point on this journey I started to fade out again and Iggy stopped the car and dragged me out onto a deserted Hollywood hilltop. It was a beautiful night. LA was stretched out before us in a swampy haze of glowing neon and the sky above us was ablaze with real stars. The only sound to be heard was Iggy's voice. 'Just don't die on me, OK,' it kept repeating. Thank God he was there to play the good Samaritan. Virtually anyone else in that environment and under those circumstances would have left me to float off into the ether. Hey, it was the seventies, baby. Kindness and basic human decency were mighty thin on the ground.

We finally arrived at the party around midnight. When Rod Stewart saw me weaving uncertainly through the door, he immediately dragged me into the toilet and started throwing tap-water from one of the sinks over my face to help further revive me. It was a gallant gesture but I think now in retrospect he did it more to impress Britt Ekland, who was there by his side. The only other memory I have of that night is this: I was leaning against a toilet-cubicle door with Iggy to my immediate left and a human behemoth hovering over both of us. 'Old Kenty and Iggy fucking Pop – as I live and breathe,' the latter exclaimed in an inebriated East London cackle. 'Look at the state of you two cunts.' Iggy – who didn't recognise the guy – was looking at him with a truly disdainful expression and I knew he was about to say something deeply inappropriate like 'Who is this fat prick anyway?' So summoning what presence of mind I could muster, I reached out, placed my hand firmly over his mouth before he could utter a single syllable and said loudly and very firmly, 'It's Peter Grant, Jim.' (I called him Jim because he tended to behave more reasonably when addressed by his given name. If you called him 'Iggy', he'd inevitably behave like Iggy, and that could prove problematic.) His face completely changed when he heard those words. Iggy knew all about Peter Grant – how feared and all-powerful he was throughout the music industry. He also knew Grant could break him like a twiglet if he felt the urge. All the contempt drained from his eyes in a split second, to be replaced by a look somewhere between stark terror and awe. 'Hey, Peter, man – great to see ya,' he spluttered enthusiastically. Grant just stood there grinning madly – he was seriously drunk – and laughing at the state we were both in. It was like two callow young punks suddenly coming face to face with Tony Soprano on a bender in a public rest room. Or two minnows confronting a whale. I told Iggy afterwards – 'Hey, listen, you saved my life tonight but I may well have saved yours too. If you had said what it looked like you were about to say to Peter Grant before I butted in, he would have crushed you like he did when he recently sat on Elvis Presley's dad.'

It was one of the juiciest pieces of gossip to have come out of the scandal-mongering seventies: Led Zeppelin get invited to a personal post-gig powwow with Elvis Presley in Las Vegas in early '75 and their manager only makes the mistake of placing his enormous girth on a chair that – he fails to notice – already contains a frail, sleeping Vernon Presley. In Chris Welch's posthumous biography of the man, Grant actually verified this improbable tale and even added embellishments. However, my wife recently interviewed one of Elvis's boys who was present when his boss met the Zeppelin entourage on the night in question – one Jerry Schilling – and he swore that the incident never occurred. Logic indicates that Schilling's version is the easier to believe; after all, Grant could have broken every bone in the poor man's body if he'd descended on him from behind. But that doesn't stop me from wanting it to be true.

I know a thing or two about how gossip is formed and then spread about. I've dished it out in my time and felt its boomerang effect as a victim of scurrilous and unfounded rumours myself. It's usually 30 per cent truth mixed in with 70 per cent wilful misinformation. Most of the time, it's mean-spirited and unreliable. But in this case, it's so ludicrously funny it deserves to be written into the history books. Elvis would have killed your ass if you'd have stepped on his blue suede shoes but he didn't seem to mind when Peter Grant sat on his dad. Maybe he was just too stoned to notice. (Strange rumours were starting to circulate about Presley all around LA. They were saying that the King was a hopeless pillhead junkie. At first it seemed absurd, too implausible to even contemplate. Elvis on drugs? No one could believe it.)

Or maybe the King felt chastened and genuinely taken aback by the sheer power Led Zeppelin wielded throughout the country of his birth at the time of their meeting. By the mid-seventies America had become their own personal fiefdom. No other act was remotely as popular. And in LA particularly the mania surrounding them was so vast and volatile it seemed capable of setting off earthquake-like tremors throughout the community whenever they played there. Zeppelin and their music had a strange, unearthly effect on the region that had to be felt and seen to be believed. The natives went stark staring mad just knowing they were in the vicinity.

Zeppelin and their touring retinue arrived in Hollywood – just as the Faces were finishing up there – in order to play a series of concerts booked all over the West Coast that March. They even had their own private aeroplane waiting at the local airport to wing them to the venues. In the past, the town had played host to the group's highest times whilst out on the road. But the high spirits of yore were much harder to locate this time around. Cocaine was largely responsible for this hardening of Led Zeppelin's spiritual arteries. There was far too much of it freely available: dealers would literally line up to share their wares and curry favour with the group's principals. And the groupie situation surrounding the band had lately gone into a state of red alert. Valley girls were prepared to tear each other limb from limb in order to beat the competition and bed a Zep member. Jimmy

Page told me about an incident where one deranged female had placed razor blades in a hamburger bun one of her rivals was about to eat as a way of eliminating her from the competition. The story had helped inspire the lyrics to one of their most recent songs – soon to be available on *Physical Graffiti* – 'Sick Again', Robert Plant's disapproving ode to these self-styled she-creatures of the Hollywood Hills.

In fact, both Plant and Jones made a point in '75 of steering well clear of all the groupie hysteria by renting accommodation in quiet mansions near the beach, far away from the Sunset Strip. The rest of the touring party though were happy to install themselves in Hollywood's Continental Hyatt House hotel in the Strip's centre, an establishment renowned for turning a blind eye to any outbursts of rock 'n' roll excess.

Yet even Jimmy Page had grown tired of being fought over by scantily attired LA jailbait. In '75 he initiated a new sexual pursuit: celebrity wife-swapping. He'd lately been seen enjoying the company of Bebe Buell, Todd Rundgren's leggy consort, but had chosen Chrissie Wood as his 'special friend' throughout this West Coast stopover, a situation that didn't best please her husband, Ronnie. Page spent practically all his down time sequestered in his suite on the hotel's top floor. I visited him on several occasions there and found him holding court with a number of other acquaintances, all of us seriously wired on the voluminous quantities of cocaine that were readily available. Heroin was just starting to creep into the picture too. One night, he treated us all to an impromptu screening of Kenneth Anger's *Lucifer Rising*, the film he intended to create a soundtrack for later in the year. It lasted for about half an hour and consisted of amateurish home-movie footage shot by Anger of an extremely stoned Marianne

Faithfull in black robes silently stumbling down a staircase embedded in the mountains of Egypt, holding a lighted candle.

Page may have been ever-increasingly drawn towards the dark side of life but he didn't let these preoccupations interfere unduly with his professional responsibilities. He could still detach himself from the madness when he chose to. John Bonham, however, wasn't so lucky in this respect. Los Angeles brought out all his most disturbing character traits and magnified them to a degree that made him a very frightening individual to be in close physical proximity to. He drank all the time partly as a way to counterbalance all the cocaine he was inhaling continuously. He'd even taken to placing an ounce bag of the stuff between his legs during their live shows and could sometimes be seen placing his hands inside the bag and throwing handfuls of the drug into his nostrils whilst still behind the drum kit. Mick Hinton, his personal roadie, told me once that the entire road crew would very carefully dismantle the kit after each concert's conclusion and then tip his drum mat over a large sack in order to capture and share the large deposits of cocaine the drummer had spilled onto it during each show.

However, his escalating excesses were turning him into an increasingly tortured figure. One night that week, he ended up spending an evening in the company of Bryan Ferry, the suave Geordie crooner whose Roxy Music were also touring the LA area at that point in time. Ferry later recalled Bonham repeatedly bursting into tears and pleading to return to the relative calm of his home and family back in the Midlands, so terrified was the drummer becoming of his own insatiable appetites whilst on the road.

I made my own escape from LA in early April, just in the nick

of time. I returned to London with an unsightly sunburnt face –
I'd fallen asleep at an outdoors Beach Boys concert I'd attended
two days prior to taking the plane homeward – and no apprecia-
ble healthy glow to my features. I'd made few friends during the
two months I'd been resident there and was now pretty much *persona non grata* in the region. Someone had even alerted the local
police to have me placed under arrest if I ever returned there (it
must have been rescinded; I flew back five years later without
incident). The folks over there just didn't understand kamikaze
journalism. The place gave me the fucking willies anyway and I'd
rubbed up against enough of its weird scenes and fame-
worshipping grotesqueries to last me a lifetime. The way I saw it,
California was doing me a favour banning me from its borders.
I'd almost died out there but had still managed to tunnel my way
out. Plus I had a couple of hot stories to peddle to the *NME* and
its readers. All was not lost – at least not yet.

London hadn't changed in the time I'd been away from it – it
was just as grey and glum-spirited as ever. Glam rock had brought
some fleeting colour to its streets and music venues two or three
years earlier but now that trend had petered out, all the blokes at
gigs and in clubs had gone back to dressing like roadies and the
women didn't look much better. I was still flouncing around in
my Beau Brummell phase and was generally mortified by the lack
of sartorial flair being exhibited by my pop-picking compatriots
that year. But then 1975 was another watershed year in rock and
youth culture, and watersheds are generally gloomy places to be
stuck in.

It was the last year that old-school rock 'n' roll values still held
the reins over young music-lovers around the world. Throughout
the sixties the music itself had grown in structure and complexity

in a genuinely forward-thinking fashion, but by the mid-seventies it had become stagnant and far too besotted with its own perceived past. A case in point? John Lennon's musical output over the two decades. Simply play 'I Am the Walrus' from 1967 and then follow it up with 'Whatever Gets You Thru the Night' (a US no. 1 hit for him in '75). The first track is a glorious, mind-boggling sonic lurch into the unknown whilst the second is an unimaginative regurgitation of late-fifties Brill Building popcraft complete with a double-corny sub-King Curtis sax solo. Rock was still hopelessly Yank-fixated, which meant that the vast majority of English acts were still singing with pronounced American accents and name-checking American towns and cities in their songs instead of being true to their real roots and writing about their own experiences and regions. Punk would change that, of course. But punk as we now know it was still a full year away from unleashing its fury.

In its absence, UK-based rock was being hijacked once more by the testosterone brigade – lusty-voiced blues-cliché-spewing lead singers in gonad-constricting loon pants who were always using the medium of music to bray on about their two-fisted manliness and rambunctious hard-loving ways. Ex-Free singer Paul Rodgers – lately a rising star again with Bad Company – was the kingpin of this hirsute studly mob. Legend had it that Rodgers was so manly he could start a show clean-shaven and by the end of the set he'd have grown a full beard before the audience's very eyes. But a capacity for sudden facial-hair growth is ultimately scant compensation for the lack of musical adventurousness he and his ilk instilled in the mid-seventies rock landscape. I could see it in the rapture-free stares of their London audiences. Everyone looked just as jaded as I still felt.

A lot of good music had come out of the early seventies and I'd been there to hear it all. But by mid-decade, inspiration was scarce on the ground. A few gifted mavericks like David Bowie, Steely Dan, Joni Mitchell and Neil Young still released new music of real consequence and artistry but the rest had mostly gotten bogged down in aimlessly parroting whatever they wrong-headedly perceived to be 'the new contemporary trend'. This was when the musical abomination known as 'white reggae' started to materialise. And if rock bands weren't making complete fools of themselves trying to appropriate rhythms best left to the likes of Toots and the Maytals, they'd be loitering in studios under the influence of too much cocaine attempting to play funk with equally desultory results. What a sorry state contemporary music was in. Two years earlier, I'd returned from the States with my suitcase laden with new records I'd heard whilst there and fallen in love with. When I'd flown back this second time, I hadn't bothered to take any vinyl whatsoever from my LA sojourn with me. The only piece of music in my luggage had been a master tape James Williamson had made for me of a Stooges gig in Michigan just prior to their final break-up. On it you could hear Iggy being heckled and then physically attacked by a biker gang in the audience. I told James and Iggy I could sell it for them and get them some (much-needed) advance cash in the process, and they'd happily complied. I then flew to Paris and gave it to my pal Marc Zermati, who was the only punk-related person to have his own independent record label – Skydog – at that time. Marc paid them and then received another live Stooges tape by mail from Williamson. The two low-fidelity tapes were sequenced together and released the following year under the title of *Metallic KO*. The record went on to sell surprisingly well and became a seminal soundtrack for UK punks, who gleefully aped the unruly aggression of the audience response captured within.

Stepping back into *NME*'s Long Acre office that spring felt strange. Business was booming – the paper was selling more than ever – but morale was low within its ranks. It felt like most of the staff and contributors had suddenly grown detached and cynical about what we were supposed to be doing. Few of us now felt the continued urge to push the envelope and take rock journalism into ever more provocative areas. I was unhappy about this state of affairs and duly vented my spleen on the subject to the guilty parties. And then – just three weeks after waving my unfond farewell to California – I got the sack.

In strict point of fact, I was fired for someone else's fuck-up. My bosom buddy Pete Erskine was supposed to deliver a cover story one week but missed the deadline because he chose to down a full bottle of cough medicine instead of applying himself to the task at hand. He was so comatose he also neglected to hand in a singles review I'd completed and was counting on him to deliver to one of the editors due down at the printers. This review's non-appearance was the reason for my sacking. Erskine got off with just a few stern words.

This not unnaturally threw our friendship into a state of some turmoil. I loved Pete dearly – he was my closest friend at the time – but lately he'd become something of a liability. Ever since heroin had come into the picture our relationship had tended to mirror the one later shared by the two protagonists in the film *Withnail and I*. Pete had left his wife and child and moved into my squalor-ridden Archway retreat (he'd lived there whilst I was off on the West Coast). Suddenly he had no family to keep him

in check and got swept up in hard drug use instead. It scared me
to see how quickly and how intensely he fell under the lure of
heroin. It was like standing next to someone you care about
whilst that person is being sucked into quicksand. It hadn't
escaped my attention that I was a bad influence on him: our relationship just ended up bringing out the worst in each other. At
first I felt responsible for his worsening state. But then he started
screwing up in the workplace and I found myself having to cover
for his mistakes. Now I'd been given the boot from the *NME*
over something that was essentially his fault. That's when I
stopped feeling responsible for Pete.

The sacking not only seriously compromised one friendship
but also annihilated whatever feelings of camaraderie still lin-
gered within me vis-à-vis the rest of the *NME* staff. That cher-
ished sense of a shared goal – that 'all for one and one for all'
high-spiritedness – had left the building back in 1973 or early 1974
at the latest. In its place a mood of divisive complacency had
taken over the premises; it increasingly felt like I was one of the
only writers who'd stayed committed to upping its level of
impact, subject range and journalistic standards. To that end, I
was still prepared to risk death, ridicule, deportation and even the
wrath of the entire music industry. My colleagues weren't nearly
as gung-ho though. They generally preferred the age-old 'anything for an easy life' approach, clocking on and off between 9
and 5 and then stealing away to the comfort zone of their private
leisure-worlds outside of pop culture.

Tony Tyler, the paper's features editor, had basically given up
on popular music the day the Beatles broke up and had come to
loathe the seventies and its rock musicians with a fierce passion
(in the eighties he actually gave vent to this hatred in a slim tome

entitled *I Hate Rock & Roll*). After making it his personal crusade to belittle Bryan Ferry whenever possible in print, he'd turned his disapproving gaze on me. He then persuaded Ian MacDonald that I needed to be put in my place and that the best way to achieve this was to kick me out of the *NME*. These two then went to Nick Logan and told him I'd become too arrogant and loose-cannon-like and needed to be given my marching orders. This he did – in a short letter he handed me one day in the office. I read it before exiting the premises in high dudgeon.

The weeks that followed are grim ones to recall. They took my name off the *NME* masthead and acted as though I'd just vanished into thin air. Rumours started circulating throughout London that I was unemployable. Back in the seventies rock journalism wasn't something the daily papers wished to incorporate into their pages, so career alternatives for me meant signing up with one of the lesser music weeklies – something I wasn't prepared to do. So I did the only thing I knew how to do when placed in extreme, emotionally depleting circumstances. I went back on the smack.

A month passed before I was struck by a rare moment of lucidity. One night I managed to compose a heartfelt letter to Nick Logan protesting my innocence and generally giving my side of the story. Once he'd read it, he got in touch and asked me out to lunch. During the meal he invited me back into the *NME* fold under somewhat reduced conditions, and I agreed to return. But things were never the same again for me and that paper. Before I'd viewed the *NME* as 'us'; now I saw it as strictly 'them and me'. Any illusions that we were basically all on the same page and fighting the good fight together went straight out of the window.

I had one ace left up my scribbling sleeve – the Brian Wilson story I'd been researching over the past months. I had enough material for a book but decided instead to have the 40,000-word text I was working on serialised over three separate *NME* issues. More people would read it that way and I'd be able to show the world, his wife and my in-house persecutors who the real 'man with the plan' was when it came to extending the paper's cutting edge. I went to work like a soul possessed, which was handy as I only had a month to turn it around. The first 20,000 words were a dream: I'd sit there and the prose just flowed out onto the page. I could stay focused and scribbling for up to twenty hours at a stretch. But then – halfway through – something snapped inside my mind and I started losing momentum after that. I'd sit for hours struggling over a single sentence. By the end I felt utterly drained. Nowadays I'm inclined to think that this was because of all the heroin running around my brain and bloodstream but at the time I saw it as something more supernaturally catastrophic, a potentially terminal condition.

Real inspiration – particularly in so-called pop culture – almost always comes in notoriously short spurts. Even Bob Dylan enjoyed only three years as a bona fide creative groundbreaker ('63 to '66). I'd enjoyed three uplifting years too. From '72 to mid-'75 my writing talent had been on the rise. It reached its peak with the Wilson investigation. After that it went into free fall. I still contributed to the paper but I don't think anything they printed with my byline attached during the rest of the decade was up to snuff. Partly it was the drugs, partly it was simple burn-out, but a lot of it was because I'd grown to actively despise the way the *NME* chewed up and then spat out virtually anyone of substance that came into its orbit – contributors and musicians alike. I no longer trusted anyone who worked there and felt little affinity with their tastes and editorial policies.

As soon as my writing talent began to go on the blink, I realised I needed to start investigating new avenues of gainful creative endeavour, if only to help pay for the drugs I was now addicted to. I tried being a DJ for one night at a Camden Town club called Dingwalls but the bloke running the place told me I wasn't up to the task because I hadn't played enough disco. There was only one other halfway viable option open from that point on. I needed to get a group of my own together and make my living as a professional musician.

I'd harboured this particular fantasy from even before reaching puberty. As a child, I'd been forced to study classical piano and had actually learned how to sight-read music in the process. Then I'd fumbled through my teens groping to master simple barre-chord shapes and finger-picking techniques on a crappy acoustic guitar with strings like curtain rails I'd somehow inherited. By the time I'd reached nineteen, I could play both instruments – after a fashion. But I didn't really know how to play what then constituted rock 'n' roll in any way, shape or form.

Amazingly, this didn't prevent me from recklessly offering my guitar-playing services to Iggy Pop the first time I met him back in 1972. That was my dream gig back then – to actually play in the Stooges. Thankfully he rejected my offer pretty much on the spot. I say 'thankfully' because had he arranged an audition for me in a rehearsal studio I'd have come out looking like a prize oaf: I'd never actually played an electric guitar up to that point in time. Later that same year the Flamin' Groovies invited me to be their keyboard player even though I don't recall us ever playing a note of music together. I was tempted but turned them down mainly because I didn't want to relocate to San Francisco.

The following year I finally got my first electric guitar. Michael Karoli out of Can sold it to me – a flashy-looking Plexiglas affair that he'd picked up over in Japan and soon tired of. I strummed away on that until – a further twelve months later – I acquired the stolen Fender from Steve Jones. By mid-'75 my living quarters had become overtaken by the six-stringed buggers. You couldn't move without bumping into a fretboard and knocking the thing to the uncarpeted floor. But my attempts to make music specifically for the public arena up until then had been tentative at best. There were a couple of sessions at Brian Eno's home studio at Maida Vale. I'd also tried to work with a guy called Magic Michael – an acid head with his own unique personal magnetism who sang like Frank Sinatra and often performed in drag or stark naked. You can catch a glimpse of Michael in full deranged performance flow – replete with shrunken genitalia – in Julian Temple's Glastonbury film. As you can probably imagine, we went nowhere fast. Michael went on to work as Can's singer for a couple of months and even moved to Cologne for a while, before resurfacing in London and becoming one of the first signings to Stiff Records. He could have been a massive star but just didn't have the focus and ambition to make the journey.

At one point, the *NME* started to take an interest in my musical dabblings. In early '74 Nick Logan offered to set me up with some esteemed Tin Pan Alley Svengali who'd then be employed to groom me as a performer and recording artiste. His one proviso was that I write about the whole experience and then continue turning out copy for the paper even if my pop-star career were to actually take off. It sounded like a sad old caper to me. Pop stardom really wasn't something I'd ever craved. And when he went on to suggest that my Svengali could well be Jonathan

King, I nipped that idea smartly in the bud without further forethought. The idea of being moulded and talked down to by some self-styled pop pimp was not one that I cared to entertain. So what did I go and do in the summer of '75? Only link up career-wise with another glib-tongued shyster who dreamed of exploiting and then discarding impressionable young boys with stars in the eyes.

It had been eighteen months since I'd first encountered Malcolm McLaren in Paris and in that time I'd come to view him both as a cultural ally and caring friend. In my darkest hours following the Chrissie Hynde bust-up I'd poured my heart out to him and he'd always listened sympathetically and offered sound advice. But we'd spent most of our times together verbally plotting out the revolution we both recognised that rock music needed to undergo in order to be truly relevant again. Looking around sleepy London town in 1974 though we'd quickly concluded there were no authentically wild young stars-in-waiting to heed sedition's call. So we turned our attentions to America and its two struggling punk-rock forefathers. I'd recently tried – and failed – to persuade the Stooges to regroup. During the same time line McLaren had moved to Manhattan in order to attempt to reverse the down-bound fortunes of his beloved New York Dolls. During the first six months of 1975 he took on the self-appointed role of being their personal style and image consultant. He dressed them in red vinyl costumes designed by him and then sewn up by Vivienne Westwood and also managed to coerce the group's principals into writing a batch of new songs. But then he took up with the wrong-headed notion of persuading them to embrace Marxism and quote passages from Mao Tse-tung's little red book during their live sets. Americans throughout the ages have always taken a distinctly dim view of Communist propagandists and certainly weren't about to tolerate it coming from a down-at-heel group of three-chord-playing cross-dressing drug addicts. Sensing their jig was well and truly up, the quintet splintered apart in the middle of a US club tour, leaving McLaren to pack up his tent and scurry back to London.

The day after his return – it would have been sometime in early June – he and Westwood came to visit me in my soon-to-be-vacated Archway lair (the landlord – distressed at my lack of domestic skills – had found a loophole in our leasing agreement and was booting me off the premises). For several hours he ranted at the expense of the lately departed Dolls. They'd vomited over the clothes he'd had made for them. They'd sniggered at the Marxist manifestos he'd tried to impress upon them. The singer was a social gadfly, the bassist a raging alcoholic and the lead guitarist and drummer were so junked up they were perpetually half-asleep. He'd started out with high hopes but the group had let him down at every turn. They'd run out of ambition and moxie and their individual shortcomings had turned them into failures who deserved to fail. He was well rid of them – or so he kept saying.

Trying to change the subject I asked McLaren if he had any projects or plans now he was back in London. That's when he told me he'd decided to commit his future energies to shaping and guiding the group that our teenaged reprobate colleagues Steve Jones and Paul Cook – as well as his old shop assistant Glen Matlock – had been struggling to launch. They were young and malleable – unlike the Dolls – and could be counted upon to kick up enough of a storm to rudely awaken the sleeping metropolis from its post-hippie coma. I'd yet to hear them play and so was initially sceptical. But he was already grandly scheming out their fate. He'd even come up with a name for his new wards whilst out in the States. He was going to call them 'QT Jones and the Sex Pistols'.

A few weeks later, he returned to ferry me over to witness a group rehearsal. We drove to a huge building somewhere in White City that had – until recently – been a functioning BBC studio. But the TV company had moved its staff, cameras and audio equipment to another location, leaving the old premises empty and guarded over by one none-too-vigilant caretaker. This caretaker had a son called Warwick Nightingale, who happened to be one of Steve Jones's little gang and who'd been assigned the lead-guitar duties in his group. Warwick – better known as 'Wally' – had either persuaded his dad to let them turn one of the rooms into their very own rehearsal space or else he'd simply stolen the keys to the building and opened it up to his colleagues.

The four of them were lurking at the entrance as McLaren and I drove up. Then we entered the premises, walking through one spacious stripped-down room after another until we reached one that possessed a makeshift wooden stage on which several amplifiers were placed. I complimented them on their choice of equipment – it was all very state-of-the-art – and they told me it had all been stolen, every last stick of it. The microphones – they then revealed gleefully – had been heisted from David Bowie's 1973 farewell to Ziggy Stardust concert. Jones and Cook had hidden under the chairs after the audience had left the London venue and stayed there for several hours. During that time, the onstage equipment had not been dismantled. Instead a roadie had been elected to keep an eye on it but he'd fallen asleep on a chair next to the drum riser. Jones and Cook eventually tiptoed around the slumbering roadie onto the stage itself and stole the microphones by clipping them from their leads with a pair of garden pliers.

In due course they plugged their guitars in, Cook sat down behind the drum kit and the four of them performed their entire repertoire to McLaren and me. It mostly consisted of songs first recorded in the mid-to-late sixties by hit-making London-based pop groups of that era, like the Small Faces' 1965 debut single 'Whatcha Gonna Do About It' and a lesser-known album track called 'Understanding', followed by the Who's 'Call Me Lightning' and 'Substitute'. After that their song choices became distinctly ill-advised. They struggled through a wooden rendition of 'Everlasting Love', the old Robert Knight soul classic that had also been covered back in 1968 by a UK act called the Love Affair, before segueing unconvincingly into the Foundations' cheesy pop classic 'Build Me Up Buttercup'. Contrary to later legend, they could play quite well. Matlock and Cook had already bonded into a tighter and more energetic rhythm section than the New York Dolls had ever boasted in their ranks whilst Jones's singing style was a straight – but not unimpressive – copy of Steve Marriott's classic larynx-strafing hollerings. But there was nothing remotely radical about them. They were marooned in a musical past they'd barely known.

But then – after some coaxing – they decided to unveil the only two songs they'd managed to write amongst themselves. One was called 'Scarface' and the other 'Did You No Wrong', and they were exactly the same piece of music with different words. 'Scarface' was about a gangster and boasted a lyric written by Jones's profligate stepdad, a retired boxer. Steve pulled out a piece of paper at one point and showed me the verses written in their author's own halting scribble. Almost every word had been grievously misspelt. Still, I wasn't looking to these lads for tips on good grammar. At this point I just wanted to hear them play something that sounded reasonably contemporary and 'Did You No Wrong' finally managed to fit the bill. It's the only self-penned song from their early repertoire that they later went on to record for posterity and that later studio version – still available for all to hear – isn't so different from what I heard that day. Sure, John Lydon's recorded vocal is more sneerfully adenoidal than Steve Jones's gruff, hectoring original delivery but the lyrics – written prior to Lydon's arrival but still credited to him – are pretty much identical. Ditto the riff, chords, groove and sense of lurching unbridled menace. All I knew hearing it for the first time was that – in a year filled with cocaine muzak and pretentious sonic blather and smoke – it was like suddenly breathing fresh air after being trapped down a mine shaft. I hadn't heard straight rock 'n' roll sound this spry and impactful since the Stooges were still firing on all cylinders back in 1972. At the end, McLaren and I exchanged meaningful glances. The little red-headed bastard might actually be on to something here, I remember thinking.

In due course, the group downed tools and looked to us for some kind of verdict on what they'd just been playing. I told them I was enthusiastic about their self-penned stuff but warned them to banish 'Everlasting Love' and 'Build Me Up Buttercup' from the repertoire, ditch the underwhelming mid-sixties déjà vu vibe and start listening and learning from the more current US-based punk-rocker elite. McLaren then took over the discussion in heated tones. He immediately turned on poor Wally Nightingale, telling him he didn't belong in the group, couldn't play well enough and that he should just take his guitar and vanish: he was fired. This was a bold move on McLaren's part. Wally held the keys to the rehearsal space after all and was also probably the most proficient player of the lot of them. But McLaren couldn't abide the fact that he wore glasses and was the most overtly sweet-natured of the bunch. He was already thinking in terms of image at the expense of musical prowess. I'd rarely seen anyone behave in such an overtly ruthless and tactless way towards another human being. Nightingale's eyes were moist with tears as he exited the building: with no forewarning he'd just been viciously exiled from the gang he'd mucked around with since childhood. Not that his old cronies appeared to give a damn. A minute after he'd gone, both Cook and Jones started running him down, calling him a 'cunt' and ridiculing his teary-eyed departure. That's when I got my first serious insight into what a bunch of flint-hearted little back-stabbers they really were.

But the surprises weren't over yet. Nightingale's sudden sacking meant there was now a big hole in the group's sound. Steve Jones had worn a guitar around his neck when they'd played but – as he'd only started actually learning how to play the thing three months earlier – he'd employed it as a convenient stage prop rather than a musical instrument. 'Who's going to play guitar then?' Glen Matlock asked McLaren. McLaren turned in my direction: 'Nick plays guitar. He can be your new member.' He didn't ask me if I was interested in taking on the role – we'd had no prior words on the matter whatsoever. It was just presented as a fait accompli. Suddenly I was a Sex Pistol.

'Well, why not?' was my first and foremost reaction. At that exact moment in history, I wasn't doing much with my time apart from hunting down heroin. At least it would make a change from lying horizontally on a broken-springed mattress and staring dreamily at the ceiling. But there was a lot of work to be done.

And they were still kids. There was only a four-year age difference between us but when you're a worldly twenty-two-year-old and you're suddenly thrown into the company of eighteen-year-old artful dodgers, relationships are never going to be balanced. It was a challenge – but a worthwhile challenge to take up, whatever the outcome. I'd never been in a group before and a part of me relished the experience of now being part of a music-making gang. Plus I sensed that – with or without me – they would become a successful act because they were still so young and so cocksure. At the very least, it would be something to tell the grandkids in years to come.

My Sex Pistols sojourn lasted roughly two months, possibly throughout July and August '75. I can't say for sure because time lines tend to become unreliably elastic when you're as stoned as I was throughout that period. But that's how it feels to me now, looking back from the vantage point of relative sobriety. We didn't rehearse every day – more like once a week. We still used the old BBC building for these sessions. God knows how they'd squared this with spurned Wally and his caretaking dad but they managed to hold on to the space until autumn, when McLaren found them a basement in Denmark Street to work in. At first I busied myself working out the guitar parts of their existing repertoire. I made sure both 'Everlasting Love' and 'Build Me Up Buttercup' were given the heave-ho. McLaren then coerced us into covering two singles that were part of the oldies collection on his shop's jukebox. Both songs were B-sides. One – 'Don't Give Me No Lip, Child' – had first been recorded in the mid-sixties by an English singer called Dave Berry. The other – 'Do You Really Love Me Too? (Fool's Errand)' – was a pop song performed by McLaren's personal fetish object Billy Fury. Neither number did the band's evolving set list any great favours – to me they were just more wrong-headed retro tomfoolery – but at least learning and then struggling to rearrange them was more gratifying than just aimlessly jamming.

The most productive moments between us happened when Jones and Matlock came round to my place separately and I'd play them records and tapes in an attempt to locate new material and a new direction. Matlock wasn't like the other two, which is to say he wasn't particularly tricky or light-fingered. He was more middle-class – about to enrol in art college – and he'd actually read a few books. Jones, on the other hand, had been a borstal boy and was completely illiterate – unable to decipher a single printed word or even write his own name. That didn't make him a fool in my book. What he lacked in basic schooling he'd more than made up for in accumulating street-survival savvy throughout his teens. But he was at a crossroads in his young life with only two career options open to his lack of qualifications. He could either follow the path he was already on and become a serious hard-core criminal robbing banks and the like. Or he could chance his arm and try and make it as a rock star. For the time being, the two roads were intertwined: he'd already stolen all the group's equipment and continued to filch and then sell guitars – and other musical equipment – from various central London instrument stores. In fact, no one in Britain at that time had a greater talent for hiding guitars inside a large coat and then vanishing from the scene of the crime than Steve Jones. Now it was time to find out if that talent extended to actually playing them as well.

That's why I was seeing so much of him *chez moi*. We'd sit around and work on our hopefully intertwining guitar parts.

McLaren had decided that the group needed a new singer and that Jones should just play guitar in the line-up from now on. As I just mentioned he'd only started three months earlier. But he was an incredibly quick learner. What had taken me literally years to put into practice on a fretboard he managed to master in a matter of weeks. Actually, that was the most exciting aspect of being in the Sex Pistols musical boot camp – watching Steve Jones find his own voice as a guitar player. Once his fingers could form a few rudimentary chord shapes he was off and running because those chords finally offered him a language to express himself in that had nothing to do with his nemesis, the written word. I tried to show him some minor chords but he wasn't interested in them: they sounded too pretty and soft-laddish to his ears. He preferred just the big brash major barre chords. They better conveyed his inner spirit, I soon realised. Steve after all wasn't given to introspection, musical or otherwise. He wasn't the sort of bloke you'd try and introduce to the music of Nick Drake. I bombarded him with Stooges thug rock instead. 'Forget the Small Faces – listen to Iggy and his boys. Adopt what the Stooges are doing on their records and make it the integral part of your sound' became my mantra to the group. (I even phoned James Williamson's LA phone number to tell Iggy about the Sex Pistols and attempt to persuade him to fly over and be their frontman. That was when I learned the news that he had in fact just been incarcerated in an LA mental hospital.) I also force-fed him and Matlock a cassette tape John Cale had given me of some studio recordings he'd produced for a Boston band called the Modern Lovers. Matlock became greatly enamoured of two tracks on that tape – 'Pablo Picasso' and 'Roadrunner' – and started pushing to feature the latter in the Pistols' repertoire. I in turn became increasingly insistent about covering 'No Fun' from the Stooges' first album. That was my contribution to their musical development really: stripping away all the retro silliness and pointing them squarely towards the future.

McLaren meanwhile was focused on finding that elusive new singer. For reasons only he can tell you, he refused to go down the conventional route and place an advert in the 'musicians wanted' back pages of the weekly music comics. Instead he chose a more unorthodox approach: he'd hear about a group of teenagers who were performing at a minor social event being held around the outskirts of London and then drive to the event – with the rest of us in tow – to see if they had a singer worth poaching. I'll never forget him guiding us to what turned out to be a bar mitzvah celebration out in Hemel Hempstead in order to check out the musical entertainment, which consisted of five spotty youths sleepwalking their way through the Bay City Rollers' recent hits. After they'd finished playing, McLaren strode up to their singer – who looked and sang like a junior bank clerk – and went into his pre-rehearsed pitch. 'I'm the manager of the Sex Pistols, the most exciting group to ever come out of London, the greatest city in the world. We're the Rolling Stones to the Bay City Rollers' Beatles and we're looking for a singer. Do you fancy coming down to our rehearsal place and giving it a shot?' The kid looked at him and the rest of us with a kind of clueless scepticism. 'No thanks, mate' was all he muttered before sidling off to a table on which several unopened beer cans were still loitering.

Undeterred, McLaren abandoned the bar mitzvah circuit and chose to continue his quest by frequenting the various gay London nightclubs that had sprung up over the past five years. One afternoon he turned up to the rehearsal room accompanied by an extremely timid young man who stuttered whenever he spoke. McLaren immediately demanded that we audition him, insisting that this nerve-wracked youth might well be the answer to our prayers. Like good foot soldiers we did as we were told but I could tell that none of the group were happy about this latest turn of events. Malcolm then gave the lad an earnest pep-talk and told him to stand in front of the microphone stand and sing some notes. He got him positioned between Jones and me and we all started playing. But the youth just stood there silently trembling. This was someone who would have had difficulty saying boo to a goose, never mind fronting the Sex Pistols. McLaren started going ballistic. 'Try putting a guitar round his neck,' he suddenly demanded. 'He can't play anything but it might help put him in the mood to sing.' So we hung a guitar around his neck – but it only made him look more awkward and ill at ease. Malcolm meanwhile was berating the guy for being so timid and Jones and I were looking at both of them with angry eyes. We tried one more run-through but it was evidently too much for our callow vocalist. He remained mute, staring into space with a stricken look in his eyes whilst a puddle of urine began to appear from out of his left trouser leg. If Jones hadn't moved the mike stand, the poor chap would have probably been electrocuted for losing control of his own bladder. McLaren gave the weeping youth with the damp trousers cab fare home and we never mentioned the incident again. But it indicated to me at least that he didn't have a clue about how to gainfully extend this outfit's career trajectory.

Steve Jones nursed similar doubts. It was his band, after all – his gang, his equipment. But McLaren had suddenly elected himself as the boss-man and had told Jones he was no longer the singer. This would have been more acceptable if McLaren actually had a red-hot vocalist waiting in the wings, but he didn't and his attempts to drag any juvenile Tom, Dick or Harry into the role were becoming more and more excruciating to observe. Jones and I would discuss McLaren's increasingly wacky approach to group management when he'd come round to visit. I'd know he'd arrived when I heard the window to my first-storey garret creak open and saw him climb through. Being an inveterate cat burglar, Steve rarely entered any building through the front door – it was against his religion. Anyway, one evening a guy called Alan Callan who lived one street away and who worked for Led Zeppelin's Swan Song record label called up and invited us to record something at his home studio. Jones and I wrote a song on the spot – I played guitar and he sang. It was a slow number called 'Ease Your Mind'. I haven't heard it since the night we recorded it so I can't give you an objective take on its merits. Ultimately it was just a fun way of passing the evening and nothing more. But when McLaren heard about it, he saw the session as me trying to undermine his control over the project. He banded the other three together and told them I was a disruptive influence that needed to be exiled forthwith. He then sent Glen Matlock round to give me my marching orders.

In all honesty, I wasn't that surprised or upset. It had always been something of an uphill struggle trying to find common ground with those guys, musically and socially speaking. It wasn't just the age discrepancy: I was a middle-class druggie fop and they were working-class spivs who'd steal the gold out of their mothers' teeth. The fops had owned the first half of the seventies but the spivs would take it over in 1976 lock, stock and barrel. In other words, for the Sex Pistols to be accepted as an authentic working-class rebel youth phenomenon they needed to rid people like me from their ranks. But I already knew that virtually from the moment I stepped into their web. What we had was never going to be a long-term relationship. I didn't want it to be. I knew from the outset that these were the kind of people that you couldn't trust on any level whatsoever.

But the scales fell from my eyes with regard to McLaren. For eighteen months I'd viewed him as a trusted friend. I'd been wrong. The guy was just another control-seeking snake in the grass. I'd underestimated the ego that lurked within his Machiavellian mindset. For a couple of months following my firing it was amusing to hear the stories about how the group's career was developing. Malcolm found them a singer: himself. A little-known event in the early Sex Pistols career, it was also extremely short-lived and ended abruptly after he imprudently suggested they cover a Syd Barrett song from the early Pink Floyd repertoire.

It must have been sometime in October when I found myself walking down Charing Cross Road and suddenly turned to see him sidling up alongside me. There was a spring in his step and gleam in his eyes. He excitedly began telling me that the Pistols were now rehearsing in Denmark Street and had just achieved the seemingly impossible: they'd found the singer who was destined to make them all immortal. 'He's this really weird kid . . . looks a bit like a spastic . . . and he's on acid all the time. But he's the best thing in the group. He came in the other day with the lyrics to a song he'd just written. The title's "You're Only Twenty-Nine – You've Got a Lot to Learn". Absolutely bloody brilliant.' And we both laughed out loud because indeed it did sound brilliant. The 'really weird kid' of course turned out to be John Lydon and it's fair to say that the Sex Pistols didn't really become the Sex Pistols until he came into the frame. I'd been involved in a work in progress in other words – a project yet to reach full fruition. I can't help thinking now of that line uttered near the end of Roddy Doyle's book *The Commitments* when the old-timer trumpet player says words to the effect that being in a group is mostly about dull routine but the early days are the ones to cherish – the ones filled with poetry. Well, there wasn't much poetry in the Sex Pistols' early days as far as I was aware. A lot of ducking and diving, bad manners and brute force, certainly – but no grace-filled epiphanies or magic moments to wax nostalgic over. It's funny looking back: none of us knew just what we were unleashing on the world. The rest is history of course – or 'my story' as both McLaren and John Lydon egocentrically like to view the 1976 punk-rock explosion throughout Great Britain. I'm just glad I got out when I did. I don't think my nervous system could have withstood being a Sex Pistol right to the end of the line.

So poor old Wally Nightingale became their very own Pete Best and I became their Stuart Sutcliffe. That's one way of looking at it anyway. Of course, Stuart Sutcliffe died shortly after leaving the Beatles. I managed to keep breathing, though with some difficulty. Since the summer I'd become a twenty-four-hours-a-day full-bore junkie. That's probably another reason why the Sex Pistols no longer wanted me around. When I'd started tentatively using a year earlier, it had transpired in relatively luxurious surroundings – cosy, well-heated, sultrily lit Chelsea apartments, big colour TVs with the volume dimmed, cool sounds wafting from the stereo. Not any more. Now it was a case of taking your life in your hands and stepping into squalor-ridden squats with rats scurrying across the floorboards and an equally scary clump of human debris starting to experience the first pin-pricks of drug withdrawal standing around waiting for the dealer to return with the stuff. I was in the deep end now – sucked out into a sea of screaming bloody madness. I'd tried to stop again and again but each time grew more horrendous until my spirit had been broken. Now I simply couldn't stop. I'd exhausted the willpower to fight the addiction. It's a scary sensation to realise your life is going down the toilet and you can't do a thing about it except to hang on, try to remain breathing and keep feeding that habit.

The winter of '75 was a particularly cruel season – bitingly cold and bleak, bleak, bleak. I was holed up in an otherwise empty house awaiting demolition somewhere in Islington that Hermine had found for me, God bless her. And there was a heroin famine in the city: I had to spend practically all my waking hours walking around the metropolis in search of a ready source. But the worst of it was the music I'd always be hearing wherever I went. One song reigned supreme over Britain's airwaves at year's end: Queen's 'Bohemian Rhapsody'. Every home in the British Isles seemed to own a copy. Walk down any street and you could hear it wafting out onto the sidewalk like the smell of bad drains. Pub jukeboxes played nothing else. If anyone dared pick another selection, they'd have probably been ejected. The omnipotence of 'Bohemian Rhapsody' made it official: prog rock was still the opium of the masses. Hearing it echo around me on my daily travels, I felt utterly defeated. Queen's record shamelessly paraded everything I'd fought against as a rock commentator: it was theatrical, pretentious and meaningless, faux classical music for high-brow poseurs with low-brow attention spans, kitsch masquerading as art. I couldn't see a way out of it. I was doomed and so was rock 'n' roll. Heroin was killing me and Freddie Mercury and his fruity chums had just seen off the latter. It was one of those 'darkest hour before the dawn' extended moments. I couldn't conceive then that my recent dancing partners the Sex Pistols would actually ride in like the cavalry and save the day for rock just a few months hence. And I couldn't – in my wildest imaginings – foresee them stabbing me in the back the way they were about to.

1976

Working within the media is rather like being employed as a snake handler. Sooner or later it's going to bite you back.

Judge not unless you're prepared to be judged yourself: the Bible is very clear on this point. Yet journalists instinctively feel compelled to make extravagant judgement calls on their subjects – endlessly measuring their talent, their political and moral agendas, calling into question their public images, belittling their fashion sense. Whilst this approach often results in widely read copy and the promise of a highly paid column in the dailies, it also tends to set those who initiate the process onto the rocky road towards karmic retribution.

Of course, most news hounds become so gung-ho ambitious and intoxicated by their power-playing status that they conveniently misplace any residue of conscience that may have once lurked within them. Without conscience there can be no awareness of consequences; thus no awareness of the forces of karma. But ignorance doesn't prevent it from working its own mysterious magic at all times.

Like Burt Lancaster's sociopathic columnist in *Sweet Smell of Success*, the hard-core media breed make their bones taking indelicate pot-shots at the cultural movers and shakers *du jour*, become – briefly – ersatz celebrities themselves, lose all

perspective as a direct result, turn arrogant and lazy and cultivate many high-powered enemies. Then they almost inevitably
become the victims of a scandal of their own making and have
to suddenly be put out to pasture by their long-suffering
bosses, their twilight years eked out in bitter alcoholic reclu-
sion.

This is karma in full effect – powered by greed, riddled with
hubris, ending in drunken recriminations and unholy isolation –
and it hits worst when least expected. I was only in my early twenties, with little knowledge of Buddhist theology to back me up,
but even I could sense its intricate sway over the very scheme of
human existence, if only as a form of divine superstition. People
in the seventies talked about karma as though it was as obsolete
as the kaftan but I knew I was still somehow under its tricky spell.
My charmed life was running out of blind luck. My playhouse
was about to get burned down.

Still, I had no ready clues about how or when my judgement
day would manifest itself exactly, though there was always the
distinct possibility of having my legs broken by revenge-seeking
aggrieved recording artistes who'd fallen foul of my critical faculties. 'You need to watch what you write, young Kent,' a disgrun-
tled manager once informed me in a London nightclub. 'You're
making too many enemies in this business.' He wasn't alone in
this view. From day one, I'd been actively looking for trouble in
one form or another. It was only a matter of time before trouble
came looking for me.

In mid-'73 a tabloid reporter informed me that the Bee Gees
were planning to beat me up because of an unflattering review I'd
penned of one of their singles. Put yourself in my place: you are
suddenly told that the Bee Gees intend to break you limb from

limb at an undisclosed place and time in the immediate future. How do you react?

Well, if you were me, you'd make a point of heading to a nearby record store and studying the sleeve of the trio's most recent album in order to see exactly what kind of physical shape your opponents might be in. Scanning the cover I quickly surmised that I might be in for a terrible thrashing. Two of the Gibb siblings, Robin and Maurice, were reassuringly pasty-faced but big brother Barry was clearly the one in the family who'd inherited all the testosterone and muscles. He was also sporting more hairs on his chest than you could count nestling against loud golden medallions at a New Jersey convention for mafia capos. If he and I ever crossed paths, I knew I was wheelchair-bound.

The *NME* threw a party in August at the Speakeasy to further trumpet the fact that we'd lately become the biggest-selling music weekly in the known universe, and the Bee Gees' publicist duly let it be known that the trio would be turning up specifically to extract their pound of flesh. My co-workers at the paper all thought this was tremendous fun and never wasted an opportunity to tweak my paranoia further on the matter. But as the evening progressed in a blur of alcohol and back-slapping bonhomie, it became increasingly apparent that the three Bee Gees would not be gracing us with their six-fisted presence. Only little Maurice put in an appearance and he was so drunk he needed two minders to keep him from falling over.

At one point, he stood about two yards away from me and attempted to look menacing, but to scant avail. His face was flushed like raw beetroot. His pair of human crutches quickly encircled my would-be tormentor, shepherding him to the exit of the club, and that was the end of that. In the battle between myself and the Bee Gees, I had somehow ended up the victor by default. Still, it was a pyrrhic victory at best. Four years hence, the trio would become one of the biggest-selling and most influential acts of the seventies – experiencing a second coming that even Lazarus might envy. I meanwhile would be occupying the same period of time as a homeless junkie barely staying alive.

The fates were certainly frowning on me a full year later when I found myself in Island Records' Basing Street studios in Ladbroke Grove watching Brian Eno record a track for his *Taking Tiger Mountain* album in the company of John Cale. Cale and I had been consuming cocaine quite liberally just prior to this and so everything in the studio felt like it was somehow alive and humming with diabolic energy.

Feeling fragile, I went looking for a toilet, hoping it would prove to possess a more soothing atmosphere. I opened the door to a dimly lit room fitted out with a urinal and several separate cubicles and realised that I wasn't its only occupant. Six or seven strange-looking black guys were standing by the urinal. One of them was holding the largest joint I have ever seen in my entire life. It looked like a smouldering tree limb wrapped in countless rolling papers. An entire pack of Rizlas must have gone into its construction. The guy had to hold the thing aloft with both his hands in order to get a hit off it. He was a wiry arrogant-looking little fellow with angry eyes blazing out of an enormous head topped off by a humongous mass of braided hair, and he and his cohorts were clearly none too happy to see me suddenly in their midst. It was Bob Marley and the Wailers taking a break from recording tracks for their album *Natty Dread* in the adjacent studio.

Although I'd briefly lived in a Jamaican community in Ladbroke Grove two years earlier, I'd never seen a fully fledged

Rastafarian with ample dreadlocks in the flesh before. Now I was suddenly being confronted with a whole gang of them. I felt like Bob Hope in *Son of Paleface*, in the scene where the comedian as prissy, citified dentist 'Painless' Potter – having ventured west – comes suddenly face to face with a tribe of homicidal tomahawk-wielding Apaches in full warpaint. If I hadn't been so looped, I would have simply turned on my heels and found an alternative location for the emptying of my bladder. But cocaine has an irksome habit of decimating presence of mind and so I hurried to a cubicle, locking it behind me in shocked surprise.

The next two minutes were awkward in the extreme. I was so nervous I pissed all over my boots. There was loud derisive laughter coming from the urinals. I steeled myself to make a quick exit but knew I was doomed to experience an impromptu lesson in what happens when different cultures clash in awkward circumstances. As I edged towards the door, Marley started moving towards me, flanked by his grinning accomplices. He had a cut-throat grin on his face. He stood about three inches away and spat out the word 'Rasclaat' directly into my worried face. Apparently, it's Jamaican for 'scumbag' or something equally demeaning. I bowed my head and departed in haste. This was my first-hand introduction to Jah Bob's supposedly all-inclusive 'one love' philosophy for mankind and all I could think was, 'Oh well, at least I didn't get lynched.'

In the years that followed, Marley and his media enablers would convincingly fashion a public image of the man as a quasi-mystical deity that millions would unquestioningly buy into, but my brief encounter told me he was as deeply flawed as any other ambitious little man slouching arrogantly around the planet. I'd never written a word on him or the Wailers. He didn't know me from a hole in the ground. He just took offence because I was dressed flamboyantly and was sporting traces of eye make-up. It was obvious he had a serious problem with men who were unafraid to exhibit their feminine side in public. To Marley's hard-eyed Rasta-centric mindset spiritual salvation was not attainable to Southern Jessies on hard drugs. He may well have been right too.

Now fast-forward to eight months later. I'm floating around the Roxy, the music-industry watering hole on Hollywood's Sunset Strip, when Led Zeppelin's John Bonham and Richard Cole suddenly decide to hurl their drinks at me and declare – according to the notorious Zeppelin biography *Hammer of the Gods* – that my life 'isn't worth piss'.

This wasn't something to be taken lightly. Bonham was a great big brick shithouse of a man who habitually became transformed into a psychopathic farmhand out of Sam Peckinpah's *Straw Dogs* when over-inebriated, and Cole had the reputation of being able to kill a man or woman with a single karate blow. I got out of there as quickly as possible before any real physical damage could be done.

The next morning, Peter Grant phoned me – all sweetness, light and profuse apologies: 'I've spoken to both Bonzo and Coley . . . they're very sorry . . . you're still our ally.' To further mend fences, he invited me on the group's private jet to take in a Zeppelin concert in nearby Oakland later that day. A sobered-up Bonham and Cole were duly apologetic when I arrived at their hotel.

Later that night – at around 3 a.m. – me, Grant, Bonham and Cole were all in Grant's suite, snorting yet more cocaine – Jimmy Page was in an adjacent room with a young woman – and listening to a white-label copy of Bad Company's second album when the large bay windows that opened onto the suite's fifteenth-floor balcony suddenly burst open and Keith Moon appeared in our midst as if conjured out of thin air. He'd just climbed down the side of the building from the roof of the hotel attached to some sort of mountaineer's winch and had narrowly escaped falling to his death. His eyes were bulging out of his face like huge mischievous saucers and he wasted no time in making his unruly presence felt in every corner of the room. 'I tell you what, playmates – that Raquel Welch was on the blower to me again. She won't bloody leave me alone. It's always the same old line. "Keith, I need you so desperately. You're the only man who can fulfil my needs." I had to tell 'er right there and then, "Raquel, love, you're barking up the wrong tree. Keith Moon can't be tied down to just one woman. I've got to play the field. Go buy a dog instead. Buy yourself a three-piece suite."'

Everyone fell about laughing. And I got to spend several hours in the company of the two greatest drummers in the history of rock 'n' roll. Bonham absolutely adored Moon, and Moon clearly loved Bonham back. But he didn't seem to like himself much. His moods shifted chaotically and without due cause. One minute he'd be the life and soul of the party, performing his side-splitting Robert Newton-as-Long John Silver impersonation to everyone's delight, the next he'd be talking glumly about his aimless life in Hollywood and the difficulties of getting the other three Who members interested in more group activities.

His face and torso that night were both extensively padded with an unsightly strain of toxic bloat and behind his customary shield of berserk bravado you could catch glimpses of a man struggling to make sense of his own insanity whilst trying to kid himself that it wasn't somehow all linked in with his continuing descent into full-blown alcoholism. No wonder he and Bonham were soulmates: they shared the same terminal disease. Moon had only three more years to live, Bonham five.

The early-seventies rock scene had its share of violent outbursts but that violence was usually ignited only in hotel rooms, backstage facilities or small VIP clubs when too much cocaine and alcohol were mixed together. It rarely spilled over to the public sector. Paying audiences were never targeted for a pummelling. Even the early punk bands didn't physically abuse those who'd come to see them. They'd abuse themselves instead.

This became apparent to me when I flew to New York in April '76 for a forty-eight-hour stopover whilst en route to cover a catastrophe in the making: a tour of the US Midwest being undertaken by UK bubblegum glam rockers the Sweet, who were then trying to pass themselves off as virtuoso hard rockers, a kind of poor man's Deep Purple with permed hair and shiny jumpsuits.

The three days and nights I got to spend with that sorry bunch are forever etched on my mind. Imagine *Spinal Tap* without the punchlines. The high-or-low point was reached one morning in the lobby of a Holiday Inn in Cleveland we were checking out of. The jazz legend Count Basie was also in the vicinity and – being a friendly, non-judgemental soul – wandered up to the group members at one point and offered his best wishes for their continued success, even though he obviously didn't have a clue who they were. 'Fuck all that, mate,' tartly responded the Sweet's Neanderthal singer, who'd evidently mistaken the venerable big-band maestro for a hall porter. 'Help us load our baggage into those limousines outside the door instead.'

Returning to New York I felt an immediate urge to get high once more. Richard Hell phoned me out of the blue and offered to set up a meeting with his heroin dealer. I jumped in a yellow cab and hightailed it down to his grungy-looking apartment.

We'd never met before but struck up a lively rapport nonetheless. Malcolm McLaren had told me all about him, anyway. His real name was Richard Meyers and he'd been born in Kentucky: he and a school friend named Tom Miller had moved to New York in their late teens intent on becoming published poets. That's why they'd both changed their surnames: Miller called himself 'Tom Verlaine' in homage to Arthur Rimbaud's dissolute literary sidekick. Both were equally taken with the idea of forming a rock group and Verlaine was already a more-than-accomplished electric guitarist. Hell learned some rudimentary bass lines and the pair duly instigated their first line-up – a quartet known first as the Neon Boys and then as Television.

Unfortunately they soon developed vastly different visions about what their group should be sounding like. Hell favoured shorter, more dynamic songs that gave extensive vent to his nihilistic world view. Verlaine felt intrinsically drawn to the dreamy improvisations of late-sixties West Coast rock and his lyrics often read like LSD hallucinations transposed into text. Their club audiences around Manhattan during the early months of 1975 soon split into two camps: those who came to lose themselves in Verlaine's ethereal guitar solos and sensitive 'starvation artist' persona and those who came to cheer on Hell as he boisterously leaped around the stage singing in a grating voice about being part of 'the blank generation', his chosen appellation for the emerging seventies youth mindset.

Malcolm McLaren and the New York Dolls were part of the

latter crowd. McLaren in particular was utterly smitten by Hell. He loved his look: the short self-cut electric-shock hairstyle, the ripped T-shirts and thrift-store suits held together by safety pins. His rampant magpie instincts for kick-starting a possible future fashion explosion were suddenly detonated the very moment he first espied the Television bassist in the flesh. Hell's whole appearance was too radical to make an impact on torpid mid-seventies American culture, but take the same ingredients, repackage them first as costly designer garments to the lovey fashionistas of London and then find a young impressionable rock band to model them and turn those same designs into compulsory high-street rebel-wear for youngsters throughout the British Isles *et voilà*! Of course, he would only really be stealing someone else's ideas but basic moral considerations never seemed to invade McLaren's devious mindset. He was a little man with a big destiny to fulfil and woe betide anyone who underestimated the fact.

For his part Richard Hell saw McLaren as a bit of a con artist but essentially harmless. No one in New York could imagine that the nervous little red-haired Limey who'd briefly convinced the New York Dolls to become Marxist sympathisers – a move that utterly torpedoed their career – was actually going to rob them of everything they were working towards.

At that exact moment in time, the New York scene around CBGBs was ablaze with talent. Patti Smith was about to start recording her debut album, but almost everyone else from Television to Talking Heads was still unsigned and therefore financially reliant on performing live in small clubs. The three acts mentioned had nothing to do with punk rock, however. Smith, Verlaine and David Byrne were all worshippers at the altar of the art-rock aesthetic that came into play in the late sixties with the advent of the Velvet Underground and the Doors, and were now attempting to find new creative avenues for its expression within the dilapidated context of mid-seventies Manhattan club-land.

There were only two real punk bands on that scene. The first was the Heartbreakers, who'd been formed after Richard Hell had been evicted from Television at the end of 1974 by his old school pal Verlaine, and Johnny Thunders and Jerry Nolan had walked out of the New York Dolls shortly afterwards. This three-some already shared one common bond: drug addiction. At first when they played around Manhattan everyone had dubbed them 'the Dooji Brothers', 'dooji' being one of many local slang terms for heroin. 'Catch them while they're still alive' became the group's catchphrase whenever they were advertising one of their shows.

Hell and Thunders – the group's two leaders – had enjoyed a brief honeymoon period of mutual admiration but soon fell into open dispute about the Heartbreakers' creative development. Hell wanted to make edgy art rock based around his bleak poetic insights whilst Thunders wanted to play simple-minded three-chord rock that tallied well with his newly assumed image as a scrappy Italo-American cross between Keith Richards and Arthur Fonzarelli, the hero of mid-seventies TV show *Happy Days*. Their musical alliance would end in tears by mid-'76, but in April Richard was still a Heartbreaker struggling to keep his band-mates attuned to his artsy sensibility when all they really wanted to do was further promote their own junkie lifestyle to a small, like-minded clique of followers.

Quite sensibly, no one remotely affiliated with the US music industry at the time – or even the incestuous CBGBs scene – felt they had much of a future. Instead all eyes were on a younger act – a quartet from Forest Hills who'd suddenly made a big impression on downtown Manhattan. The Ramones were the real punk-rock deal: four deeply dysfunctional young men who had never darkened the towers of higher education and who therefore felt absolutely no affinity whatsoever with the prevailing 'rock goes to college' aesthetic of the early seventies.

Their music wasn't about intellect; it was all about instinct: geeky three-chord bubblegum rock played with authentic primordial savagery. They sang about their aimless lives as well as their often-morbid fantasies but did so with a kind of understated drop-dead humour that immediately became hugely endearing to anyone hip enough to get the joke. It also made them an instant paradox. How could four guys who seemed so many bricks shy of a full hod still write lyrics so exquisitely laced with deadpan irony?

This was an enigma I found myself confronting during my April sojourn in Manhattan. The Ramones had caused such a sensation in so short a space of time that they'd actually been signed up to a record deal with Seymour Stein's local Sire imprint by the very beginning of '76. In fact, they'd just finished their debut album. It hadn't taken long to record. I was invited up to Sire's headquarters one afternoon to hear the finished product as it was being mastered.

Only the record's producer, one Craig Leon, was present in the tiny listening room. After several minutes of superficial banter, he placed an acetate – or maybe it was a tape – onto an extremely expensive piece of recording equipment and cued the first bars of 'Blitzkrieg Bop'. The opening chords suddenly roared out at us at an ear-shredding volume. And then just as the vocals came in, there was a sudden explosion. One of the speakers had literally been blown out by the sonic bombardment of the music. Leon and I looked at each other approvingly: rock music that shattered everything in its path – it seemed like a good omen for the future.

And the Ramones themselves? Deeply weird, every last one of 'em. Tommy the drummer, the oldest, straightest one, was their leader back then and had elected himself the group's spokesman in a misguided attempt to play down their general lack of cerebral sophistication. Tommy would go to great pains to promote his group's 'normal, blue-collar rock' agenda and became increasingly frustrated when other members like Johnny and Dee Dee would interrupt him with offhand comments that inevitably showed just how bizarre they really were.

Dee Dee Ramone was already a legend of sorts around downtown Manhattan. I remember walking around the Bowery one afternoon with Richard Hell and seeing Dee Dee on three separate occasions – each time in the company of a different middle-aged, effeminate-looking man. 'Uh, this is my uncle,' he'd tell us with a shameful expression on his sweet young face. He was really turning gay tricks to feed his drug habit – everybody knew this. He even wrote a song about his experiences – '53rd & 3rd' – that was included on the Ramones' first album. But in reality he was anything but proud of his part-time vocation. Johnny Thunders in particular used to needle him about it mercilessly. 'Hey, Dee Dee Ramone – where's your fucking uncle?' he used to shout at the Ramones bassist whenever their paths crossed.

Looking back, the New York scene in 1976 had everything going for it: a diverse range of groundbreaking young bands, a sense of (fragile) community, novel alternatives to style and basic rock charisma and a new attitude for youth at decade's end to consolidate themselves around. Yet they were still grievously deficient in two key areas: management and media coverage.

Most of the managers floating around the CBGBs bands seemed to be older gay men more interested in coercing young boys into acts of sexual congress than in advancing careers. And media interest in America was minimal at best, especially from national publications like *Rolling Stone*. The US has never had a weekly music press – apart from industry tip-sheets like *Billboard* and *Cashbox* – and the few monthlies available were too stuck in the immediate past to recognise that a new era was dawning under their very noses.

That's fundamentally why the English punk scene exploded with such deadly efficacy, whilst its more creative New York counterpart – and forerunner – spluttered around like a damp squib pinned to a tree trunk. London is a small city inhabited by a media always ravenous to glom on to anything new and potentially provocative and splash it over their pages. Chas Chandler understood this implicitly when he took Jimi Hendrix from New York clubland anonymity in late 1966 and transplanted him to London, where his extraordinary guitar-playing and exotic image could be more effectively assimilated first by the press and then by a mass audience. Malcolm McLaren understood this too. It was one of the few smart insights he ever had as the Sex Pistols' manager. Another bright ploy he capitalised on was to involve the Pistols' grass-roots following, the so-called Bromley Contingent, in the group's early media coverage, thus making it look to all and sundry as though a genuine new movement was coming into bloom. Apart from that, he was way out of his depth and riddled with wrong-headed notions.

His yuppie apologists like to throw around big words like 'situationism' and 'postmodernism' when discussing McLaren's questionable accomplishments in the realm of seventies punk management these days, terms inevitably designed to bewilder rather than illuminate. I knew McLaren throughout 1974 and 1975 and was privy to many conversations with him about his personal vision of what the Sex Pistols might represent as a potential art concept. He never once mentioned situationism to me as his guiding philosophy. It only appeared in his interviews after the fact.

No, Malcolm's real career gurus were the old-school Tin Pan Alley chicken hawks who'd controlled the late-fifties UK rock marketplace. His key point of reference in this domain was Larry Parnes, whom he quoted endlessly. Parnes was a gay man with music-industry connections who 'discovered' his acts whilst cruising local building sites looking for attractive young men he could mould into the next Fabian and then exploit mercilessly. Like a pimp, he'd first seduce his quarry with specious promises, then dress them up in a sexually provocative fashion and change their names to something preposterous like Stormy Tempest or Vince Eager. Then he'd put them to work until they literally dropped, always making sure to pocket the lion's share of whatever monies they managed to generate during their few fleeting months of fame.

Parnes and his ilk would duly be overtaken as pop impresarios in the early sixties by the likes of Don Arden. Arden showed no inclination for ever wanting to sexually molest his young male acts. He was too busy ripping them off and breaking the legs of anyone who fell foul of him. In short, the man was a sadist and a vicious thieving spiv, so warped by his own petty-minded criminality that he was fundamentally unable to see that he could actually make himself more money by treating his clients fairly than he could from robbing them blind.

This was a lesson learned by Arden's former enforcer Peter Grant – and it was one he would put to spectacular use when he came to manage Led Zeppelin in 1968. It was at this point that UK rock/pop management entered a new era – one where the musicians and performers were finally permitted to share generously in all the wealth they were generating but had previously never seen on their own bank statements.

In later years – the early nineties to be precise – McLaren would become obsessed with Grant's music-biz accomplishments to the point of trying (unsuccessfully) to produce a film about his life, but in 1976 he was way more infatuated with the ongoing career trajectory of the Bay City Rollers than Led Zeppelin's globe-straddling antics. The platinum-plated Rollers and their singularly creepy manager Tam Paton were proof enough that the Larry Parnes approach to pop Svengalism was still alive and capable of reaping big financial dividends in the seventies. To McLaren, the teeny-bopper Scottish quintet were the Beatles to his band's Rolling Stones and in the early days he endlessly talked up the parallel as a way of getting the Pistols established in the public eye.

To him – like Parnes and Paton – the whole pop process was divided into two neat sub-headings: the puppets and the puppeteers. Musicians were the puppets, born to be endlessly manipulated like slow-witted peasants. The managers meanwhile were the string-pullers, the men with the plan, the princes guiding the paupers. Jones, Matlock and Cook never questioned McLaren's basic scruples or possible hidden agenda in his dealings with them – how sweet to be an idiot – until it was far too late. But John Lydon was onto him pretty much from the get-go.

When Lydon joined the Pistols in the autumn of '75, McLaren should have sensed that he was bringing in someone who might soon turn out to be a thorn in his side. Unlike the other three, Lydon – though still a teenager – had a mind of his own. It wasn't a particularly attractive or well-ordered mind – the guy was often on acid – but he was certainly its only occupant and wasn't about to let some King's Road fashion ponce claim squatter's rights in it and then brainwash him into a state of pop-star servility.

McLaren and Lydon's relationship at the outset was strained at best. I spent an evening with them one night in October at the Camden Town club known as Dingwalls. It was the first time I'd ever encountered the future Johnny Rotten. He wasn't yet the viper-tongued larger-than-life entity we read about nowadays. He was sullen and withdrawn, an obvious victim of chronic shyness. He was physically fragile too and strangely sexless. At one point, an attractive woman approached our table simply to compliment Lydon on his (suspiciously Richard Hell-like) hairstyle. The gesture appeared to totally unnerve him. Straight afterwards he bolted from his chair and ran out of the building. McLaren and I looked at each other quizzically. How could a wallflower like this credibly front a band who called themselves the Sex Pistols?

Of course, we all know the answer to that question more than thirty years later. Lydon quickly banished all traces of post-adolescent wimpiness from his public persona and promptly rose to the occasion with a scary single-mindedness. Shortly after the Dingwalls incident, McLaren and the group invited me to one of their first-ever public appearances, at a party held by an effete artist and social gadfly named Andrew Logan.

There were only about thirty people present, amongst them Mick Jones and Brian James, both still in the process of forming bands of their own. Lydon was saucer-eyed from the LSD he'd just consumed, the other three were drunk as lords and their repertoire that night consisted of only one song – the Stooges' 'No Fun' – played over and over again until a seriously disturbed-looking Lydon began smashing up his mike stand. At this point Logan swanned over and suggested that maybe their set had reached its fitting conclusion.

It had been an odd spectacle to say the least, rather like seeing the early Stooges fronted not by a young white James Brown but a teenage version of Albert Steptoe, the miserable-old-geezer from much-loved British sitcom *Steptoe and Son*, instead. It was a mad blend to aim for and yet somehow it worked. Lydon's very sexlessness and physical fragility only seemed to make his stage presence all the more menacing. He represented a radical depar-ture from the conventional lead-singer-in-a-rock-band stereo-types of the time. His vocal range was limited to no more than three notes and its tone was instantly harsh and grating. It was an instrument that was nonetheless ideal for projecting a sense of overwhelming contempt over any subject the singer chose to sink his mangled teeth into.

Lydon loathed most of what passed for classic rock 'n' roll. He despised Elvis Presley, Jerry Lee Lewis and all the other pioneers – thought they were a bunch of gormless plooks. He disliked the Beatles too and thought the Rolling Stones were well past their sell-by date. Instead he listened intently to German avant-garde bands, even going so far as to model his own malevolent wailing on the sound made by the vocalist on Neu's debut album. He was a bit of a closet art-rock aficionado. It must have driven Jones and the others mad. But without his infuriating presence in the foreground spitting into a microphone, the rest of the group had no centre to galvanise their individual capabilities around. If he hadn't been there, they'd have still been a good – and potentially successful – little rock act but they would never have been a bona fide cultural phenomenon.

Things changed radically within the group once they started getting written about in the UK press. As soon as Lydon saw his face staring back at him from the pages of the music comics, he was never the same again. His ego suddenly exploded to sky-rocket proportions, as did his sense of personal power. But this was only to be expected: after all, he was still a teenager whose childhood had been blighted by recurring bouts of chronic ill-ness that had left him mentally disorientated until his adoles-cence.

McLaren's reaction to sudden infamy though was even more dramatic and he had fewer excuses. He was considerably older than everyone else and therefore supposedly more mature and level-headed. And yet a full personality transformation occurred within him the moment his group started getting fêted by the media. Fame lifted up her skirt to him and little Malcolm became utterly transfixed by the sight he beheld. It ruined him for the rest of his life.

At the end of April '76 he came to visit me, and his personal metamorphosis was obvious from the moment he entered my living room. Gone were the slight stutter and air of self-conscious nervousness that had so defined his demeanour in the immediate past. He now walked with the cocksure air of a young prince min-gling with his lowly courtiers.

Chrissie Hynde was with him – fresh from her native Akron to try her luck once again back in swinging London town. She didn't seem too happy to see me again but McLaren immediately came to the point of why this visitation was taking place. He'd decided to extend his pop-Svengali instincts beyond the realm of the Sex Pistols and start a second band that he was fully intent on controlling with the same steely grip. Chrissie would be the singer and I'd play guitar. Mick Jones – then known only as 'Brady' – would be the bassist and a kid from Croydon called Chris Miller would be the drummer. The three of us – McLaren, Hynde and myself – even drove to Miller's hotel room that same night somewhere on the outskirts of London to sound him out on the project. He seemed to be up for anything but was still taken aback when McLaren suddenly insisted that our group had to be called 'the Masters of the Backside'.

The guy still couldn't see past using musicians as glorified rent boys for his pimp-centric ambitions. The project was over for me as soon as he came up with that demeaning name. Plus Hynde and I were still far from comfortable in each other's company. Time had not healed the old wounds that still festered between us. She came back to see me alone a few days later and our conversation soon degenerated into an almighty row that promptly spelt the end of 'the Masters of the Backside' before we'd even played a note of music together.

It was at this time also that my girlfriend Hermine discovered that her tightrope had been stolen. This was most inconvenient as she'd just been booked to walk it at a Women's Lib festival somewhere in Cardiff during early May. Somehow this unfortunate state of affairs developed into a scenario where she would sing at the festival instead and I would back her up. It was then that Chris Miller turned up and offered to lend his musical support. He had two friends with him: a black-haired guitarist called Brian Robertson some years his senior and a maladjusted youth called Ray who'd spent much of his adolescence devoid of parental guidance, even sleeping on Brighton beach for extended periods. In a couple of months' time, Brian would change his surname to 'James', Ray would reinvent himself as 'Captain Sensible', Chris would take on the daunting sobriquet of 'Rat Scabies' – and with a horror-film obsessive who called himself Dave Vanian also in tow they'd begin playing around London as the Damned.

But before that they committed themselves to two performances as the Subterraneans – the name came courtesy of a Jack Kerouac novel I favoured at the time – in my old stomping ground of Wales's capital city. Half the show consisted of us doing the least liberating-for-women songs ever conceived in rock – nasty misogynistic numbers like the Stones' 'Under My Thumb' and the Crystals' 'He Hit Me (and It Felt Like a Kiss)'. The other half featured brand-new songs, most significantly Brian's composition 'New Rose', which was premiered for the first time ever at the two concerts we gave. Not that anyone noticed: there were only eight people present in both audiences.

Back in London, though, a fierce conflict was brewing between Malcolm McLaren and anyone he perceived to be threatening his pre-eminence as the Pygmalion of punk. Anyone operating outside of his personal radar was suddenly marked out for instant retribution. He'd lately become so caught up in his new-found power that he'd started a new trend at his group's London shows: setting members of the audience up for a bloody beating.

Lydon – intimidated by the rest of the Pistols – had opted to bring some of his own hooligan cohorts into the group's immediate entourage – proper bad boys like John 'Sid' Beverley and Jah Wobble. Watching their former school pal suddenly become the poster boy of late-seventies rock revolution had made them equally determined to make their mark on this new scene. At this exact moment their capacities for music-making were at best minimal but not to worry: little Malcolm conscripted them instead into his own private thug army. They could run wild at Pistols concerts, punching and stabbing and bloodletting with complete impunity.

When Beverley blinded a young girl during a show at the 100 Club that summer, few amongst the media chose to draw attention to the incident. McLaren had them all hypnotised like chickens. Some bright spark at *Melody Maker* had just come up with a new 'punk' manifesto. 1976 was 'year zero'. The old rock 'n' roll was dead. Punk was the new reality and anyone who disagreed was a walking fossil. A kind of mass hysteria was being conjured forth that threw the old music-industry guard based in Britain into a complete panic.

No one knew what to think of this new music for fear of being suddenly judged old and obsolete. And no one dared to directly address the savagery and barbarism of its protagonists. Like sex, physical violence isn't something the English generally feel too confident about exploring. When it erupts before them, they tend to cower back, hide in the shadows and pretend that nothing untoward is going on. Thus it was that McLaren and his bully boys were able to terrorise London club-goers over and over again and still receive a clean bill of health from the city's jobbing journos.

The first time I saw 'Sid' Beverley was on the 27th of May, 1976. He was lurking around the backstage entrance of a Rolling Stones concert being held in the huge Earls Court exhibition show-room, unsuccessfully trying to chance his way into the venue. In an ill-fitting second-hand suit and electric-shock hair, he looked like a juvenile Dickensian chimney sweep.

The second time I saw him – just two weeks later at a Pistols show at the 100 Club – he left more of an impact. The atmosphere that night was tense in the extreme. McLaren was doing his puppet-master routine, setting up more dupes for a public thrashing. Two members of Eddie and the Hot Rods' entourage – their logo designer Michael Beal and A&R man Howard Thompson – were in the house, and to the Pistols this was tantamount to a rival gang invading their turf. Just before his band started playing, McLaren stood on the stage alongside John Lydon and beckoned to 'Sid' to join them. They then pointed seemingly in the direction of the two interlopers and grinned conspiratorially. Sid pulled out his chain and immediately went to work. But I was mistaken: McLaren and Lydon hadn't dispatched him to beat up the Hot Rods intruders. They'd sent him to beat me up instead.

Sid didn't waste any words. He just lurched over and started kicking merry hell out of my seated frame whilst brandishing his bike chain just above my head. One of the Hot Rods guys intervened momentarily, only to have his face lacerated by the chain. Whilst this was happening, Vicious's accomplice Jah Wobble materialised before me. He held an open penknife and was waving it no more than two inches from my eyes. There was dried blood on the blade and a look of pure sadistic delight in his piggy eyes as though he was about to experience an impromptu orgasm at any second.

Then he stepped back, allowing Sid dead aim at my skull. He took three or four bike-chain swings but only managed to connect with me once. I was so stoned that night that I didn't even feel the blow. But I could tell that something potentially life-threatening had transpired because there was blood everywhere: on the wall behind me in a wide crimson arc and all over the back of my jacket. If two more of those chain-swings had actually reached me, I'd probably have been killed by the head trauma. And what was the audience doing whilst this was going on? Just standing there, afraid to react, taking it all in voyeuristically. Finally a bouncer grabbed 'Sid' from behind, disarmed him and dragged him towards the nearest exit. As I was being led out, Vivienne Westwood ran up and started apologising profusely for what had happened: 'The boy who did that – he's just this psychopath who's fastened on to the group. We'll make sure he's never allowed into one of our shows again.' Blah-blah-blah. McLaren told me the same thing when he phoned up a day later to try and mend fences.

Who did they think they were fooling? I knew they'd set me up, that it had all been pre-arranged and that my old buddies in the Sex Pistols were probably all in on it too. All my professional life, I'd been expecting this moment. But I'd always imagined it coming at the hand of someone I'd genuinely affronted. I never dreamed I'd be stitched up by people I'd helped and viewed as kindred spirits.

Still, I should have seen it coming. Only a year before, McLaren and Westwood had marketed a T-shirt they'd designed together. On its front was written 'One of these days you're going to wake up and discover which side of the bed you've been sleeping on' and below were two lists of names. One list was a roll call of their chosen favourites, the other of their most despised enemies. My name turns up in the pro column right next to 'QT

Jones and the Sex Pistols'. Now I'd been shunted rudely over to
the other side of the bed. That's what happens when you find
yourself mingling with the beautiful people. You've always got to
keep your back to the wall. You never know when you'll be their
next sacrificial victim.

Did I tell you I'd become recently homeless? I was now entering the most brutal hard-core phase of heroin addiction – the
phase where nothing else matters, not even a roof over one's
head – or loving companionship. Hermine had left me too. I'd
become too toxic for her to waste further time on – at least for
the moment. So I was out on my own and up to no good.

Drug addiction inevitably promotes a heightened sense of isolation within the mindset of its victims but that didn't mean I
was alone in my predicament. In May I'd spent time with the
Rolling Stones and they were slowly unravelling too from all the
chronic drug abuse around them. Their music had lost all of its
primal momentum. Bob Dylan saw them live around this time
and Ian Hunter later asked him what he'd thought of the group's
mid-seventies incarnation. 'Apathy for the devil,' he'd simply
replied with a jaundiced sneer on his cocky little face.

Something had turned distinctly rotten in the state of Led
Zeppelin too that same year. In October I went to their newly
instigated World's End headquarters to interview Jimmy Page for
the *NME*. They had a film coming out – *The Song Remains the
Same* – accompanied by a live soundtrack album but both were
deeply underwhelming approximations of what usually transpired at a Zeppelin live event.

Normally the film reels and live tapes would have been judged
inadequate and left in a closet. But Peter Grant was not fully on
top of the situation and had let them both reach completion in

order to feed the record label with new product whilst the group stayed away from the touring circuit. Grant's impending divorce had taken all the wind out of his sails and had sent him spinning into the throes of a full-blown drug-accelerated breakdown. I spoke to him on the phone for just five minutes that day: he sounded like a cross between a wounded bear and Darth Vader with a slight East London lisp. 'I just want to know if you're still our ally,' he kept asking me. It made my blood run cold.

Page looked distinctly fragile when he finally arrived. It soon became clear he wasn't too enamoured with the film and record he was supposed to promote either – and so our talk centred more on his recent adventures. He was particularly vexed about the *Scorpio Rising* film project and its director Kenneth Anger. He claimed he'd contributed the soundtrack music and even helped finance the editing, but that Anger was unable to complete the work and had generally been mistaking the guitarist's kindness for weakness.

I wrote up Page's comments only to find myself later having to confront Anger face to face. He turned up at the *NME*'s office demanding a right of reply. When one wasn't forthcoming, he held aloft his right hand puckishly. 'I just have to crook this little finger and Jimmy Page will automatically be transformed into a toad,' he informed me with due theatricality. He was also strongly implying that he could do the same trick on me. But I was unmoved. That's the one positive about being a homeless junkie: even witchcraft can't intimidate you. You're so far down the ladder anyway, nothing seems worse than where you already are.

What else was going on? Oh yes, the Clash. Bernie Rhodes had been McLaren's boy – his gofer and general dogsbody. Rhodes had been heavily under his spell, working tirelessly for whatever mad cause Malcolm had drawn him into. But devotion has its limits and – seeing his mentor suddenly neck-deep in media attention – Bernie had started developing ambitions of his own. If McLaren could become a bona fide pop Svengali, then so could he.

In the late spring of 1976 he began consorting with Mick Jones and a strikingly handsome youth named Paul Simonon who'd been briefly employed by David Bowie's Mainman organisation as a lookalike decoy to confuse fans when the star himself was out in public. Keith Levene – a prog-rock-besotted guitarist – was also in the picture as was a drummer called Terry Chimes. But they needed a frontman more than anything else – as well as a new musical direction. The latter they discovered the first time they listened to the Ramones' debut album. Then they lured Joe Strummer of the 101'ers into their web.

Strummer was already a known quantity around London's pub-rock circuit as the snaggle-toothed troubadour of the capital's new bohemian squatocracy, so his sudden defection to the cause of punk was not without personal consequences. I saw one of the Clash's first-ever London shows – again at the 100 Club. It was visually impressive but the players – still including Keith Levene – hadn't yet secured a solid rhythmic foundation to build their sound from and were basically just making a bunch of shrill, overamplified noise. Afterwards I saw Strummer in a state of advanced inebriation and close to tears remonstrating with Bernie Rhodes. 'I've sold out, Bernie,' he kept saying over and over again. But it was only a fleeting moment of uncertainty on the singer's part. As soon as the glowing reviews started getting published, the former John Mellor – the upper-middle-class son of a former British government diplomat turned self-styled king of the proles – knew he'd made the right decision when he ruthlessly rejected his old squat-rock cronies in order to throw in his lot with the new breed.

By the end of '76, his group were out there on the cultural barricades alongside the Pistols and the Damned as part of the Anarchy package tour, getting banned and/or publicly demonised almost everywhere they played. The tour should have compounded a sense of genuine unity within this fragile punk community but instead only contributed to its ongoing fragmentation. The managers were all at each other's throats and the groups began to get coldly competitive with each other. An even more divisive element had been imported into the mix: Johnny Thunders's Heartbreakers had been invited over from New York to take part in the tour. Thunders's arrival in the London punk milieu that winter would have grievous consequences. The guy was a walking advert for heroin and many impressionable young scene-makers were suddenly seduced into sharing the high with the guitarist.

But was I really any better than him? Junkies are junkies, after all. Sordid people leading sordid lives. It's the nature of the beast. I wasn't consciously endangering others in my thirst for junk but in the past twelve months it had managed to turn me into a pitiful public spectacle. There's one photograph that sometimes turns up in punk-related tomes that was taken at year's end 1976. John Lydon is sneering triumphantly next to a high-spirited Brian James whilst I stand to their immediate left looking like I've just been liberated from Dachau concentration camp.

Even more alarming to behold were the few articles I managed to eke out during this spell. Reading them now is like watching a man trying to swim his way through an ocean of mud. At Christmas time I made my annual pilgrimage to visit my parents, who now lived in Morecambe, Lancashire. My mother burst into tears when she opened the door and saw the state I was in. That's when I knew I was truly in hell.

Death-dealing druggies and psychopaths to the left of me. Chicken-hearted chicken hawks and yuppie violence-groupies to the right. Stones in my pathway every step of the way. I felt like I'd suddenly taken up residence in one of Robert Johnson's most godforsaken compositions. 'The valley of the shadow of death' wasn't just some grim reference from the Bible any more; it was my new postal code.

If I'd had my druthers, I would have been making radical New Year's resolutions to redeem my situation, but I simply couldn't summon the required willpower. The worst was yet to come.

1977

This is how 1977 started for me.

On the 28th December 1976 I left my parents and returned south in a state of some urgency. The drugs I'd taken there to tide me over the Christmas season had run out and it was only a matter of a few hours before I'd be feeling the withdrawal symptoms. I had no actual London home base as such to return to – I was still effectively *sans domicile* – but the dealers would probably still let me pass out on their floors and that was all the roof I needed over my head at the time.

Stepping back into the city I looked around and the streets seemed virtually deserted. Everyone had left to see in the new year with family and friends out in the provinces. I immediately made some phone calls and checked out some addresses but all my former drug connections were out of town as well. My bones were beginning to ache and my eyes were watering like a lovesick girl's. In desperation I visited the surgery of a well-known London 'croaker' – a registered doctor who was known to prescribe strong pain medication, tranquillisers and pill-form speed if the price was right. I told him my problem – I was a heroin addict on the verge of withdrawal – and he tut-tutted and played the armchair moralist for five minutes. Then he wrote out a script and handed it to me, though not before pocketing £20 of my dwindling personal cash flow. I took it straight to a pharmacy, only to discover that he'd prescribed me nothing for the physical pain I was about to experience, just some mood-altering medication I'd never taken before.

Now I had to attend to a second pressing concern: finding myself some form of temporary accommodation. I ran into a girl I'd sometimes seen on the smack circuit in the streets of Westbourne Grove and unburdened my tale of woe on her. She then took me back to her squat and said I could sleep in the spare room. Her boyfriend lived in the building too – a big Scottish guy, hard as nails. I think his name was Trevor. He'd been a well-known and justly feared fixture on the local junk scene for some time – shaking down users and dealers alike, stealing and swindling his way around the metropolis. But then he'd gotten addicted to a drug even stronger than heroin – a pink pill they gave only to terminal cancer patients the name of which now escapes me. It was manufactured in such a way that it was extremely dangerous to attempt direct injection. The chalk in the pills wouldn't dissolve and would then be mainlined straight into veins as well as muscle tissue and bone marrow and start spreading disease. But this hadn't stopped Trevor. He'd started shooting up the stuff in his left leg. Now he couldn't walk. He just lay there in bed and got his girlfriend to do everything for him – cook his food, change his bandage, cop his dope. The first night I moved in, he showed me the infected leg; from the toes up to the knee, everything was swollen green. 'Looks like gangrene,' I muttered, albeit cautiously. 'Aye, I know,' he'd replied. 'It's only a matter of time before this bugger' – indicating the infected leg – 'gets amputated. I'm nae worried, though. I'll get a ton of gear free off the NHS as a result – maybe a lifetime's supply. Giving up a leg for a deal like that is the best thing that's happened to me in a while.'

By and by, I retired to the room they'd let me crash in for a few days. Drab drawn curtains, one naked light bulb, no heating, one raggedy-ass mattress awash with the aroma of stale joss sticks. It was like taking up residence inside a Hieronymus Bosch painting. For two whole days and nights I lay there trembling, sweating and cursing. Upstairs someone kept playing the same record over and over again. It was a weird jazz instrumental with a free-form sax solo that slurred in and out of concert pitch, like a form of musical water torture. It was one of the rare times in my life when I genuinely feared for my sanity. I tried taking these mood-altering pills my doctor pally had thoughtfully prescribed for me but they only made things worse.

Now I was shaking so hard I was scared I'd go into epileptic convulsions, whilst my brain seemed to have suddenly turned to quicksand. I looked at the name on the pill bottle again: Tryptizol. I'd heard that name before. Then it slowly dawned on me. This was the same drug that had killed Nick Drake and he'd overdosed on just three of the treacherous capsules. I'd been given a potentially life-threatening drug by a registered physician without being advised beforehand on the quantity I was supposed to take. A year later, this same physician took on Keith Moon as one of his patients and prescribed him a drug called Heminevrin to combat the drummer's alcoholism. Again, he failed to alert his patient to the dangers of taking too many and Moon died as a result. The point being – you had a hard road to hoe if you were a drug addict in the seventies. There was no Narcotics Anonymous or Priory-styled detox facilities to escape into. Most medical professionals wouldn't touch you with a bargepole. And almost everyone else treated you like a leper. It was all down, down, down. You'd think you'd hit the bottom rung of the ladder and then the ground would open up and once again you'd be in free fall, blindly grasping the air around you.

When would I wake from this nightmare? Not any time soon – that was for sure. I still couldn't see any righteous alternative. The real world outside felt even more inhospitable than the junkie world I was trapped in. And just as insane. A power-crazy greengrocer's daughter was about to take over the country. And Sid Vicious had just joined the Sex Pistols.

Glen Matlock was the one who informed me that January. He wasn't well chuffed by the turn of events – as you can probably imagine. But Lydon – feeling threatened by Jones and Cook's evil Siamese-twin-like closeness – had wanted one of his own bully-boy accomplices in the line-up to balance their internal chemistry out more evenly. And then McLaren had fallen in love with the idea of an authentic sociopath joining the group. No one bothered to question the musical wisdom of replacing Matlock – a powerful bassist and key songwriting source – with someone who could barely play a musical instrument and who was incapable of contributing to new material. Ever since the group had sparked a national tempest by swearing at a drunken oaf called Bill Grundy who was supposed to be interviewing them on the telly that winter, the Pistols had been trading on a policy of outrage over proficiency at every turn and the yield to date had been singular to say the least. Their name was on everybody's lips but they were banned from playing live throughout England and kept getting signed and then abruptly dropped by record labels. Bringing Sid into their mix was like adding fire to a leaking pool of gasoline. A terrible explosion was bound to transpire as a result. People would get badly injured, some would lose their lives. It was a disaster just waiting to happen and I was just glad I'd been exiled when I had; at least I was out of the eye of their latest hurricane.

Only I wasn't. McLaren chose to broadcast the arrival of Sid Vicious into the Sex Pistols by sending a series of telegrams out to the music – and daily – press on which a single curt message was inscribed. Sid was now a Sex Pistol, the missive stated, and the main reason he'd been picked was because 'he gave Nick Kent just what he deserved at the 100 Club'.

Reading that in the *NME* and everywhere else certainly jolted me out of my junkie stupor for at least five minutes. The thoughts that flooded through my head in that moment of ersatz clarity were distinctly unpleasant ones. I'd been victimised once – by people I'd helped and befriended – and now I was being victimised and slandered again in the public forum – by the same vampiric morally bankrupt preening scumsuckery backstabbers. This was war. But a war I was never going to be able to win. What was I going to do? Buy a gun on the black market and cap the little red-haired prick? He wasn't worth the angst, the effort or the expense. Nor did I have the time to even plot a feud. The moment-to-moment fabric of my life was tied up in far more pressing issues – like 'Where will I sleep tonight?' and 'How can I stay loaded for the next twenty-four hours?' Revenge was a luxury I couldn't afford to cultivate at this stage in my life.

One evening either two or three weeks after McLaren's poisonous telegram had hit the presses, I made my way up to Dingwalls for some social distraction. I was scarcely through the door when I turned to my right and saw a figure approaching. He had ink-black hair and a big village-idiot grin breaking up his features like a split coconut. Once again I found myself face to face with Sid Vicious.

My first thought on seeing him advance before me? 'Oh boy, here we go again. Look out for that bike chain.' But he just stood there grinning and offered me his hand to shake. 'Listen, mate,' he said, 'I want to say sorry about what happened at the 100 Club. I was out of my head that night. It was nothing personal.' He then told me that he and Lydon 'felt bad' about what McLaren had written about me in his press statement, that it was 'well out of order'. I just stood there drinking in his words, thankful that my cranium wasn't again under siege. 'He doesn't seem too bright,' I remember thinking. But he sounded sincere. And borderline contrite too. I accepted his apologies, we shook hands and that was that. He sloped back to the bar presumably to cosh some unlucky music-industry shill whilst I went in the opposite direction in search of anyone who might give me free drugs. It was just a brief encounter of the 'ships passing in the night' variety – but it would not be our last.

Meanwhile, it would be fair to say that 'what happened at the 100 Club' and McLaren's later glorification of the incident in the media had a truly calamitous effect on my life. Whenever I attended punk-themed events around London throughout all of 1977 and most of the following year, someone I'd never met before would walk up to me and try to start a fight. It was like suddenly having my very existence turned into the script for a bad Western, the kind where the star-crossed wandering hero has to confront some new trigger-happy inebriated ruckus-raiser in every saloon bar in every town he stumbles through.

Actually I'm overstating the menace a little: I never actually got threatened with a gun. But knives and other sharp wounding

objects were sometimes waved provocatively in my face. My tor-
mentors just wanted to earn a bit of instant punk cred for themselves and maybe even a mention in the music comics. Some
misguided person with orange hair tried to stab me in the toilets
at the Roxy whilst my back was turned. He failed to pierce my
flesh with his blade but cut the jacket I was wearing to ribbons in
the ensuing mêlée.

Mostly though it was just verbal violence. I'd be standing there
minding my own business and some ferret-eyed mouth almighty
flanked by the inevitable pair of gormless-looking sidekicks
would sidle up and begin harassing me. 'You think you're it' –
that was always the first line out of their lips. 'You think you're it.
But you're not. You're just a piece of shit.' And so on. Usually I
was so stoned that the invective being evoked at my expense
splashed over me like water off the proverbial duck's back. That's
one of the only good things about using narcotics – it can shield
you from having your senses too infiltrated by the slings and
arrows of outrageous fortune. But it was still a draining process to
have to withstand these assaults on my flesh and general character time after time.

Did I truly merit this sorry, sorry fate? Well, yes and no. Much
of my bad fortune – specifically drug addiction and homelessness
– I'd brought upon myself. They were nobody's fault but mine.
And I'd done a lot of bad things over the past three years. I'd been
too arrogant and too vain, too immature and too judgemental,
too wayward and too goddam hot-headed – and that was just the
short list. But I never ever let myself become one of those all-the-
way bad people who lose all sense of personal humanity and conscience. My heart just wasn't in it. My inner moral compass was
still halfway functioning throughout this whole wretched era.

And yet to suddenly become an all-purpose whipping boy for the emerging punk hordes – that was unjust and plain wicked. Shit, I'd been running around in the music press like a headless chicken talking up punk rock as the next big thing back when Joe Strummer had still been a folk-singing Woody Guthrie wannabe, Malcolm McLaren a fifties rockabilly haberdasher and John Lydon a bloke with long red hair who sometimes sold LSD at Hawkwind concerts. And then to be victimised by the very thing I'd helped bring into being – that was cold.

But at the same time there was no way out. What could I have done? Retreat to the provinces, get healthy and become a librarian? That wasn't my idea of a viable lifestyle alternative. I just had to keep brassing it out and stay breathing.

After seeing in the new year at the House of Gangrene, I'd spread my junkie wings and moved on to other druggy crash pads in the immediate vicinity as a source of temporary refuge. One shelter from the storm was a first-floor apartment on All Saints Road just two or three doors along from the notorious Mangrove restaurant, a well-known local hotbed of friction between Jamaican potheads and the local constabulary. A guy called Nigel lived there – white, well-spoken, Oxbridge graduate, held down a straight job on weekdays, took loads of drugs on the weekend. He was one of the few genuinely soulful yuppies I've ever crossed paths with. He was also homosexual, as were his two flatmates, one of whom was a journalist for *Gay News*. He'd let me sleep on his floor when I had nowhere else to go. He and his co-inhabitants never tried to foist their sexuality onto me. They were out in the margins of society too – down by law and circumstance – and kind-hearted enough to invite a sad specimen like me in from the cold to share their frugal living space.

One afternoon I wandered in and Nigel was talking to an alarming-looking young American woman with dyed blonde hair and a nerve-jangling voice. The subject of their increasingly heated conversation centred on a recent drug deal gone wrong. Nigel had given this harpy money to secure him some heroin and she'd come back with a tiny packet full of brick-dust. 'Money for old rope,' he kept muttering darkly. 'Fuck you, you simpering faggot,' the woman – who'd obviously just robbed him – fired back. She then turned on her heels and exited the building, leaving only a trail of insults in her wake. It was my first encounter with Nancy Spungen.

I'd be at Nigel's place for two or three days at a time and then – not wishing to outstay my welcome – scoot across the road to a hard-core junkie crash pad on a small street parallel to Portobello Road. This place was the closest I ever came to frequenting one of those Victorian opium dens where the clientele would all be splayed out on the floor in states of shared horizontal stupefaction. It was really a ground-floor flat that had been lately squatted by a guy called Gary, who'd fitted the main space out with some mattresses he found on a nearby skip and then opened up the premises to any junkie who might share his dope with him. He was a pretty typical example of what passed for a heroin addict in the more downtrodden areas of London during the late seventies: a nice guy – too sweet-natured to become fully criminal-minded – who'd stumbled into a deadly lifestyle and who was trying to just keep his head above water. His big problem – apart from the dope – was his girlfriend Amanda. Amanda was as grey as a ghost and she babbled incessantly – a semi-comatose, deeply disturbed human ragbag of rampant neurosis. Nobody could stand her apart from Gary, who was utterly besotted with the ungrateful woman and who saw himself as her knight-in-shining-armour protector. She didn't deserve him: the love he felt for her was pearls before swine. Later in 1977 she left him to move in with a psychotic dealer working out of North London and Gary had committed suicide the night he found out.

Another of my junkie 'homes away from home' was up in Maida Vale, close to Little Venice, where a Persian youth named Attila (it was his real name) was dealing from a basement squat that due to lack of electricity looked more like a cave than a bed-sit. Attila was a rich oil sheikh's son but daddy had promptly disowned him when he'd discovered his son courting a drug habit and exiled him from the land of his birth. The boy – who looked about seventeen years of age – had landed in London and was now connected with some heavy-duty Persian gangsters who used him to sell their product from his extremely humble outpost. He was not long for this world but at least he had an older companion from his homeland with him to keep an eye on the business.

Engin, his Persian compatriot, was a real box of human fireworks: long, thinning hair, a beard from straight out of the Old Testament days, yellow skin, emaciated, cadaverous features, mad terrorist eyes – he looked like a smack-addled Ivan the Terrible and he talked like the ultimate soothsayer of doom. Even when stoned out of his gourd, he'd be mumbling darkly about the impending apocalypse and the godless nature of mankind. It was just as well he devoted all his energies to using and selling heroin or else he'd have probably been out and about putting bombs in tube stations.

Engin dealt from a tip of a squat he shared with a rail-thin, comatose Irish hippie girl called Siobhan down on Castellain Road, only two minutes' walk from Attila's abode. One late afternoon I had cause to visit the place and found myself ambling towards the building in question when something else caught my eye. A youth was lying horizontally, half of him on the pavement, half of him on the road directly in front of Engin's. He looked to be in a lot of pain. My first instinct was 'Oh shit – maybe he's been shot. Maybe Engin's just been robbed by some heavy-duty villains and there's been some kind of massacre.'

But then – as I approached the prone form – I recognised who it was: Sid Vicious – again. Moreover, a Sid Vicious undergoing extremely nasty physical contortions. 'What the fuck are you doing laid out like that?' I asked him. He was crying and moaning – literally – babbling on about how he had to get some smack because the Pistols had a show that night and he was too sick to make the date. He'd heard that someone was dealing on this street and so had gone from door to door, getting them slammed in his face at every turn. He'd gotten so frustrated – he said – that he'd taken out his knife and started cutting up his chest. He then showed me the wounds. I'd never seen the results of self-mutilation before. It was an alarming sight. Anyway, I helped him up off the ground and guided him to Engin's door. Sid after all was breaking the number-one commandment in the drug addict's Bible – never needlessly draw attention to yourself in public – and had to be removed from the sidewalk before the police were called in.

When he opened the door, I could see Engin was not elated by the thought of seeing Sid about to cross his threshold. Apart from being a full-time harbinger of gloom, he also fancied himself as a prog-rock drummer. His drum kit took up most of the living room where he and his true love spent all their time. You'd be nodding out on a sofa and suddenly be rudely awakened by him bashing away on the thing as he tried in vain to keep time to a Mahavishnu Orchestra record blasting from the stereo. Engin had heard about punk and reckoned it was the music of the Antichrist. Now the Antichrist was about to step into his home and hearth. Suffice to say, it took all my powers of persuasion to get him inside. Once in, I asked Engin to help Sid out, and after some grumbling he supplied him with a five-quid bag of heroin. Sid dug a syringe out of one of his pockets, cooked the stuff up, drew the residue up into the syringe's barrel and then – without tying off to find a vein – just drove the needle into his arm, sending blood spurting onto the floor before him. Thirty seconds later, his eyes were as tiny as pinwheels and he was weaving uncertainly about the room with a beatific grin on his face. He couldn't stop thanking me and Engin for our generosity, and with good reason. Nothing bonds junkies closer than when one helps another in time of sickness.

Four days later I returned to Engin's Castellain Road sink-hole only to find him sharing the space with two new tenants. Sid Vicious and Nancy Spungen had taken up squatter's rights there too – just strong-armed their way into his living room with all their worldly possessions contained inside three or four plastic shopping bags. This was a truly mind-boggling living arrangement: Engin and his whispering girlfriend were dyed-in-the-wool hippie relics whilst Sid and Nancy were foul-mouthed barbarians who would have gladly spat on their hosts and then left them both bleeding in an alley in normal circumstances. But heroin has a curious way of bridging all social and cultural divides once one has succumbed to it. At first Engin had bristled at the idea of these two moving into his domain but Sid had pulled out a bunch of cash he wished to exchange for dope, and from that moment on he and his horrifying girlfriend had been allowed to become fixtures on the premises. They occupied a ratty old couch which they lay on in a semi-conscious stupor.

When I arrived, a black-and-white telly was already relaying the sounds and images of a live Eric Clapton concert especially filmed and recorded for the BBC. On the flickery screen, Clapton – a former heroin addict himself – stared out at us from behind a gold prospector's beard. He looked seriously liquored up and sang in a voice frayed with exhaustion and too much inhaled nicotine. There was nothing remotely dynamic about the music he and his group were making – no energy or daring. It sounded like everything that punk had lately been invented to give the bum's rush to and Spungen kept up a running commentary as she stared witheringly at the spectacle, employing language that even a sailor might have paused before using. One of Clapton's backing singers was a black woman and Spungen kept running her down, calling her 'that dumb fuckin' nigger' over and over again. I looked at Sid to see whether he shared his love interest's racist outlook but he was comatose, eyes shut tight, mouth slightly ajar. How this scabby pair ended up becoming the token Romeo and Juliet of the late seventies is something I – and pretty much anyone else who knew them – still find bafflingly hard to take into full account. Theirs wasn't even what you would call 'love' per se – more an intense mutual neediness.

Both of them were damaged goods and bad apples and each saw in the other disturbing qualities they craved for themselves. Sid was initially drawn to Nancy because she was stronger, bossier, more abrasive and even more morally vacuous than he was. Nancy glommed on to Sid because he was a rising star with a malleable, still-not-fully-formed personality that she quickly recognised she could exploit in a way that could help her realise her one burning ambition – to become a celebrity herself.

Heroin did the rest – tied them up together in nasty little knots and fabricated the love-dust they claimed to see in each other's eyes – and now heroin had thrown them into my orbit too. Almost everywhere I stayed throughout most of 1977 Sid and Nancy would somehow end up there too. I crashed at Johnny Thunders's Mayfair flat for two weeks that summer until the pair dropped by and never left. You couldn't pass out around either of them because they'd start frantically ransacking your pockets for drugs and money whilst you slept. That was an occupational hazard for any socialising junkie in the seventies and I soon found a way to circumvent it – I'd Sellotape my drugs to my body when it came time to turn in.

Later that summer, Hermine found me temporary accommodation in a large Dockland warehouse complex also frequented by the sculptor Andrew Logan and film-maker Derek Jarman. My new living quarters were one large unfurnished room overlooking the Thames. It was an ideal place to lie low in, reflect on recent events and try and change my disastrous way of living. But then – just three days after I'd moved in – Sid and Nancy turned up without prior warning too and everything promptly turned to shit. I'd just been to the local shop and had arrived back in time to find Sid pissing against my front door. I immediately pointed out to him that if he'd just turned around and walked three steps forward, the stream of his urine would now be sailing into Father Thames instead of befouling my new hidey-hole, but he didn't seem able to grasp the point I was making.

The evening we spent together was like all the others: Sid nodding out whilst Nancy sat around maliciously cursing out the rest of mankind for hours on end. Apart from Iggy Pop and Johnny Thunders, she never had a good word to say about anybody – and she had a real bee in her bonnet about Sid's soul-brother Lydon. 'He thinks he's such a fuckin' star – but he isn't. Sid's the real star in the Sex Pistols. Aren't you, Sid?' She'd then whack her boyfriend in the ribs, causing him to stir from his coma. 'Yeah, Nance, you're right,' he'd mumble before promptly falling back into the arms of Morpheus.

Late in the night Nancy decided it was time for her and her intended to get some actual bedrest. There was only one bed available – the one I was using – but she bitched and moaned so much about sleeping on the floor that I let them pass out on it instead. The next morning I noticed the pillow had a rancid-looking yellowish substance stained all over it. I reached out to touch it and it felt moist and greasy. Sid noticed my growing consternation. 'Sorry, mate,' he said. 'I didn't have any hairspray yesterday so I stuck a bunch of margarine in my hair to get it to stand up. It must have melted when I was sleeping and messed up your pillow.'

How was one expected to react to situations like this? My solution was not to react at all. Just let them run wild until they find another strung-out fool to leech off. A couple of days later they'd vanished, leaving behind a touching memento: a torn plastic bag full of used, unwashed syringes that they'd hidden under the mattress. I'd tolerated their company for days and nights on end but I can't say I ever enjoyed a single second. Sid had a certain goofy charm when he was on his own but let's not kid ourselves here please – they were both supremely unlikeable people who tainted every setting they stumbled into. Only twenty years old and already they had the smell of death in their young pores. That's not something that deserves to be romanticised down through the ages.

Whilst I continued to languish in junkie-land, my relationship with the (relatively) straight world outside grew more and more tenuous. My visits to the *NME* throughout the year were infrequent at best. There had been changes afoot in my absence, none of them for the better. The office had moved from Long Acre to the twenty-first floor of a multi-storey high-rise near Waterloo station where it now shared space alongside all of IPC's other printed outlets. This relocation led to a sharp dip in office morale that everyone involved was affected by in one way or another.

Nick Logan – still the editor – started showing the symptoms of a looming nervous breakdown, whilst his former second lieutenant Ian MacDonald appeared to be engulfed in a mental meltdown all of his own. Ian had actually resigned from his assistant editor post in late '75. In '76 he decided to experiment with LSD for the first time. By 1977 he'd given up his worldly possessions and rented Maida Vale apartment and moved in with a Sufi commune living in a squat off Little Venice. (Two of his cohabitants had been the gifted singer/songwriter Richard Thompson and his wife Linda.) Later in the decade, he returned to his parents' neck of the woods back in Gloucestershire, where I believe he remained until he took his own life in 2003. For me, Ian and Nick had been the best and brightest of the *NME*'s golden-age hierarchy. The three of us had been the ones in the engine room feeding the furnace and steering the train. But the stress and friction involved had finally drained us all and sent us spinning each into our own lonely orbit.

It was a sad way to end a winning streak, even more so because no one else in the paper's then workforce had the requisite gumption to take over the weekly running of the enterprise with a genuinely inspired new game plan. The punk explosion then being detonated throughout the British Isles had rattled the *NME* writers' cages too, leaving the majority of them scared and uncertain about how they ought to react. To better cater to this new trend, two new staff writers had been brought into the fold the year before. One was a young man who dressed much like Frank Sinatra had in the fifties – pork-pie hat, dark suit, white shirt with black tie hung loose around the collar. His name was Tony Parsons and even though he was only twenty-two or thereabouts, he'd already managed to have his first novel published – a tome entitled *The Kids*.

He talked like a young East End scrapper and looked like he could be handy in a fist fight, something that couldn't have been said about any other male in the office. The other new recruit was a strange teenaged girl with a pronounced West Country twang to her accent, sullen eyes and a vibe about her that could best be described as 'Myra Hindleyesque'. I liked the idea of Julie Burchill coming aboard – she certainly knew how to shake things up – but the reality was often hard to stomach, particularly when one found oneself in close physical proximity to the young woman. Soon enough they became an item and their romance speedily turned into one of those classic 'you and me against the world' kamikaze affairs. The repercussions of this union were felt clear through the London music industry in '77 but most especially at the *NME*'s headquarters, where older staff members began developing stomach ulcers as a consequence of having to coexist alongside the Parsons–Burchill juggernaut. My so-called colleagues still apparently bear the psychic scars from the time the pair decorated their combined desk space with barbed wire, dubbed the area 'the kinderbunker' and then basically declared war on the rest of the paper. I don't recall personally witnessing that particular episode but, like I said, I made it my business to frequent the *NME* as little as possible during this period. I'd simply drop in from time to time and stick around long enough to steal as many albums as I could from the 'reviews' drawer and then go off and sell them at a local record exchange to get money for more dope.

But I had the misfortune to be lurking there the day Burchill goaded Tony Parsons into beating up Mick Farren, and that was an ugly and disturbing sight to behold. Farren was a friend of mine – one of the few non-junkies who still let me visit his apartment during my lost years. He and his then girlfriend Ingrid von Essen would often feed me and let me sleep on their cushions when I had nowhere else to go. Mick had been another punk pioneer – back in 1967 he'd been insulting audiences and generally inciting mayhem as the singer in a three-chord thrash act who'd called themselves the Deviants – but was now having a hard time connecting with this graceless new breed more than ten years his junior. He made the mistake of locking horns with Julie Burchill and – kaboom! – ended up getting his face flattened by Parsons's fists of fury.

Looking back now it's clear to me that amphetamines were at the root of this and most other outbursts of punk-related bloodletting. Bad speed was the stimulant of choice for London youth in 1977, specifically a product known as amphetamine sulphate, a white powder often fabricated in the bathtubs of provincial biker gangs that burnt nasal membranes, destroyed brain cells, promoted paranoia and aggressivity and generally transformed its adherents into emaciated bug-eyed wack-jobs. When you inhaled a line of the noxious substance, your nose stung for a whole minute and your sense of smell was engulfed by a rank Ajax-like odour that left you temporarily cross-eyed with nausea.

It was cheap though and could keep you so wide awake you'd be grinding your teeth together until your gums started to bleed. Then, several sleep-deprived days and nights later, your bones would be aching and you'd feel like something a stray dog had just vomited up. You'd also have only the slightest recollection of what had actually transpired during the prior seventy-two hours. That's why most reminiscences by UK punk musicians of the time are generally so unreliable: they simply don't have the brain cells required to reactivate the past objectively any more. Thus the era gets rewritten and turned into a myth without due reference to the driving poisons – the mindless violence, bad drugs and Tin Pan Alley ponces – that would so quickly nip its momentum in the bud.

Those who gleefully recast the time as one long happy-go-lucky punky reggae party evidently weren't present at the same events that I beheld. Or maybe it's just that we come from such different perspectives. Take for example the Slits. Others viewed them as a bold and liberating feminist clarion call. I thought they were a bunch of talentless exhibitionists. Watching them in the early days shrieking and stumbling cack-handedly through their tuneless repertoire was as grim an experience as going to get my wisdom teeth removed by an incompetent dentist. How had this concept that you could legitimately stand onstage holding a musical instrument even though you couldn't actually play the thing taken root and why was no one else viewing it as a musical version of the emperor's new clothes? The lunatics had now taken over the asylum that doubled as the late seventies' rock landscape. The seditious youthquake that had started in the fifties with James Dean had ended up being co-opted into a wretched hail storm of spit, safety pins and bathtub speed: from *Rebel Without a Cause* to rebels without a clue.

The only old-school punk pathfinder to benefit from the generational tumult of 1977 was my old pal Iggy Pop, who pulled off a major comeback coup that spring. The last time he appeared in this book it was back in 1975 and we'd left Iggy languishing in a Los Angeles nuthouse. But then clear out of the blue he received a surprise visit. 'I was in a mental hospital and Bowie happened to be there for another reason,' he would later recall. 'And he came up one day, stoned out of his brain in his little spacesuit, with Dean Stockwell the actor. They were like "We want to see Jimmy. Let us in." Now the strict rule was never to let outsiders in: it was an insane asylum. But the doctors were star-struck [laughs] so they let them enter. And the first thing they did was say "Hey, want some blow [cocaine]?" I think I took a little, which is really unpleasant in there. And that's how we got back in touch.'

When Bowie toured America in spring 1976, Iggy was his travelling companion. The former Stooge was also close by when Bowie made what appeared to be an ill-considered fascist salute to fans as he re-entered Britain via Victoria train station. Standing in the wings and watching the stick-insect Duke with his taut hair and stark black-and-white *Station to Station* stage show, Iggy later recalled feeling 'miserable, lost, lonesome and nostalgic . . . [Yet] I had been offered an opportunity in that David Bowie offered me the chance to make solo records, basically with him as my band. And at the time that he offered me that, the guy was a white-hot talent.'

In June, a month after the *Station to Station* tour had ended – without further incident – Bowie and Iggy began recording an album together at the Château d'Hérouville studios near Paris. Bowie wrote the music, played almost all the instruments, directed the vocal performances and suggested many of the several lyrical themes. 'To work with him as a producer,' Iggy now claims, 'he was a pain in the arse – megalomaniacal, loco! But he had good ideas. The best example I can give you was when I was working on the lyrics to "Funtime" and he said, "Yeah, the words are good. But don't sing it like a rock guy. Sing it like Mae West." Which made it informed of other genres, like cinema. Also, it was a little bit gay. The vocals there became more menacing as a result of that suggestion.

'He has a work pattern that recurs again and again. If he has an idea about an area of work that he wants to enter, as a first step, he'll use side projects or works for other people to gain experience and gain a little taste of the water before he goes in and does his . . . And I think he used working with me that way also.'

Whilst completing *The Idiot* at the Château, Bowie began work on *Low*, the record that would become his follow-up to *Station to Station*. At exactly the same juncture, *Playboy* published a lengthy interview conducted by Cameron Crowe and dating from Bowie's recent mad sojourn in LA. 'I'd adore to be Prime Minister,' the singer stated provocatively. 'And yes, I believe very strongly in fascism. The only way we can rid ourselves from the sort of liberalism that's hanging foul in the air at the moment is to speed up the progress of a right-wing, totally dictatorial tyranny and get it over with as fast as possible. People have always responded better under a regimental leadership.' And then came the punchline: 'Rock stars are fascists, too. Adolf Hitler was one of the first rock stars.' Seeing such sentiments uttered in cold print must have given David Bowie serious pause for thought. If they didn't, he needed only to stand in front of a full-length mirror and study his skeletal physique to see that all was not well in his fame-insulated world.

Vowing never to live again in Los Angeles, he remained in Europe, staying briefly in Switzerland (where his faithful assistant Corinne Schwab put him in touch with a therapist) before heading for Berlin with Iggy Pop. Moving into a seven-room flat at 155 Hauptstrasse in the city's downmarket Schöneberg district, he mingled anonymously with the area's mostly immigrant population and found inspiration for several instrumental pieces he planned to record with the recently recruited Brian Eno. 'The first side of *Low* was all about me,' Bowie later explained. 'Always crashing in the same car and all that self-pitying crap. Isn't it great to be on your own; let's just pull down the blinds and fuck 'em all . . .'

The record shocked listeners at first. Bowie sounded withdrawn and down in the mouth throughout his five vocal performances, as though his personality was deflating before our very ears. 'Deep in your room / So deep in your room,' he intoned, like some crooner peddling Valium via a television advert. Today, Bowie likes to claim that *Low* and its two follow-ups *Heroes* and *Lodger* were conceived and recorded in a largely cocaine-free state of being, but other sources insist this wasn't exactly the case. Certainly he was taking far less of the drug in Berlin than he'd managed in LA, but there was also a lot of alcohol being consumed. Iggy would later recount that in a typical

seven-day week he and Bowie would spend two days in some
form of intoxication, two days recovering from the hangovers,
and three days straight, 'which is a pretty good balance for musicians'. Of his months as Bowie's Berlin house guest, Iggy still
remembers the basic routine. 'Get up in the morning on the
fourth floor of a cold-water building and take a sponge bath. Cut
a little brown bread and cheese, and eat. Then walk over the city,
which hasn't changed since 1910: organ grinders who still had
monkeys, quality transvestite shows. A different world. By
evening, I'd go have dinner with Bowie, see a film or watch
Starsky and Hutch – that was our big thing. If there wasn't enough
to do, I knew some bad people and I'd get stoned and drunk.
Sometimes I'd do the bad stuff with Bowie and the good stuff
with the bad people.'

In March 1977 Iggy played his first-ever 'solo' concert in a
venue called 'Friars' out in the English town of Aylesbury as the
official unveiling of a world tour booked for that spring. Only it
wasn't really a solo deal because David Bowie was part of his
backing band, supplying the keyboard accompaniment and backing vocals. The Duke remained out of the stage spotlight and had
certainly dressed down for the occasion. In an anorak and flat cap
he looked more like a registered taxi driver than a rock star. Still,
his everyman attire and dimly lit profile hunched over a keyboard couldn't detract from the soon-drawn realisation that he
was the one who was really in charge of Iggy's new direction.

As a result, the singer's own performance felt oddly con-
strained in its desire to exhibit a higher grasp of professionalism.
He still moved and danced like a whirling dervish but he wasn't
interacting with the audience, wasn't stirring up the communal
frenzy any more. Bowie was midwifing him into a new career

phase – that of the performer in control of himself and his surroundings – with a pre-arranged set and precious little room for
any kind of spontaneity or 'sonic jazz'. The London punk
cognoscenti came out in force to savour the moment and Johnny
Thunders stood next to me through much of the show. But
before the end he was turning on his heels. 'I can't watch this shit
any more,' he'd murmured. 'Jim's just Bowie's bitch now. I can't
believe he sold out his rock 'n' roll side to go cabaret.' I thought
his reaction was small-minded and told him so. I actually liked
some of the music they were playing. Not the brace of ill-advised
Stooges covers but the new material that no one in the audience
had ever heard before: songs from *The Idiot* and *Lust for Life*. I saw
what Bowie was essentially trying to pull off – rehabilitating his
'wild American friend' whilst enlarging his own musical frontiers
and gaining some handy punk cred in the process – but my heart
still went out to the guy because his patronage was an act of genuine kindness that had probably saved Iggy's life and such acts
were desperately hard to come by in the seventies, particularly in
the music-making marketplace.

The Idiot got released at the end of March and promptly
polarised its audience. Lester Bangs wrote one of his last truly
worthwhile pieces of criticism on the subject in a *Village Voice*
article entitled 'Blowtorch in Bondage'. He lambasted the
album's contents with a vengeance; 'the person singing on *The
Idiot* sounds like a dead man', he wrote disparagingly. But he and
other Stooges hardliners were missing the point. Iggy and Bowie
were just taking the whole dank vampiric vibe of the seventies to
a further sonic and conceptual extremity. Too remorselessly bleak
and experimental-sounding to snare any kind of mainstream hit
momentum, the record nonetheless held a rising new demo-

graphic – most notably creative young Mancunians such as Ian Curtis and Howard Devoto – spellbound with awe and the accompanying tour turned out to be a stirring standing-room-only success everywhere it played.

At its conclusion, Iggy and Bowie promptly deployed their working unit – Hunt and Tony Sales as the rhythm section plus a Scottish guitarist named Ricky Gardiner – back to West Berlin, where they all entered a recording studio known as Hansa together and commenced work on a second album project. It was at this juncture that Iggy started to rebel against his European patron's grip on his own creative destiny. 'Bowie's a hell of a fast guy,' he'd later reflect. 'Very quick thinker, very quick action, very active person, very sharp. I realised I had to be quicker than him or whose album was it going to be?' By the end of the summer sessions, he'd managed to wrest back control of his core musical identity – *Lust for Life*, the resulting record, was brim-full of inspired autobiographical lyrics that dovetailed neatly into Bowie's generally more uplifting-sounding backing tracks. Indeed it was such a tour de force that many were predicting that it would provide Iggy with the elusive cross-over hit that would finally transform him into a bona fide superstar.

But then just as the record was being shipped into stores that September, news broke that Iggy's more prestigious RCA Victor label-mate Elvis Presley had died and the company promptly suspended the further pressing and distribution of *Lust for Life* in order to cope with worldwide demand for the King's back catalogue. The curse of Osterberg was still in full effect. His career had been sidelined yet again, this time by a fat bloke dying on the toilet. He tried keeping a stiff upper lip but became seriously unglued just prior to going out on his second world tour that year, booked – without Bowie's presence this time – to promote a new record that was barely available in the shops.

One afternoon in September I wandered into the *NME*'s drab Waterloo headquarters only to hear a familiar sound coming from out of Nick Logan's office – a deep-voiced American baritone that suddenly see-sawed into a high-pitched cackle whenever its owner came to the punchline of the tale he was telling. From a distance, I could just about make out the form of a strange little man in thick, frameless glasses and sporting disastrously short hair and a nondescript trench coat, slacks and golfing shoes who looked disconcertingly like the kind of character Jerry Lewis might have played in one of his early movie romps. Only the voice gave him away: it was Iggy.

I went over to greet him but couldn't get past the fact that his appearance and general demeanour were those of a completely crazy man. I took him to one side and asked what on earth he was doing on the premises. 'I'm trying to get hold of some crank,' he replied – 'crank' being US slang for speed. 'And I heard there might be some here. Can you help me out?' Oh boy – Iggy Pop on uppers: the most hyperactive man on the planet under the sway of the most hyperactive drug on the planet. It was a recipe for utter bedlam. He then invited me to join him for a ride around London in his limo parked outside. I told him I couldn't help him obtain any amphetamine but followed along anyway simply to further our sudden reacquaintance. I ended up spending the rest of the evening in his company and wishing I hadn't. He wasn't unfriendly but he was so bizarrely different from the guy I'd known back in the Stooges that it felt like he'd assumed a whole new personality in the interim – a personality moreover that was bewilderingly hard to actually like. He'd strut around like a little banty rooster marshalling his troops – his tour organisers and general personnel – like the drug-deluded ghost of General Patton. Then I joined him on an impromptu midnight trek to the Roxy, London's most notorious punk niterie, only to watch him behave there with such a haughty sense of self-entitlement he almost got punched out by the barely pubescent drummer of X-Ray Spex.

Still, Iggy managed to get two great albums out in 1977 and build a lucrative solo career for himself as a live act hither and yon, and these positive accomplishments ultimately far outweighed any negative energy and tricky karma still dogging his tracks. By any reckoning he'd be able to look back on the year as a providential one – a time of growth and dreams fulfilled. Other rock stars I'd known back in the early seventies wouldn't be so lucky.

1977 came down like a jackhammer even on big boys like the Rolling Stones and Led Zeppelin. Keith Richards got busted in Toronto that February by some Mounties who discovered enough heroin and cocaine in his hotel room to put him behind bars for several years. Many strings had to be pulled – many favours called in – but the Stones organisation somehow managed to keep him out of jail and out of Canada until an actual trial date was set. A rehab stint was set into motion but it evidently failed to have lasting results. In Ian McLagan's autobiography *All the Rage* the former Faces keyboard player recalls doing sessions with the group in a Paris recording studio later the same year and witnessing the guitarist 'jab a needle straight through his jeans into his bum and leave it there, the syringe sticking out as he walked around the room laughing loudly'.

With no fresh product to promote apart from a ropey in-concert album entitled *Love You Live* and a key member in big trouble, the group wisely opted not to tour that year. Led Zeppelin also had no new recordings to release during the same time frame, a singer still recovering from an auto accident in Greece eighteen months earlier that had come close to crippling him for life and two other band members in the early stages of heroin addiction. Even more alarmingly, their manager Peter Grant had just been put through a painful divorce by his once-devoted wife Gloria and was numbing the extensive emotional wounds brought on by no longer having a family to counterbalance the craziness of being at the helm of the world's biggest rock attraction by consuming far too much cocaine for a man of his gargantuan girth. His mood quickly darkened and he began making bad business decisions, the most far-reachingly ill-conceived being his green-lighting of a huge Zeppelin tour booked into all the major cities in America throughout the spring and summer months of '77.

To the group's credit, they managed to perform well through most of the forty-nine shows despite ill health, frayed nerves and escalating levels of chemical refreshment. But the tour would end up going down in the history books not on its musical merits but for a single grotesque incident that will haunt the group for an eternity. In Oakland Coliseum just prior to the first of two Zeppelin concerts being presented by Bill Graham, the most powerful promoter in America, Peter Grant, bookended by John Bonham and Richard Cole, had savagely beaten up one of Graham's security team, a young man named Jim Matzorkis. 'Grant said "Hold him,"' Matzorkis later testified, 'and just started punching me in the face with his fists and kicking me in the balls.' The victim then recalled a fourth accomplice of

Grant's 'trying to rip my eyeballs out of their sockets. I think my lawyers found later that there was some incident where he did rip somebody's eyes out. That scared the hell out of me.'

The identity of this fourth accomplice was made available under the banner headlines that prevailed in the world's press when he, Grant, Bonham and Cole were formally arrested at Graham's instigation in their San Francisco hotel two days after the attack and all charged with grievous assault. It was John Bindon, a well-known London-based career criminal who'd dabbled in acting – he played the slow-witted enforcer Moody in *Performance* – and improved his circumstances by becoming one of those colourful East End villain types that sections of the seventies aristocracy liked to adopt and invite to their soirées. Bindon wasn't short on colour: he was supposed to be equipped with the largest penis in the whole South of England and was known to be a close personal friend of Princess Margaret, the Queen's wayward little sister. But those bored rich folk who fell under his earthy charm generally preferred to remain blissfully ignorant of his shadow self and its gleeful ongoing involvement in murders and acts of bodily harm too gruesome to itemise here. In the same way that human excrement like Charles Manson could only make their homicidal mark in the LSD-drenched late sixties, someone as brutish and bloodthirsty as Bindon could only rise up and get himself integrated into the worlds of glamour and prestige that fell under the dark voyeuristic penchants of the seventies. When Grant and Richard Cole elected to have him be part of Led Zeppelin's security staff that year, they unwittingly unloosed real demons within their organisation that were far more deadly and disruptive than anything Jimmy Page could have possibly conjured up in Aleister

Crowley's old lair with his occultist books and spells.

Why on earth did they embark on such a foolhardy collaboration? It was the drugs again. Everyone was so coked up they'd convinced themselves that the lives of the members of Led Zeppelin were under threat and that the only way to combat a possible assassination attempt whilst touring the States was to hand-pick the most vicious brutes known throughout the whole Western world to be on their team. When you think about it, it was a distinctly 'punk' way of reacting, particularly for a bunch who'd lately been branded 'tired old farts' by the same demographic. After all, back in London, Malcolm McLaren was behaving in an identical fashion and making out like a bandit on the publicity. His thugs just hadn't killed anybody yet.

But razor-boys and the violence groupies who enable them were generally less tolerated in the American music business of the late seventies. Bill Graham had Grant and co. (briefly) jailed and fingerprinted and then went on the radio to denounce Led Zeppelin and their management as the closest thing in rock 'n' roll to Nazi Germany. This must have sounded like serious fighting talk to Grant's ears – he was Jewish after all – but he was still too chemically looped to fully comprehend the consequences of what he'd set into motion in Oakland. As Richard Cole later recalled, 'Once we got out of jail we rounded up the troops, jumped on a plane and got the hell out of town. We went to New Orleans where we were going to be given the keys to the city! Led Zeppelin was to be the first group to play at their new stadium.' The group hadn't even had time to book into their New Orleans hotel when a phone call came to the reception area requesting the presence of Robert Plant. Plant – who'd apparently been unhappy about John Bindon being on the tour and who'd also been the only Zeppelin member to try and talk reasonably with Bill Graham on the day of the aggression – then learned that his six-year-old son Karac had suddenly died from a mysterious viral infection.

From that moment on, Led Zeppelin was never the same again. In his sorrow Plant turned away from the life he'd been living for the past ten years and even considered giving up music as a career and becoming a teacher instead. He was also apparently deeply hurt when Page, Jones and Grant failed to appear in person to pay their respects at his son's funeral. But Grant had already exiled himself away deep inside his warped head-space. One of Bill Graham's assistants, Nicholas Clainos, was in conference with his boss in their San Francisco office the night the news came through. The phone rang. 'Bill's secretary said, "There's a guy on the line who says he's Peter Grant,"' Clainos later recalled. 'Bill and I picked up the phone. Bill said "Hello." The guy was speaking real low. He said, "I hope you're happy." Those were his exact words. Bill said, "What are you talking about?" He said, "Thanks to you, Robert Plant's kid died today." And he hung up the phone. We found out later . . . [Led Zeppelin] had to go home. They cancelled New Orleans and they never played again in America as the original Led Zeppelin. In their eyes, it was all karma and all tied together. Whether Robert Plant ever thought that or only Peter Grant, I don't know.'

The above testimony is just one eyewitness quote from a whole grizzly chapter dedicated to the Oakland incident and its repercussions that appears in *Bill Graham Presents*, the famed promoter's posthumous autobiography. Published in the nineties, a copy of the book fell into the hands of Grant himself not long before his own death from heart failure in 1995. According to a friend whom he contacted as soon as he'd finished reading its contents, the revelations in the chapter entitled 'Led Zeppelin' caused the big man to weep uncontrollably. 'Is it all true though?' asked the friend, who happened to be Ed Bicknell, Dire Straits' manager. 'Yes,' replied Grant through gulping tears. The truth had clearly mortified him. 'I don't want to be remembered as a bad person,' he kept saying. But it was too late. History was about to shunt his positive accomplishments into the margins and portray him for the ages as some fearsome ogre who hired known killers to help further his omnipotence.

Virtually everyone in the rock 'n' roll hemisphere seemed to be adrift in troubled waters during 1977. It was that kind of year. You might look enviously across the Atlantic at groups like the Eagles and Fleetwood Mac raking in the cash, hogging the top slots in the hit parade and racking up multi-platinum sales for their latest output, but when you actually listened to either *Hotel California* or *Rumours* it became numbingly apparent that it was just more high-grade cocaine music for the masses. Bruce Springsteen, the country's big hope, was out of action for most of the year, tied down by legal proceedings that threatened to jinx his future recording career. And the US heartland was generally unresponsive to the first New York-based punk recordings being made available. The Ramones still weren't getting played on the radio and the debut albums by Talking Heads, Television and Richard Hell and the Voidoids were all destined to attain only meagre chart placings in their homeland. A few disaffected kids in every major city would cherish these records but there was no discernibly 'mainstream' youth shift towards all things 'punk' like there was that year throughout Britain.

It was still some kind of freak-show cult out there in the land of shopping malls and sagebrush. Some elemental galvanising force needed to arrive in the country much like the Beatles had in 1964 and then take the nation completely by storm. Iggy Pop was too old and the Ramones didn't really have the right personalities for the job. The only logical candidates were the Sex Pistols. In late autumn of 1977, Bill Graham, Peter Grant's new worst nightmare, contacted Malcolm McLaren and offered the band their very own San Francisco showcase at an old hippie venue he still ran known as the Winterland. McLaren eventually took him up on his offer and scheduled a small tour of other US states to precede the show. And that – as history now clearly indicates – was the end of the Sex Pistols. America has a habit of decimating English groups on their first tour of the colonies and such was the case with Shepherd's Bush's finest. In the end they had the bollocks but lacked the stamina. If the New York Dolls were too much too soon, the Pistols were too little too fast.

I saw Sid maybe two weeks before he was due to 'invade' the United States. I was walking out of a dope house on Powis Square as he stumbled into the courtyard. He was wearing a black patch over his right eye like a pirate. 'Is that for theatrical effect then?' I asked him. It wasn't, he cheerily insisted. He'd lately lost the vision in his right eye. It was all to do with him shooting up something he shouldn't have and going temporarily blind as a consequence. Then he mentioned – apropos of nothing – that he'd overdosed thirteen times in the previous twelve weeks. He was grinning as he said it, like he was waving around some kind of junkie badge of courage. 'Way to go, son. Way to go,' I mumbled back. And then we went our separate ways. I knew I'd never see him again. The smell of death coming off him had become way too pungent.

It's funny though – when Sid got booked for murdering Nancy over in Manhattan a few months into 1978, his mother, whom I'd never met before, sought me out at the *NME*'s new office in Carnaby Street. She was a well-spoken, small, birdlike woman – pencil-thin, quiet-natured, noticeably intelligent, younger-looking than I'd expected – and she asked me to help her in drumming up support for her son in his darkest hour. By chance, the Clash were having a record-company-sponsored knees-up for their latest recording only a few streets away and so I shepherded her over to the festivities and introduced her to Mick Jones and Paul Simonon. I think they actually ended up playing a special benefit show for Sid not long afterwards. In the brief time we were together, I pondered asking Ann Beverley how she felt now about having used heroin whilst her son was still in her womb. And what had actually transpired in their home environment to create such a monster – but left the questions unspoken. I didn't want to cultivate any kind of relationship with the woman. I just wanted to be rid of the whole sordid Sid scenario and the hateful, barbaric time frame that had seen its rise and fall.

Did anything good happen for me in 1977? Well, I managed to obtain a pre-release tape of Television's *Marquee Moon* album sometime in spring and played it incessantly on the crummy little cassette player I took with me on my travels around London's smack shacks. I quickly concluded that I hadn't heard new music this compelling in years and wrote a long review to the effect that ended up netting the New York quartet their first *NME* cover. This exposure actually gave Television a handy springboard for instant recognition in a country where no one had yet heard them play a note. Upon its release, *Marquee Moon* penetrated the lower echelons of the UK album top 30 and even the notoriously prickly Tom Verlaine thanked me later for having aided its commercial momentum. At least it indicated to me that whilst my own writing might have become stilted and flawed of late, my instincts for recognising other people's talent were still safe and sound.

The only other worthwhile assignment I pulled off for the *NME* that year was to instigate the first interview the paper ever ran with Elvis Costello. I'd known his manager Andrew Jakeman, aka Jake Riviera, for more than three years and had watched him formulate and then boldly put into practice an independent record label he'd called Stiff, which began releasing singles in '77. I'd also steered the Damned onto his management roster a year earlier. Jake started out pinning his main hopes on developing Nick Lowe from the underrated pub-rock stalwarts Brinsley Schwarz as a hit-making singer/songwriter and record producer but secretly lusted to find his very own Bob Dylan to play Albert Grossman alongside. When a former roadie of Lowe's old group sent in a demo tape to Stiff, he sensed he'd struck gold dust. There was a compelling urgency in Declan MacManus's beseeching voice and an eloquence and trickiness to the lyrics of all his self-penned compositions that were astonishing to hear from one so young. The twenty-year-old MacManus had lately been gaining experience as a struggling UK Bruce Springsteen clone with a group named Flip City but was now ready to assume a musical identity of his own. Riviera renamed him Elvis Costello but MacManus was otherwise firmly in control of his own destiny.

The newly rechristened Costello was as young as any of the other punk upstarts making merry that year and could instinctively relate to their rage and youthful audacity. But his music drew from a deeper well than the one containing just the Stooges and a bit of reggae. He'd already digested the works of the real masters of pop songcraft – Burt Bacharach, Brian Wilson, Lennon and McCartney, Bob Dylan and Randy Newman – and was determined to create songs of his own that stood up to their exacting standards. He was a big talent and big thinker blessed with a canny knack for self-packaging. 'The only motivating points for me writing songs are revenge and guilt,' he'd seethed at me during our first encounter. It was a great line that was destined to appear many times hence in banner headlines over other articles on the guy. He knew it and I knew it too. He was using me to construct his very own media profile for future exploitation.

But he was still very young and not a little drunk and so when he slipped out of his Mr Angry routines and started to reveal a sweeter, more playful nature, I warmed to him. He ended up paying me two of the nicest compliments I've ever received. The first was something he told me in an alcoholic semi-stupor. Just before making music his full-time profession, Costello had been working in the office of a company engaged in the creation and upkeep of early computers. On his last day there, he went to clean out his desk and found my old Brian Wilson articles from 1975 lurking at the bottom.

And he wrote part of his song 'Waiting for the End of the World' about seeing me almost get attacked by fellow passengers on a tube ride out towards Middlesex. I'm the guy in the first verse – or at least that's what its composer told me. I don't mean to brag but I've been the subject matter of several tunes penned by the great, the good and the indifferent. Chrissie Hynde lyrically re-enacted our ugly break-up in a dirgey ballad the Pretenders released in 1994 called '977'. Adam and his wretched

Ants wrote and recorded a sneer-driven early B-side called 'Press Darlings' that featured the refrain 'Nick Kent – he's the best-dressed man in the town'. And Morrissey's supposed to have penned a particularly vituperative attack on my person that I've never bothered to listen to – a song called 'Reader Meet Author' that appeared on 1996's *Southpaw Grammar*. Being a 'rock muse' may be the secret dream of many but believe me, hearing your name and likeness sullied in song isn't all it's supposedly cracked up to be. I could've certainly done without the exposure. But I always liked the Elvis song and hearing him play it live that year with his Attractions was always a moment to cherish. It told me that even in my current shabby state, I was somehow still having an impact on the way rock culture was developing.

But the best thing that happened to me in 1977 occurred in late autumn, when I finally succeeded in becoming a registered drug addict at an NHS-sponsored facility in Westbourne Grove. It was actually just a small wooden hut that had been recently constructed on the grounds of the local hospital to deal with the growing heroin epidemic in the region. A young doctor and a nurse were in charge. Their job was to determine whether anyone who came through the door seeking their aid was a real addict or some joker trying to feign dependency in order to ponce off the system. If – after countless urine samples – you'd proven to them that you were one of the former breed, then they'd prescribe you daily dosages of a drug called methadone – almost exclusively taken orally in liquid form – which you could then pick up legally and free of charge from an obliging chemist's.

I liked methadone. A lot. It gave me the same warm inner glow and skewed sense of dreamy invulnerability that heroin had provided at the beginning. In fact, there didn't seem to be much difference between the two drugs – they were equally addictive on a purely physical level and interacted pleasingly with the same parts of the brain once they'd invaded the bloodstream. Ultimately I was just substituting one bad form of chemical dependency with another.

But there were still immediate upsides aplenty for me to gloat over. First and foremost, it broke the spell smack had me under for the past four years. This was a miraculous occurrence in itself: another few months of struggling through the life I'd been living of late and I'd have ended up a corpse decomposing inside a condemned building. Everyone I'd started out using heroin with was now dead, near death or facing jail time. We all should have known better. We'd all read the stories. Heroin is bad karma in powder form and it killed loads of jazz musicians so what chance did the flakier rock generation stand under its influence? We were all like sheep being led to the slaughterhouse. But then just as I reached the killing floor, salvation – in the form of a methadone script – plucked me away from death's merciless blade. I had a lot to be thankful for. I was now getting high daily on a drug that was both legal and free. That was my definition back then of heaven on earth.

And I no longer had to spend 80 per cent of my waking hours wasting time in increasingly dangerous hot spots looking to score a drug that was sucking up 100 per cent of my income. For the first time in ages, I had money in my pockets again. That winter I moved into a hotel in Kilburn and rented a cheap room there throughout the next twelve months. I started bathing regularly and taking better care of my physical appearance. Let's just say that personal hygiene hadn't been too high on my list of priorities during those hard-core junkie years. I started eating again too. Before that, I'd been subsisting on a daily diet of bread and soup. When I could afford it, I'd sometimes buy a can of baked beans to tide my intestinal juices over, but now the prospect of eating from a plate full of warm, solid, nutritious food was a luxury I could once more afford. I must have felt like I was back in the high life again even though I was really still just chicken-scratching around in the outer margins of abject poverty.

If you'd been living in or even commuting to London during 1977, you'd have more than likely seen me promenading through its streets. Every postal code in the metropolis had its pathways stained by my shadow that year. I was always on the move, scurrying from one dilemma to the next. My presence often provoked verbal abuse from other passers-by – I may hold the seventies record for being called a poof the most times in public by complete strangers – but at least it had never escalated into the realm of actual bodily attacks.

But then in mid-December I found myself strolling alone through King's Cross late one evening when I suddenly felt a sharp pain in the back of my neck. I turned slightly and realised someone was directly behind me holding a knife. As this sank in, three more individuals surrounded me, pointing their knives at my face.

There was a sort of open field next to where we were all standing – a dismal-looking patch of parched grass and brown rainy mud. They propelled me onto this stretch and began beating and slashing my skin with their weapons. They were more punk wannabes who wanted to do what Sid did. I'd never seen them before in my life. But boy, did they leave a lasting impression. They had this ritual of first cutting me and then kicking me in the same place their knives had just been. My face was such a bloody pulp from the attack after three minutes I could barely see in front of me and strongly sensed I was about to be stabbed to death. Somehow I struggled to my feet at one point and screamed at them 'Just kill me. Get it over with' over and over again. It seemed to stun them momentarily. Then I felt a boot connect with the left side of my lower torso and, as I started to fall to the ground again, another boot drove into my skull, effectively knocking me unconscious.

When I came to, my assailants had vanished into the night, leaving me spreadeagled like a piece of human debris in the drizzling rain. For a while I didn't have the strength to pick myself up off the ground. But at the same time I could feel my blood seeping into the mud around me and I knew that if I didn't get back on my feet there and then I'd never ever be getting up again.

I managed to negotiate the several streets needed in order to collapse in a nearby drug house of recent acquaintance. A junkie girl living there bathed my wounds with a damp cloth whilst her boyfriend fed me with lashings of Valium, pain pills and reefer. An hour later, I was blissfully high and laughing out loud at some inane spectacle playing itself out on the tiny black-and-white TV they had in their room. A very, very bad thing had just befallen me but I'd not been left traumatised by its occurrence. This moment would stay with me because it was the moment I realised that whatever vile circumstances fate might still have in store for me, I'd somehow find a way to survive them all. Over the past two years, I'd been beaten by chains, stabbed with knives and had my very lifeblood drained by drugs and homelessness. All I needed now was to be visited by a plague of locusts and an outbreak of boils and I could have set myself up quite credibly as a seventies fop son of Job figure. But my recent travails had left me stronger in spirit than I'd first imagined. I'd become battle-tested.

I was just counting the days now until 1977 reached its expiration date. I couldn't wait to be shot of it. Rastafarians had put forth the theory that the year would be one of mighty, life-altering mystical portent. When the two sevens clashed – so they preached – an apocalypse would be ignited. Either that or some momentous messianic visitation – I was never quite sure which. But of course nothing remotely like that actually came to pass.

On the white side of the tracks, though, the grim reaper had been hard at work. By year's end, the obituary lists were overflowing. There was Elvis checking out on the commode and Marc Bolan the fatal victim in the passenger seat of a car that crashed into a tree. 'Who's dead this week then?' Mick Jagger had asked me that summer over lunch in a Soho-based Chinese restaurant. 'Hard to tell these days innit. Pop stars! They're dropping like flies. Droppin' all over the place, mate.' He was being flippant but the point was still clear. That dark vortex he and his henchmen had helped open up in the Zeitgeist of a dawning decade was now reaching critical mass and getting darker and more omnivorous with every ticking second. Anyone who tells you 1977 was a bright and bountiful year wasn't really living in the belly of the beast. Those of us who were deserve a medal for simply having stayed the course. Meanwhile, 1978 lay ahead, grinning like a lazy crocodile. Old Blighty was about to get royally pussy-whipped by Mrs T and her political enablers. To paraphrase Shakespeare's Macbeth – what fresh hell was all this going to set into motion?

1978–1979

I'm stringing these last two years into one hold-all chapter because that's the way I see them now – as one big hazy splurge of time. For me all the seminal seventies stuff occurred in the six-year period between the birth of Ziggy Stardust and the death of the Sex Pistols. What came afterwards was really just a prelude to the eighties.

1978 and 1979 were most emphatically 'changing of the guard' kind of years in Great Britain. Labour were slain by Margaret Thatcher whilst punk choked on its own vomit and new wave became its less menacing pall-bearer. The spivs had trounced the fops midway through the decade but now the spivs were being side-lined by a new breed – the yuppies. Yuppie rock was what tickled the public's fancy all of a sudden. It had a little of the primal 'short sharp shock' dynamism of early punk but buttered things up with more sophisticated chord progressions, real singing and superior musicianship. The people who played it gave cursory lip-service to the so-called punk aesthetic but were generally more interested in upward mobility rather than dead-end-kid authenticity.

The Police were only one of many bandwagon-jumping outfits to make a big impact during this time frame. The trio was com-posed of musicians who'd been playing music separately long before 1976. The guitarist had worked with Eric Burdon's Animals and the Soft Machine in the late sixties, the drummer in a bush-league seventies prog-rock act called Curved Air and the singing bassist in a fusion-jazz combo working out of his native Newcastle. But they'd all managed to stay relatively youthful-looking with the help of a shared bottle of platinum-blond hair dye and were still clued-in enough to comprehend that a big pay day could result from upgrading punk's root ingredients with steroid-like injections of a higher musical proficiency.

Their lucky break came when the drummer turned the bassist on to reggae. When punk bands tried their hand at aping the rhythms of Jamaica, it was usually a disaster, but the Police brought something new to the white reggae synthesis by making the 'on' beats generally more fluid, supple and rock-friendly. And the singer – nicknamed Sting – had it all: Aryan good looks, an instantly recognisable multi-octave-range voice, an eclectic song-writing talent and a limitless sense of personal ambition.

I interviewed him in early '79 in between a couple of his group's many arduous club tours of America. The money hadn't started rolling in yet and he was still making ends meet in a dingy basement flat somewhere in London with his then-wife, the actress Frances Tomelty. Upon arriving at their address, it became apparent that all was not well with their relationship. Tomelty only stayed five minutes but made it abundantly clear in those minutes that she was seriously vexed at her husband, who sat for-lornly in the living room like a scolded infant. I believe the cou-ple broke up not long after this.

Sting was at a crossroads in his life anyway. Mega-success was suddenly there within his grasp after years of struggle and dreary straight jobs, and from the way he spoke, I sensed he wasn't about to miss out on any of its many perks. He reminded me of another Geordie go-getter – Bryan Ferry. There must be something about having once been poor and resident in Tyneside that really stimulates a status-seeking gene in some men. And yet Ferry was an oddity: he craved public adulation whilst feeling noticeably ill at ease whenever bathed in a spotlight. By contrast, Sting was an old-fashioned trouper who took to the spotlight like a swan to a lake. In this sense, he was far more of a Paul McCartney-styled old-school 'beloved entertainer' than a thorny new-school ranter like Lydon and Strummer. In fact, you could go so far as to call him the anti-Lydon of the late seventies. One was ugly and – relatively – shiftless, the other was an industrious pretty boy bent on self-improvement and self-empowerment. Charter members of the Bromley contingent all wanted to chop off Sting's peroxide-soaked head and burn his band-mates like witches but the Police's singles during this period were still a tonic for the times – infectious and upbeat without being air-headed and crass. They helped fill the post-punk void with a certain panache. But these guys certainly weren't threatening anyone or anything like the punks had. Rock at decade's end would become a much tamer place to eke a living from.

All the wind had gone out of the punk movement's sails in mid-January of 1978, when the Sex Pistols had splintered apart in San Francisco. Lydon had weathered the ensuing media storm by promptly moving into *NME*'s Manhattan office, which also doubled as the apartment of Joe Stevens, the paper's photographer and a trusted amigo of the singer. Lydon apparently had no other choice – McLaren had just abandoned him in America with no money for a hotel. The Pistols were dead, punk was dead and Lydon's career was dead too – at least for the moment.

It would come alive again later in the year once he'd recruited two old mates of his as well as an eager young drummer. The two mates he chose to provide stringed accompaniment raised many eyebrows in the London community. The bassist – Jah Wobble – was known far and wide throughout the region for his sudden outbursts of violence whilst the guitarist Keith Levene was equally notorious for being an unreliable hard-to-work-with junkie. It's like Lydon went purposefully looking to replace Sid Vicious in his affections by hiring the only two people he knew who were even more potentially disastrous to form a group with. The Lydon–Levene–Wobble axis managed to record two albums and perform a few iffy concerts but never quite managed to summon up the required get-up-and-go to really promote their cause. From what I've read, it seems like Lydon was plagued by an undiagnosed case of chronic ennui after the Pistols split that left him gloomy and withdrawn for the rest of the decade. The music he released during that time certainly seems to bear this out.

To his credit, Lydon never tried duplicating the four-to-the-bar hard-rock attack of his previous band. He and his dubious cohorts were looking to invent a new musical hybrid: post-punk art rock, do-it-yourself prog with reggae bass lines and krautrock in place of virtuoso noodling and ever-changing time signatures. This meant that the singer discarded the lyric-writing perspective he'd invented for the Pistols which involved picking a controversial subject and then railing against it with an over-intensity that was as comic as it was scathing. When it came to writing texts and then vocalising them for Public Image, Lydon replaced the comedy and pithy put-downs with obtuse impressionistic blather that he felt compelled to deliver in a strange adenoidal wail that hovered over the backing tracks like a wasp besieging a fat man in a deckchair.

When Lydon found a subject to stir his emotions – as was the case with 'Death Disco', a demented re-enactment of his beloved mother's recent ordeal with terminal cancer – he was still a force to be reckoned with, but the artsy mood pieces his new group were bent on forging mostly forced him into asserting himself in pretentious and overreaching ways, and becoming pretentious was not ultimately a sensible career path for the former Johnny Rotten to wander down. Once he'd figured out which side his bread was buttered on, Lydon stopped trying to impress the chintzy art-rock set and went back to inhabiting the pantomime-horse role that would ultimately net him the most income from reality-show appearances and advertising campaigns.

With Lydon off cavorting with the avant-garde, it was left to the Clash to keep punk's young dream solvent for the rest of the decade. Whilst the Pistols had been alive, Joe Strummer's bunch had been very much in their shadow. But being second-best only made them work that much harder to create their own kind of impact. This in turn gave them a much greater shot at career longevity. The Pistols were like some blinding spectacle doomed to short-circuit at the earliest opportunity but the Clash had more staying power. And they also possessed the only other charismatic punk frontman in town: Joe Strummer.

I'd first encountered Strummer when he was still a teenager named John Mellor. In August of 1969 I attended the Plumpton Jazz and Blues Festival and on the Saturday evening had been one of maybe thirty people who'd chosen to leave the main-stage viewing area to step inside a makeshift tent at the side and witness an early performance taking place there by Robert Fripp's breakthrough prog act King Crimson. A curly-haired youth I'd never seen before stood next to me throughout the set, shouting enthusiastically when not swigging from a bottle of cider which he offered to me at one point. It was a young work-in-progress Joe Strummer, and we would have both been seventeen at the time.

The next time our paths crossed was five years hence. Somehow I got coerced into checking out a new group who'd literally just come into existence. The venue they'd chosen to showcase their set in was actually a Soho record store that had allowed them to set up and play on its premises one Saturday afternoon in late 1974. Maybe the establishment thought the live entertainment would attract more record sales. If they did they were sorely mistaken. The group were beyond shambolic. A bloke with hippie hair and a grimy Afghan coat noodled away on guitar whilst two extremely suspicious-looking types to his immediate left tried unconvincingly to master the art of becoming an interactive rhythm section. Only the singer stood out. He had the voice of a ruptured seal and a surly 'Bill Sykes's dog' type of persona that seemed to be chained to an invisible chip on his shoulder so monumentally large he could have stepped out of a John Osborne play. Unlike his hippie playmates, he wore his hair relatively short in a badly groomed duck-tail and sported a suit that might have once belonged to a hobo during the Great Depression. I asked Ted Carroll – the rotund, jovial capo of Camden Town's Rock On record store who was one of the only five people there constituting an audience – what the singer's name was. Carroll – who had the amusing habit of calling anyone he encountered by their Christian name prefixed by the word 'rockin'' – 'Hi there, rockin' Dave' – 'What's new, rockin' Nick?' etc. – replied, 'That there is rockin' Joe – rockin' Joe Strummer. He's got a big future ahead of him.' 'Yeah, but not with that cowboy group he's fronting,' I remember countering.

It must have been one of the 101'ers' first-ever gigs. I saw them playing pubs and support spots several times over the next twelve months and they never really improved. Everyone who saw them was pretty much of the same opinion: the singer was something special but his supporting players were a bunch of deadbeat buskers. I don't recall ever conversing with him during his years as the king of squat rock but we certainly scowled at each other frequently enough. He lived in a squat on 101 Walterton Road and I often frequented a heroin connection dealing out of the building next door to his at no. 99. He never acted like he was particularly at ease with this state of affairs: oftentimes he'd be outside his building staring coldly at the junkies entering and leaving his neighbourhood. Mind you, he was always on the piss back then so he wasn't best placed to be voicing any kind of disdain for other substance-abusers. In fact, I never saw the man sober until the end of 1977.

But something evidently changed within Strummer shortly after the release of the Clash's debut album because he cut down drastically on his booze intake and became noticeably more health-conscious and career-focused. My guess is that he was shaping up to fully embrace his new destiny as the lightning-rod conscience of punk but it was also probably to do with him having spent the end of '77 bedridden from hepatitis. Whatever the cause, it was a bright-eyed and bushy-tailed Joe Strummer I found facing me in early '78 when we were brought together for a special televised debate on the merits and shortcomings of the UK music press that took up one episode of a weekly BBC programme devoted to analysing the media in general called *Don't Quote Me*.

Nick Logan had been invited to participate on behalf of the *NME* but asked me to go in his place. It was a bold move on his part – sending his paper's druggiest entity out into TV-land to represent the troops. I made an effort to be as clear-headed as possible but the actual taping occurred early one morning and I've never been what you'd call a morning type of person. As a result, I became uncharacteristically subdued as the three musicians booked to speak their minds on the subject of their treatment in the music comics ran down their list of grievances, expecting me to stand up for all their media persecutors. What a thankless task! Rick Wakeman of Yes was one of the three – Roy Harper the other one – and stared at me throughout our exchanges like he was trying to will me into a pillar of salt.

Only Strummer talked any real sense during the half-hour we all bantered back and forth. He paid homage to the power of the press whilst calling to attention its tricky, duplicitous side. He didn't have an axe to grind or old scores to settle and was smart enough to view the subject under discussion from an informed perspective unclouded by petty grudge-bearing. Witnessing him redeem this otherwise dreary spectacle made me realise once and for all that he was a force to be reckoned with.

I saw a lot of Strummer after that. Throughout 1979 he was living off Edgware Road near the chemist's I frequented for my daily medication and we'd often bump into each other at a local greasy spoon where we'd pass the midday hours together eating a belated breakfast and discussing the issues of the day. He had a real missionary zeal about him and took his job as punk's resident Moses very, very seriously indeed. He wanted to get his demographic politically motivated and more in sync with the questing bohemian youth mindset of the fifties and sixties. He didn't want what he'd helped instigate to go down in history as some brief fashion-driven season of silliness. He reminded me in many ways of the underground press guys I'd worked and lived alongside back in 1972, with their incessant diatribes against 'the man' and their fervent embrace of a multiplicity of fringe causes. But Strummer had far more personal magnetism and restless energy than all the rest of the country's disaffected post-hippie advocates for social revolution put together and had a far better platform to spread his message with: the Clash.

Much has been written since his untimely death about the fact that Strummer's upper-middle-class origins were so blatantly at odds with the working-class prole firebrand role he assumed in young adulthood. That may be so but his reinvention was so all-encompassing and his drive to project that reinvented persona out to the world so unrelenting that he literally became what he'd dreamt of becoming since adolescence – Che Guevara with an electric guitar. History may now indicate that he wasn't a particularly brilliant political theorist or any kind of God-given musical talent but he knew how to blend the two roles into one credible entity. And if rock 'n' roll immortality was based on physical energy alone, Strummer would be at the very top of the heap. His voice may have been a gnarly abomination, his guitar-playing just a blur of rhythmic chicken-scratching and he wasn't even particularly good-looking, but no one apart from James Brown and Jackie Wilson ever sweated more on stage in order to incite some form of rapture from their audience.

That was the great thing about the Clash: they knew they weren't the best but that just made them work harder. I remember seeing them play in some hall in Manchester in the winter of '78, not long after the release of their second album *Give 'Em*

Enough Rope, and it was like Beatlemania revisited inside the venue – kids screaming and risking personal injury to mount the stage and touch their heroes. Strummer stood aloft before them gleefully stoking the fevered response but also cannily controlling the momentum, never letting the high energy teeter into out-and-out chaos. That was his gift – the capacity to rock the house to the rafters whilst indoctrinating its inhabitants in the same breath with more than just the usual 'let the good times roll' platitudes. Thank God he and his band were there to pick up the slack after the Pistols' premature flame-out. If the Clash hadn't rolled up their sleeves and committed their efforts to furthering the range and impact of punk rock at the end of the seventies, the form would have fallen under the exclusive control of feckless thug-exhibitionists like Jimmy Pursey and Sham 69.

Pursey was a big noise in 1978 – a big, hectoring, double-ugly noise that drew punk's dimmest adherents to him like flies to excrement. Sham 69's audience was a sight to curdle the soul – skinhead behemoths with prison tattoos and someone else's blood on their Doc Martens – and Pursey had them spellbound like T. S. Eliot's ape-necked Sweeney reinvented as a punk Mussolini. Throughout '78 and '79 he made it his business to invade the *NME* offices on virtually a weekly basis and lecture us all on 'what the kids are really thinking'. You'd be trying to do your work and this malodorous brute would suddenly materialise out of nowhere and start rabbiting on about his and our responsibilities to 'the kids'. If there'd been a gun in the place, I'd have gladly shot the man. He represented everything I despised most in the late seventies: rank, vainglorious, talent-free opportunism masquerading as 'the voice of the oppressed'. Elvis Costello once remarked that the worst aspect of Thatcher's gruesome regime was the fact that she 'let all the dogs out of their cages', that she in effect empowered the greedy and heartlessly vindictive to run amok over the country's social policies and cultural landscape; punk's immediate legacy was much the same, with smarmy brutes like Pursey and his ilk suddenly choking up the spotlight and drowning everyone else out with their barking and braying.

It says a lot about the ongoing deterioration of the *NME* that such an obnoxious pest should be not only tolerated in the paper's office space but actively welcomed into its very midst. It wouldn't have happened if Nick Logan had still been the editor but in May '78 he stepped down and left the paper to be guided by other hands. IPC duly interviewed a number of possible successors and picked a candidate they felt worthy to assume the responsibilities. But then, just two weeks before he was due to take control, this 'candidate' received a visit from the drug squad, who came armed with a search warrant and uncovered enough cocaine in his home to duly charge him with dealing the drug. This charge also effectively put the kibosh on his chances of becoming *NME*'s next kingpin, which meant that IPC suddenly had to resort to solutions closer to the immediate home front.

With time running out, they had no other option but to offer the post to the fellow who'd been Logan's assistant editor since the departures of Ian MacDonald and Tony Tyler. This was one Neil Spencer, a former schoolteacher who'd first appeared in the paper in the mid-seventies as a kind of self-appointed reggae specialist. Spencer took his reggae so seriously he felt compelled to talk at all times in a fake Jamaican rude-boy accent even though he was English and whiter than a loaf of Mother's Pride sliced bread. Somehow he'd managed to get involved in the day-to-day running of the paper – editing copy, taking the train to the printers each Tuesday morning and overseeing the weekly print run – until he'd become the de facto head man during '77, when Nick Logan had often been absent.

To his credit, Spencer worked hard to keep the paper afloat in extremely trying and uncertain circumstances, and when he was formally anointed *NME*'s editorial top dog – it was made official in the May 23rd issue – it was generally assumed that he'd at least have the moxie to keep the winning team of writers at the paper's disposal in gainful employment. This turned out not to be the case, however. Spencer wasted little time in consigning the paper's more 'difficult' elements – i.e. argumentative, independent-minded writers like myself, Lester Bangs and Ian MacDonald, as well as opportunistic fire-starters like Parsons and Burchill – onto the back burner of the paper's creative oven.

In our place, he brought in a sorry selection of music-industry functionaries and groupies. One was a woman who'd been both Bob Marley's press officer and a 'close personal friend' of John Lydon's. Another had done time as the press agent for both Jimmy Pursey and Siouxsie Banshee. Joining them in the front lines were the young editor of a Clash fanzine and a bloke who happened to be sharing a flat with the singer from the Gang of Four. With these kind of industry 'insiders' on his team, Spencer felt confident he could get the paper closer to the very heartbeat of the end-of-the-seventies pop-culture Zeitgeist. What he achieved instead was to set in motion an ongoing haemorrhaging of the papers weekly sales figures.

The only one of this 'clued-in new breed' that I found in any way sympathetic was a gaunt Mancunian lad named Paul Morley who'd been a local 'stringer' for the *NME* prior to Spencer's *coup d'état* and who'd lately been drawn to try his luck as a struggling young writer in London. He was being groomed to take over the role I'd been sidewinded into assuming back in the early seventies – that of *NME*'s resident word-wielding 'gunslinger'. Spencer and the other editors were always whispering in his ear trying to mould him into their idea of the new office saviour, but I could tell Morley was growing increasingly ill at ease with their interference.

One time we were alone in the reviews room – a dimly lit space with a desk, hi-fi and a chair that was ideal for drug consumption – and I told him to ignore all the 'editorial advice', that the people now running the paper were all talentless jobsworths anyway and that he'd be far better off simply following his own instincts and writing about things that genuinely moved him. From what I've seen of his work since, he evidently took those words to heart, though not in a way I could readily relate to. At first I felt slightly protective of the fellow – he always looked like he was in the grip of some secret sorrow and soon started cultivating a scary predilection for pouring hard liquor down his throat as a way to deal with all that deadline stress. But then he decided to reinvent himself as Britain's most pretentious man – a role he's apparently proud to sustain to this very day – and I promptly lost all interest in him and his general well-being.

Morley's media ascension corresponded neatly with the way his old stamping ground Manchester had lately started to become a hotbed of home-grown music-making talent. Back in the sixties, the Northern metropolis had been something of a bad joke amongst the beat-boom cognoscenti. Liverpool had the Beatles, London had the Who and the Stones, Birmingham had the Move and half of Led Zeppelin, and all the Mancs could muster up was a bunch of mickey mousers like Herman's Hermits.

In point of fact, the city had little to boast about – popwise – until the advent of punk in 1976, when the Buzzcocks took it upon themselves to single-handedly raise local standards of group-forming and electrified music-making. As soon as the Pete Shelley-led combo burst nervously upon the national scene, the floodgates were flung open throughout the region as a tidal wave of young Mancunian dreamers determined to chance their arms on a stage or in a demo studio poured out into the public spectrum. This was UK punk's most far-reaching gift to popular culture – the long-overdue de-Americanisation of rock as a medium of expression, thus making it a vehicle for all comers. Suddenly it was cool to be English. John Lydon and Ian Dury weren't the first blokes to sneerfully sing in unadorned English prole tonalities – both Syd Barrett and David Bowie had been doing it ten years earlier – but they were easily the most influential, setting off a national wake-up call throughout the British Isles. Literally overnight, any UK group still singing in dodgy mid-Atlantic accents about rocking down the highway all the way to Memphis was rendered obsolete. Suddenly it was the 'in' thing to create lyrical scenarios set strictly in one's own neck of the woods and to be voiced in similarly Anglocentric tones, and no area benefited more from this state of affairs than Manchester. London's youth have always been by nature somewhat narcissistic and straitjacketed into a suffocating sense of their own perceived cool, but the lads and lasses up North were a lot less self-conscious and unafraid to go out on a limb even if it meant making complete fools of themselves in the process. They generally made a refreshing change from the po-faced Southern art-school wannabes who were busy scurrying aboard the new-wave bandwagon like rats off a sinking ship.

My favourite late-seventies Manc creative upstart was a pencil-thin poet named John Cooper Clarke. He was more of a beat poet than a punk per se, being older even than me, but the movement had emboldened him to stand onstage in various local pubs without the aid of musical accompaniment and fire up the punters' imaginations with his often hilarious scattershot stanzas of self-penned verse. Seeing him in action was always a sight to behold. He looked like a cross between *Blonde on Blonde*-era Bob Dylan and a willow tree in a windstorm. His skinny legs shook so much when he performed you could practically hear his knees knocking together in time with his own spoken-word routines.

In October of 1978 the *NME* sent me up to Manchester to generally sound him out. I liked him immediately – it was almost impossible to do otherwise. The guy was one of the funniest raconteurs and natural storytellers to stumble out of late-twentieth-century Britain. His life up to that date had been one long calamity stream and his recollections were all tragicomical, with the emphasis always on the uproariously comedic. For example, he had a seemingly limitless supply of woebegotten tales involving him trying to score reefer from the Jamaican community in Prestwich and being generally short-changed that – when woven together – made for an absolutely brilliant oral novel. Thirty years later, I'm still waiting for his autobiography to be published. When it finally arrives, I know it'll be a masterpiece.

I saw a lot of Johnny Clarke in 1979 because he'd often be in London and we'd stayed in touch. On a couple of occasions, I spent the evening with him and the guy who was producing his records at the time, the now-legendary Martin Hannett. I've since seen Hannett portrayed in films as an out-of-control nutcase but he always seemed pretty rational to me – passionate about music, liked to smoke pot, but no signs of inner turbulence to indicate that I was in the presence of the future 'mad, bad, dangerous to know' Phil Spector of the North. I think when he started reaping success with his production work he just opted to assume a scary image in order to mask his insecurities, and that image ended up overpowering and ultimately consuming him. The drugs obviously played their part as well. He and Clarke were still really just diehard reefer heads when I was rubbing shadows with them. But they were both ripe for further chemical experimentation – like two blokes who'd grown up listening spellbound to their Velvet Underground records and who now had the chance to live out what those songs had been talking about.

I'm trying to ransack my memory to come up with some salient scrap of detail Hannett might have told me about his working relationship with Joy Division – a relationship that would have begun not long before we met – but nothing is forthcoming. He must have at least mentioned the group to me, but nothing really registered. In retrospect it's good that Morley was on board the *NME* because he recognised something special in Ian Curtis's fledgling quartet, something that none of the older scribes was able to decipher.

I'll readily admit it – I was much too jaded to see any value in what Joy Division had to offer the end-of-the-decade pop/rock landscape. I'd been lucky enough to see both the Doors and the Stooges live in their prime and had little interest in watching a former young civil servant and his three mates trying valiantly to channel a similar sense of all-encompassing musical dread. It was only with the release of 'Love Will Tear Us Apart' that I started taking them seriously. Then I saw some TV footage of the group in concert and it all clicked. Curtis had absolutely none of the wayward sexual magnetism of an Iggy or Jim Morrison but more than made up for its absence by exuding a singular charisma born of suffocating discomfort and the looming threat of imminent epileptic collapse. I can see now that the guy was a significant talent, but by the same token whenever I'm confronted by his image I automatically think of that line Jack Nicholson delivered in *Prizzi's Honor* – 'If this guy was so fucking great, then how come he's so fucking dead?'

When it comes to Manc indie icons, I've always preferred Mark E. Smith of the Fall anyway. Not so much for his group's early musical output – which in 1979 was practically corrosive to the human ear – but because of his take-no-prisoners mega-truculent personality. I've never, ever written about the Fall but I got to know Smith quite well in the mid-eighties because we happened to frequent the same London-based speed dealer's ramshackle apartment down around King's Cross. He was just a skinny Northern lad back then who looked like his mother still dressed him but he had such a forceful personality you'd have thought he was Giant Haystacks the professional wrestler. He really is the closest thing England has ever spat out to compare with American hard-boiled rock 'n' roll cranks like Jerry Lee Lewis, and I've spent quality time with both men.

In 1994 the Rolling Stones invited Lewis to a recording session and the old bastard apparently never stopped criticising them to their faces, calling them amateurs and all-purpose soft lads until steam was coming out of Keith Richards's ears. In 1987 I once found myself in a room with the Fall leader as well as Nick Cave and Shane MacGowan and witnessed Smith do much the same thing to his two peers, mercilessly nit-picking at their music and respective images and even making untoward remarks about their countries of origin. They just sat there and took it, much like the Stones had done with the Killer.

He was generally quite civil to me though, maybe because I was well known as one of Iggy Pop's early champions and Mancs generally look up to Iggy like born-again Christians tend to revere Jesus Christ. The only points of conflict we ran into revolved around my unstinting admiration of the Smiths. Let's just say that Mark Smith wasn't a big fan of the group's lead singer and never let an opportunity pass to verbalise his contempt. The last time I saw him was in a pub practically adjacent to King's Cross station at the close of 1987. He'd just finished touring America with the Fall and had talked witheringly about the new 'health consciousness' craze supposedly sweeping the country. 'Fat blokes in sweatbands jogging down highways, women with huge biceps and skin like old leather handbags.' He then paused and looked around at the pallid forms and grey faces collected together in the main bar with real joy in his eyes. 'I can't tell you how good it feels to be standing next to really unhealthy-looking people again.' He was another one who followed Lester Bangs's dictum – the more you slowly poison yourself the more illuminated your creative output becomes. 'I read the other day that your pal Morrissey has started working out at a gymnasium each day before he goes in the studio to record,' he remarked to me at one point with a suitably sardonic grin on his face. 'Aye – all creative inspiration sweated out of the man before he can even get close to a microphone.'

Looking back at the end of the seventies, there's surprisingly little that's managed to last the test of time for me. For every Fall and Joy Division, there were a thousand careerist drones like Simple Minds and the Boomtown Rats infiltrating *Top of the Pops* and generally hogging the spotlight. Dire Straits – pub rock for the rising young homeowner demographic – were suddenly hugely popular on both sides of the Atlantic. The two least impressive acts to have come out of the mid-seventies Manhattan proto-punk clubland explosion – Blondie and Talking Heads – both managed to build lucrative, chart-busting, internationally successful careers for themselves during this period whilst the trailblazing likes of Television, Patti Smith and Richard Hell all fell by the wayside. And then came the rise of synth pop: blokes with dodgy haircuts hunched over keyboard-operated machines stuffed with wires and do-it-yourself tone oscillators making sounds like a brood of geese passing gas in a wind tunnel. Whoopee! This was the way the seventies ended: not with a blood-curdling bang but with a cheap, synthesised, emasculated whimper.

Not even the old sixties guard could forestall the sharp dip in musical standards that prevailed at decade's end. With Mick Jagger once more at the helm, the Rolling Stones managed to record and release their last real album of consequence – *Some Girls* – in 1978 but the record's subsequent success only set into motion yet another long creative slump. By 1979 Jagger and Richards had fallen into open conflict over key issues regarding the group's general direction, and Ronnie Wood was busy introducing himself to a new and extremely costly form of drug dependency then emerging from the West Coast of America: freebase cocaine. Keith Moon's death in September '78 robbed the Who of their unpredictable engine. The other three continued for a while with a new drummer but all the zany energy and sense of spontaneous combustion that had typified the group in live performance suddenly vanished from their repertoire.

Led Zeppelin eventually regrouped after the death of Robert Plant's son but Plant was increasingly disturbed to find two members of his old quartet and their manager still addicted to hard drugs. A final album was laid down mostly in Abba's Stockholm studio at the end of '78, but the singer and the bass player liked to work mostly during daylight hours whilst the guitarist and drummer tended to only come alive after dark. This conflict in personal schedules ended up destabilising the group's precious human chemistry. The resulting album *In Through the Out Door* lacked the authority, drive and inner cohesion that Jimmy Page had brought to previous sessions as player, co-composer and producer.

Led Zeppelin then performed two colossal shows at Knebworth in August '79 – their last hurrah on British shores – followed by a short European tour in the summer of the following year. An American tour – their first since the Oakland debacle – had been negotiated to commence during October of 1980 but then on September 24th John Bonham – apparently ill at ease about his upcoming duties in a country that always seemed to bring the worst out in him – calmed his nerves during a group rehearsal at Jimmy Page's house by downing some forty measures of vodka mixed together with a 'mood-altering' medication he'd been prescribed known as Motival and then falling asleep. He somehow choked to death in his slumber and never woke up again.

The repercussions were enormous. The biggest band of the seventies had lost an irreplaceable component and suddenly had no other option but to splinter apart. Another major creative player over the past ten years, Neil Young, was also stricken by grievous tidings during this period: he and second wife Pegi gave birth to

a son named Ben on November 28th 1978 who was duly diag-
nosed as suffering from acute cerebral palsy. Young committed
most of his energies in the following years to tending to the wel-
fare of his immediate family and guarding them from any kind of
public scrutiny. In the process, he closed himself down emotionally to the point where 'I was making it, doing great with surviving – but my soul was completely encased. I didn't even consider
that I would need a soul to play my music, that when I shut the
door on pain, I shut the door on my music.'

And then there was the matter of Bob Dylan's sudden religious
conversion. 1978 was the year the Bard of Beat chose to release
Renaldo and Clara, the cinematic disaster zone he'd filmed on the
fly and then painstakingly pieced together over the previous three
years. It lasted more than four hours and generally left viewers
with the sensation that they'd been watching paint dry. Everyone
was hoping the most mysterious presence in popular music would
finally strip aside his many masks as the camera rolled but all he
ended up revealing was a taste for plot-free, scattershot surrealism
and auteurish self-indulgence that had mercifully fallen out of
vogue in the film world by the end of the sixties.

'Dylan's folly' as it quickly came to be known was hauled over
the critical coals hither and yon upon its release and the catcalls
kept coming throughout the rest of '78, mainly in America.
Dylan released a new album that year – *Street-Legal* – and
embarked on a lengthy world tour, his first since 1966. The
Japanese and European dates were well-received but the 110 US
dates that followed were often savaged by the nation's media
pundits. Bruce Springsteen and Neil Young had lately been
ordained rock's new reigning messiahs and all of a sudden the
taste-makers were openly insinuating that the man who'd first

inspired Springsteen and Young to actually write songs was no longer worthy of being talked about in their lofty pantheon.

Dylan has always nursed a fairly jaundiced view of the media in general and probably took these latest harsh words in his usual stride. But a far darker cloud hanging over him during this period was all the emotional and spiritual fallout from a painful recent divorce. In 1977 the singer/songwriter had even been accused of spousal abuse in the nation's tabloids. Now he no longer had a family to anchor himself to, and with only a gruelling tour schedule to focus on, he fell into a deep depression. One of his backing singers, Helena Springs, suggested he try prayer as an antidote to his inner suffering. Another musician friend, T-Bone Burnett – a recent convert to Christianity – read Bible passages to Dylan late one night out on the road at the latter's request. When Burnett came to the line about those who place their faith in astrologers and other spokespersons of 'the dark arts' being automatically doomed to lose their families, Dylan reacted as if a lightning bolt had just struck him. And then on December 17th 1978, after a show in Tucson, Arizona, he experienced a full-blown spiritual 'awakening' whilst alone in his hotel suite. 'There was a presence in the room that couldn't have been anybody but Jesus,' he later recalled. 'Jesus put his hand on me. It was a physical thing. The Glory of the Lord knocked me down and picked me up. It's like waking one day and being reborn. Can you imagine turning into another person? It's pretty scary if you think about it.'

Dylan's conversion was so dramatic that in 1979 he put all his back catalogue in the closet and set out on another long US tour, this time determined to perform only brand-new self-composed material, with all the lyrics exclusively slanted on his sudden embrace of Jesus Christ as the King of Kings and Lord of Lords.

An album of such songs named *Slow Train Coming* was recorded and made available before decade's end to a generally perplexed world reaction. His vocal cords may have been gainfully loosened up by the son of God's impromptu visit but godly surrender hadn't brought his singular gift for songcraft any blessings. In point of fact, it robbed him outright of his wicked sense of humour and – worse yet – made him small-minded and a bit of a bigot. 'You've either got faith or you've got disbelief. And there ain't no neutral ground,' he railed out on one track. It was just too weird for most of Dylan's core following to readily accept.

At least his European fan base was spared the jarring spectacle of him addressing audiences between songs like some curly-haired Elmer Gantry preaching hellfire and brimstone to the disbelievers as he did during his US shows throughout the year. Several of these rants were tape-recorded and then transcribed to print by audience members. 'I told you "the times they are a-changin'" and they did,' Dylan informed one crowd. 'I said the answer was "blowin' in the wind" and it was. I'm telling you now that Jesus is coming back and He is! And there is no other way of salvation.

'You know we're living in the end times. The scriptures say in the last days, perilous times shall be at hand. Men shall become lovers of their own selves. Blasphemous, heavy and high-minded.'

The 'Jesus saves' banter may have come off as cranky and depressingly out of character but Dylan's quasi-apocalyptic depiction of the seventies as vanity-driven, drug-sodden 'perilous times' was pretty spot on in retrospect. The sixties had been so tumultuous for him that he'd spent the last third of that decade in a state of reclusive semi-retirement. But surviving the seventies had finally sapped his will and brought him so low that he could only react by subjugating his very spirit to some supposed higher power. Ultimately it would get marked down as just another of Dylan's bewildering 'phases', but at the time it left many deeply estranged and unable to reconcile themselves with the man.

Out on a boat navigating the Bahamas in the autumn of '79, John Lennon, Dylan's old creative sparring partner back in the mid-sixties, heard the song 'Gotta Serve Somebody' on the radio and suddenly felt the urge to pen a song of his own on the subject of spiritual servitude. A cassette recording he made of the impromptu composition is now available for all to hear on a posthumous box set. It's called 'Serve Yourself' and it's more of a rant than a song per se, a sustained howl of derision at his greatest rival's desperate clutching at the most inflexible straws of orthodox religious dogma.

Lennon had never been visited by Jesus Christ personally but in the LSD delirium of the late sixties had briefly toyed with the idea that he might indeed be the living reincarnation of God's only son. He apparently even tried to summon up a press conference in May '68 in order to inform the world of his Christ-like status until wiser heads prevailed and dissuaded him from this course of action. Yet he still managed to factor his Jesus complex into the lyrics to 'The Ballad of John and Yoko' the following year, addressing the Messiah as though he were Lennon's own personal Siamese twin. At the end of the day, though, a ferocious intellect like Lennon's was never going to be cowed by fairy stories involving a humble carpenter from Nazareth changing water into wine. Lennon had his own living, breathing higher power to prostrate himself before: her name was Yoko Ono.

In 1975 they'd reconciled and conceived a child, Sean, an event that prompted Lennon to stop making music and concentrate on a new vocation instead, that of house-husbandry. Apart from the creation in 1970 of his last real musical masterpiece – the primal-scream-driven *Plastic Ono Band* – the first half of the decade had been one long bad dream for Lennon in the shape of drug problems, FBI wire-taps and one highly publicised Hollywood meltdown. He'd had to do battle in court with money-hungry bloodsuckers like Allen Klein, work alongside egomaniacal nutcases like Phil Spector and live with the scary sensation of being constantly spied on by US government agents in the pay of Richard Nixon. Facing off adversaries like these would have been enough to take the fight out of any man.

How comforting it must have been then to hear the love of his life soothingly inform him that he didn't need to record another record or have any further contact with the music industry and the outside world in general. With her career in the avant-garde at something of a temporary impasse, Yoko Ono had become intrigued by the idea of launching herself as a businesswoman. She calmly informed Lennon that from now on she would be the family breadwinner and that he would simply concentrate on rearing their infant son.

It was evidently a sweet deal to his way of thinking because he fell into the new routine like a newborn babe into slumber. His fan base felt slighted and blamed Ono for brainwashing him into creative inactivity, but Lennon's escape from the vanity factory of seventies pop was still probably the coolest move he made in that whole ten-year stretch. Suddenly he was no longer just a valuable commodity, he was a free man. But as we all know, freedom is a very relative concept and this was as true for John Lennon as for any other human being.

When Lennon saw how his wife deftly managed to quadruple his finances by decade's end with a series of canny investment strategies, her word became law to him and he deferred to her judgement on all aspects of his life. That's why he was sailing around the Bahamas in '79 when he first tuned in to Bob Dylan crooning to his saviour: Yoko Ono – under the direction of several astrologers – had sent him out there without further explanation and he'd bowed to her wishes without question.

Listening to the radio on the vessel each day he felt suddenly compelled to start writing songs again for the first time in almost five years. At first he didn't know what to do with these new compositions until one night he heard over the airwaves a record by a new group from Athens, Georgia, known as the B-52's. The quintet had a distinctive danceable sound that was both artsy and garage-rock-friendly but what really piqued Lennon's interest were the weird Yma Sumac-like female voices shrieking out through the mix. They instantly reminded him of a sound he'd once been all too familiar with – the wife at full vocal pelt. Maybe – he thought to himself – the world is finally ready to embrace Yoko Ono's singular take on music-making with open arms. From that moment forward, his return to an active musical career became a done deal. But not as a solo entity. Lennon really wanted Ono to get the praise and attention this time around. He genuinely saw her as his superior and had even taken to referring to her as 'mother' at all times.

We all know what happened next. Lennon and Ono recorded their *Double Fantasy* album and Geffen Records released it on November 15th 1980 to generally lukewarm fanfare. Then on December 8th Lennon was returning home after having mixed a new track his wife had just concocted entitled 'Walking on Thin

Ice' at a local studio when a deranged fan shot him to death in front of his family's apartment building.

It's quite tempting to play up his murder as a kind of definitive 'death of the seventies' moment but on closer inspection it doesn't really hold up. Lennon was a spent force throughout much of the seventies anyway and had little direct influence on its ebbs and flows. No, his slaying felt far more like the death of the sixties instead, or at least the final nail in the coffin of the spirit of that now long-gone era of marmalade skies and endless possibilities.

I remember hearing the news whilst floating through central London. A radio announcement kept leaking out of all the shops along the way, followed by the eerie sound of Lennon's own voice recorded in an interview just prior to his passing. Everyone around me in the busy streets had the same stricken 'this can't be happening' look etched across their faces. Involuntarily my memory returned to the days of my youth when the Christmas season had always been soundtracked by the hotly anticipated release of a new Beatles album. When December rolled around, the shops would all be playing the record seemingly in rotation and the communal joy this music conjured up everywhere was both palpable and deeply infectious. But that was then – a gentler, more enchanted time – and this was now, the era when 'greed is good' was about to become the mantra of the masses.

In due course, I arrived at the *NME*'s Carnaby Street offices, only to walk into a scene of utter desolation. The old-timers there were all teary-eyed and barely able to speak. One was so distraught he kept having to go to the toilet to throw up. Even the younger scribes were all choked up as though it wasn't John Lennon but their beloved John Lydon who'd bitten the bullet in his place. But then how else were we all expected to react? It was a heartbreaker whichever way you looked at it: a gifted family man still nimble-witted and rife with rude health slain at the hand of some insane narcissist, a wife widowed, a young son left fatherless and a world robbed of the victim's physical presence and future artistic contributions. It was such a senseless scenario that almost thirty years later we're still trying to make sense of it.

But then again, maybe Lennon had received a momentary mental flash of what fate ultimately had in store for him back in 1970 when he wrote the song that became his second post-Beatles single release – 'Instant Karma!'. 'Instant karma's gonna get you,' he sang almost maliciously on the finished record. 'Gonna knock you out of your head / Better get yourself together, darlin' / Sooner or later you're gonna be dead.' People at the time thought these sentiments were directed squarely at Paul McCartney but Lennon could just as easily have been addressing himself. John Lennon knew a thing or two about karma after all. He saw it as the central guiding spiritual force in the universe.

As a young man he'd often behaved viciously and done his share of nasty, despicable things. But then LSD consumption had caused him to detach himself from his naturally violent temperament and become more peaceable and inward-looking. As his personality evolved so did his music and his quest for personal redemption from past transgressions. This he found with the arrival of Yoko Ono. But in strict karmic law the dark doings of the past have a way of impacting on the individual even after he or she has arrived at a state of some personal grace. And Lennon always had a scary knack for overstimulating the mad outer fringes of society, mainly because he was such an incorrigible weirdo himself.

Some years back, I was browsing through Mark Lewisohn's *Beatles: Recording Sessions* doorstopper, which chronicles each and every Abbey Road session Lennon's old group ever attended in impressively exhaustive detail, when a stunning hitherto unknown fact jumped out of the text to grab my attention. When John Lennon had recorded his vocal for 'Come Together' in 1969, the master tape revealed he'd prefaced the verses by repeating the words 'Shoot me!' again and again over the introductory riff. (George Martin had later wisely edited the phrase down to a spooky-sounding 'Shoo' that's still clearly audible on the finished track.) What can you say about such a brazenly insane act except to duly note that eleven years later, someone actually took him at his word?

But enough fanciful conjecture about the karmic destinies of rock's pioneer stock. Let's turn to the fate of lesser folk instead. What was happening to poor, poor pitiful me during these two dreary endgame years?

Things could have been worse. I always had a roof over my head as well as one square meal a day in my intestinal tract. I was way more productive than I'd been in the two preceding years. I was writing songs now and even had two of them recorded one night at Island's Basing Street studio, the place where I'd almost gotten into a fist fight with Bob Marley and the Wailers five years earlier. A friend of mine, Peter Perrett, played on the session and brought along two of his co-workers in the Only Ones – guitarist John Perry and drummer Mike Kellie – to further augment the line-up. Tony James from Generation X provided the bass parts. The finished tracks, 'Chinese Shadow' and 'Switch-Hitter', were never released – although someone told me they later briefly surfaced on a new-wave compilation released only in Japan sometime in the nineties – but I remember playing them to Iggy Pop shortly after their completion and him telling me they were good works and encouraging me to continue.

By the end of '79 I'd started rehearsing in earnest with a drummer named Chris Musto and an excellent young bass player known as James Ellar. Paying for the rehearsal space required me to keep contributing to the *NME*, though I was finding it increasingly hard to be in their general vicinity. Leafing through back issues from this era recently in order to further jog my memory, I was surprised to rediscover just how prolific I'd been in their pages during this stretch of time. The subjects I tackled ran the gamut from young hopefuls like a trio of teenagers from Crawley who called themselves the Cure to cantankerous old-timers like Al Green, Wilson Pickett and James Brown. But something was still evidently amiss with regard to the actual choice of words I strung together into article form to commemorate these encounters. True wit and illumination were still awfully difficult to detect within the sentences I was scribbling down. That's why I was moving over more and more towards a career as a professional musician. I'd lost the talent to do my other vocation any kind of justice.

The other good thing about writing songs and making music – I quickly decided – was that my continued drug-taking didn't impede the process in the way that it did whenever I tried to write journalistic copy. Methadone is generally viewed by the medical establishment as a chemical halfway house between heroin addiction and sobriety, but that's only true when the substance is administered in steadily decreasing quantities over a period of no longer than six months. That wasn't the case for me. The powers-that-be at my clinic provided me with strong daily dosages for an indefinite period of time which eventually stretched on to slightly over ten years.

It was decent of them, all things considered, because if they'd forcibly weaned me off the drug before I was ready to do so myself, I'd have tumbled back into full-blown smack insanity like a dead crow falling from a tree. But methadone is a funny drug. It curtailed my craving for junk and gave me a nice soothing buzz for a few months but then it began to rub up against my central nervous system with all the delicacy of a Brillo pad, making me generally down at the mouth and subject to grumpy moods. A drug buddy recommended Valium as an antidote to my suffering and I started mixing the little yellow or blue pills in with my methadone supply as a way to calm my nerves. The combination worked only too well. In fact, I became so calm it was almost impossible for me to get out of bed. So I started taking uppers in earnest – cocaine when I could afford it, speed when I couldn't – as a way to stimulate my depleted reserves of stamina. Factor in also that I'd started smoking reefer as compulsively as Willie Nelson and you'll understand that I was now addicted not just to one vampire drug but to four separate extremely potent rogue chemicals.

A typical day? Wake up around midday. Glug back my methadone. Take a piss. Put on a record. Snort a line of speed in order to fully wake up. Take a 5 mg Valium to counteract the fierce amphetamine rush. Smoke the remnants of a joint. Wait for the various substances in my system to form their synergy of mood enhancement. Once this occurred – it usually took about two hours – step out into the London streets to pick up the next day's methadone supply from the chemist's in Edgware Road. Spend the late afternoon hours in some tentative form of work-related activity. Skulk furtively around the metropolis as dusk is setting in. Make an impromptu call at places where drugs can be bought or scammed. Walk home after midnight. Play guitar alone in my room whilst smoking copious amounts of dope. Drop another Valium in the wee small hours before passing out fully clothed on an unmade bed. Wake up the next day and repeat process.

Looking back today from the perspective of a responsible middle-aged homeowner, taxpayer and parent, these days of advanced chemical refreshment and carefree floating feel like an odd form of freedom, but of course they weren't. I was a lone wolf now – out on the prowl for anything that could make me forget who and what I'd really become – and my world was getting smaller and smaller by the minute. Hermine my guardian angel had lately bid a none-too-fond farewell to my toxic hide. It had been coming for ages – she just couldn't stand seeing me fall further and further into the pit. She tried for a long time to wake me from my slumbers but I was beyond rehabilitation. Finally she snapped. It was either her or the drugs – the old 'tough love' ultimatum. I stayed with the drugs and she stayed with her husband. Without all the chemical interference we might have made it work, but I'd just become too pitiful for her to waste any further time on and by decade's end our love affair was just another painful memory. I reacted as I'd always done – by getting so loaded that I could feel nothing beyond woozy numbness. 'Drugs can break your spirit but they can't break your heart' should have been tattooed onto one of my scrawny biceps back then.

I was better off alone anyway – without emotional ties, drifting rudderless through the murk of old London town. I was well into my 'prince of darkness' shtick by this stage of the game. I loved strolling around the city at dead of night dressed in a black fedora hat, a black Edwardian coat worn over the shoulders like a cloak, black leather jacket and strides and dagger-pointed Cuban-heeled boots. In my drug delirium I probably thought I resembled Count Dracula's Limey stepchild. But the common man was generally less easily taken in by my dark cavorting. 'Fuck me, it's that cunt from the Sandeman's Port advert,' a drunk in a Maida Vale pub shouted at me as I stepped in to buy some cigarettes.

Shortly after that, a complete stranger collared me during some dismal music-industry function and told me I was the Thomas de Quincey of the late twentieth century. I didn't argue with him – he was a big lad after all and flushed with booze. But many years later I read a biography on De Quincey entitled *The Opium Eater* and learned that – though separated by a full century and a half – we still had plenty in common.

De Quincey had fallen into active acquaintanceship with the two men he most admired – the poets Wordsworth and Coleridge – at the same age I'd been when I started consorting with the likes of Keith Richards and Iggy Pop. Like me too, he'd been drawn to seek solace through the consumption of hard drugs in his early twenties. I was slightly dismayed to discover that he'd been a good foot shorter than me and also that for most of his published writing career he'd been something of a shameless hack. But when I got to the parts documenting De Quincey's unwavering struggles with creditors and chronic constipation, I immediately felt a strong mystical bond being forged between myself and the man.

In the autumn of 1821 De Quincey wrote a two-part essay, *Confessions of an English Opium-Eater*, based on his own life and drug history for the *London Magazine*, a literary monthly. The pieces were so widely read and commented upon that they were combined together in book form shortly afterwards and duly went on to become the author's only timeless contribution to the written word. Over in France Baudelaire set about translating the text, whilst across the Atlantic a young Edgar Allan Poe fell under its wayward influence.

Hunter S. Thompson many decades later would declare that the real secret to capturing drug-inspired reveries in prose form resides in the writer's own capacity for recalling all the salient details of his or her hallucinations whilst in an altered state, and De Quincey certainly remembered enough of his own 'spectral visions' to fill *Confessions* with credible accounts of his opiated voyages. His addiction to opium would ultimately cost him his physical health and seriously distort his powers of concentration but the drug still managed to fleetingly provide him with a genuine creative gift in the form of fiery visions that merged with his own natural dream-state to conjure forth the 'confessions' that would see him remembered – albeit notoriously – down through the ages.

I envied the man because heroin and methadone never bestowed any creative gifts on me whatsoever. I took them instead to erect an invisible shield around myself and to put me in a place where I could feel as little as possible. Coincidentally Pink Floyd released a song in 1979 entitled 'Comfortably Numb'. It was supposed to be about Syd Barrett's final days with the group in the late sixties but its dreamy languor spoke just as penetratingly to and about me and all the other 'strung-out ones and worse' littering England a decade later.

It's about time to call last orders on the seventies. My tale is coming to an end and I'm not sorry to see it reach its termination stage. I still get chills down my back when I remember too much from these final years. One thing I've learned from writing this book is that self-congratulation, self-justification, self-pity and plain old bitterness don't really make it as motors for good auto-biographical prose. You're always better off playing up the comedic aspects of your past, blending the light in with the dark and turning grief into laughter. That's something Hermine first indicated to me around the time she left me. 'You think your life is such a tragedy but it's more of a comedy. You're a comedian.' At the time I was mortally wounded but now I see she was right on the money.

One last parting shot then of life moments before the eighties ate us up. The scene: another London music-industry reception, this time in a club somewhere close to Curzon Street. It could have been for Ian Hunter or for Pete Townshend – both were present and taking ample advantage of the free-drinks policy at the bar. The rest of the big room was littered with fledgling new-wave luminaries, grumpy old punks and the usual gaggle of record company and media human flotsam and jetsam. Everyone was split up in tight little groups partly obscured by copious clouds of cigarette smoke, all of us engaged in poring over the usual Tin Pan Alley tittle-tattle of the hour.

I'd been a spectator at these kinds of functions for practically all my adult life and had discovered early on that they tend to lose their charm unless you happen to be a trainee alcoholic. So why I was actually there in the first place is something of a mystery to me now. Maybe the venue just provided temporary shelter from the winter cold and a crowd of familiar faces to melt into. Whatever the reason, it turned out to be the wrong one.

Before I knew it, I was book-ended by two surly youths looking for a fight. They just started in on me from both sides, drilling me with their double act of vindictiveness. 'You're a parasite,' one would begin, and his mate would echo the words. 'You're a cunt.' 'You're scum.' 'You're a worthless piece of shit.'

I'd been attacked countless times over the previous three years but this was the only time it really cut into me in a deeply wounding way. The Sid incident at the 100 Club had at least been relatively brief, as had the stabbing in King's Cross. But this – devoid though it was of physical violence – seemed to go on forever and it was also a highly public spectacle. Everyone in the place saw me getting ripped apart, which only accentuated the humiliation. Finally Cosmo Vinyl, the Clash's Robert De Niro-obsessed spokesman, came over and drew my assailants away from their prey.

After that I just remember weaving around the room like a punch-drunk boxer. There may well have been tears in my eyes. Everyone else was looking at me with pity in theirs. And then – out of nowhere – I felt someone grab me and sweep me off into a less populated corner of the place. It was Chrissie Hynde. She held me in her arms whilst I wept like a baby.

I can recall staring directly into her eyes and seeing a glimmer of the love and tenderness she'd once felt for me before things had gone so terribly wrong for us. I'd waited five years for that moment and that glimpse because though I was no longer technically in love with the woman, I'd never fully recovered from the way we'd ended up hurting each other the way we did and yearned for some sense of emotional closure to prevail between us. There in her embrace I felt safe for a second, as though the past six years of chicken-scratching my way through a world of hurt had been a bad dream that I'd suddenly woken up from.

But reality always has a way of butting in and pinpricking the air out of our pipe-dream thought balloons. After consoling me sweetly, Chrissie took her leave and moved over to the celebrity side of the room. Both Pete Townshend and Ian Hunter wanted to have photographs taken with her, and the pop paparazzi present were all anxious to oblige. 'I'm public property now,' she'd remarked ominously just as we were parting company. I watched her glide over to be engulfed in rock-star bonhomie and flashing light bulbs. It was a humbling spectacle to behold.

When the auld lang synes had all been sung and 1980 freshly minted into existence, Chrissie and her group the Pretenders would be sitting pretty right at the very summit of the UK charts with their third single 'Brass in Pocket'. The chart fireworks would repeat themselves over in America shortly after that. From that point on, she became a global superstar. There was a new decade dawning and Chrissie – with her fierce attitude, well-crafted, commercially viable songs and keen young supporting players – was destined to become one of its most successful artistes.

My musical career meanwhile was fated to quickly go the way of all flesh. In 1981 my group the Subterraneans would record an album's worth of original material and a single was picked for release. Actually 'released' is the wrong word: 'escaped' was more like it. Without radio play it sank like a stone. No manager would work with us because of my ongoing reputation as an unrepentant druggie. And I'd made far too many enemies in high places during my high-profile *NME* years to ever think I was going to get a fair break as a jobbing muso from the London-based music industry. It was all going to hell in a hand-bucket in other words

– and it would stay that way for a further eight long will-sapping years.

And the worst of it was – I mostly had only myself to blame. Do you want to know what the essential problem with the seventies really was? Too many flaky people. I should know. I ended up being one of them.

Afterwards

The eighties more or less passed me by like some big long money train that I'd been pointedly excluded from boarding. Music became a sorely diminished commodity due to the advent of mass digitalisation that heralded the emergence of the CD format. MTV was a further cultural abomination, robbing young minds of their God-given right to let music run riot with their own imaginations by force-feeding them with crass video images to appease their dwindling attention spans instead.

It was also an era that laid down strict guidelines about separating winners from losers. The winners were the home-owning human magpies, the yuppie tailgaters, the glib young professionals in their big-shouldered business suits forever lurking around wine bars and cappuccino outlets with their chintzy talk and grasping agendas. The losers were hand-to-mouth drifters like me – chemically impaired, squat-friendly, short on boundless ambition, not particularly money-hungry, not good 'potential husband' material, no semblance of Machiavellian cunning, only concern: 'living in the moment, man'.

In 1982 the *NME* sacked me for the second and final time. For the next two years, I wrote nothing. The new music I heard during that time left me feeling low and disenchanted. Then one afternoon in late 1984 a musician acquaintance played me a copy of the just-released first Smiths album and something came alive in me again. The Smiths resonated through me like an answered prayer. I suddenly felt the overwhelming urge to throw myself back head first into the old rock-crit scrum if only in order to garland the Manc quartet with further praise. Most of my old colleagues thought I was completely mad at first, but me hitching my muddy wagon to the Smiths' rising star was the key move that got me onto the road that led first to career recovery and finally to personal redemption.

By late 1987 I'd 'bounced back' – it was official. Nick Logan and Paul Rambali of *The Face* took the chance to employ me at a time when almost everyone else in media-land was determined to shun me from their doors of employment like the proverbial stray three-legged dog. Partly to repay their act of largesse, I endeavoured long and hard to make the articles I submitted to them as outstanding as possible. A long Miles Davis piece from 1986 for example took me almost six months of daily scribbling and re-editing to complete.

Still, the hard work paid off. Suddenly the yuppie hordes who'd scorned and spurned me were coming over to pat me on the back, buy me a drink and call me 'the great survivor'. They should have looked more closely. Nothing had really changed inside my private world. In fact, I was taking more drugs than ever before. And my current living quarters consisted of a tiny four-walled hovel in a drastically gone-to-seed block of flats somewhere in Kentish Town – not so much a room, more a glorified coal bunker.

That's where I first contracted a nasty lung infection due to the asbestos lined into the roofing. My immune system was on the blink due to all the dope in my system and it quickly developed into pneumonia. One day I couldn't get up off my mattress any more. Then I started coughing up blood. I'd been giving the Grim Reaper the old familiar two-fingered salute (or one-fingered salute if you happen to be American) for fourteen years but now he'd finally pinned me down. I felt like one of those poor plague-stricken peasants in Ingmar Bergman's *The Seventh Seal* lying around on thistle-strewn fields philosophising whilst waiting for Death to claim them.

Through a supreme effort of will, I somehow managed to board a train leaving London and voyaging to Swindon, where my parents now lived. After two weeks of bed rest and triple-strength antibiotics I was all patched up and ready to inhale more of the big smoke. I returned at the very outset of 1988 intent on polluting myself anew. But as soon as I was back in my old haunts, the dreaded symptoms started up again. My body was telling me in no uncertain terms that it could no longer deal with all the rigours of my addicted condition and that if I didn't change my way of living dramatically I'd be spending my remaining years in an iron lung or a wheelchair.

Sometimes you need to have things spelt out for you but I got the message eventually. In mid-January I travelled back to my parents' modest retirement flat and moved into the guest bedroom, having pre-arranged with my London clinic to taper off my methadone dosage in weekly reductions. For the next three months I underwent a self-administered withdrawal from all my old bad habits – methadone, amphetamines, Valium, you name it. The folks at the clinic told me I was being rash and that I'd be far better off entering some costly rehab facility for an indefinite period. But that was out of the question. I'd already spent all my money on drugs. I didn't have any more to dispense on trying to be weaned off them.

It wasn't that bad – all things considered. Valium withdrawal was the worst – twitching for three days and nights and a couple of full-blown panic attacks. And the methadone reduction process sometimes made me feel like I was on acid, though without the hallucinations – a common reaction, I later learned. The hardest aspect was the lack of sleep – for two whole months I subsisted on a regime of no more than one hour of shut-eye a night. It all sounds unrelentingly grim when described in stark prose but I look back on that time now as oddly exhilarating. During those two months I actually felt my soul re-entering my body. A corner was being turned. A new road was opening up for me.

Once I'd gotten over the chills and aching joints, I set about healing my body in the old-school way: when ill health looms, simply go outside and walk the ailment off. My folks lived next to a picturesque park called Coate Water, with a big pond and miles of open countryside and rolling hills behind its borders. I'd take tentative rambles through the greenery that grew more extensive as my stamina returned.

By May I was completely drug-free for probably the first time ever in my adult life and passing my days strolling through the forest alone. The activity made me feel like I was a teenager again, a child of nature. I could feel my old hippie roots a-stirring. And then one day I walked for miles and miles into countryside I'd never ventured through before until I came to a little *Finian's Rainbow* kind of village bathed in the idyllic rays of an early afternoon sun high in a cloudless blue sky. The place seemed deserted. The only shop there was shut. No activity on the streets. My gaze fell on the tiny wooden chapel partly obscured by a tree. I'd not been a churchgoer since before reaching puberty, but for some reason I felt compelled to enter the building. No one else lurked within. It was just me staring up at the stained-glass windows feeling the coloured light reverberate through the darkness of this candle-lit space I was now in.

As the light streamed over me, I was seized by the crazy urge to kneel down and pray at the altar. I asked God to help keep me away from the low side of the road. Let me begin again, I pleaded. I can change, I swear. Give me the strength to redeem myself. I have done many bad things. But I know the difference between wrong and right. I have this window of opportunity now to turn my life around. Rid me of this terrible loneliness. Restore me in the ways of grace. As I concluded my sinner's lamentation, the light from the windows engulfed the whole room in a blazing golden glow. OK, it wasn't as dramatic as Jesus Christ turning up in person to Bob Dylan's hotel room but I knew there and then that some kind of full-blown spiritual experience was visiting me. It was ironic – all that time I'd been looking for God in drugs, and then just as soon as I get them out of my bloodstream He makes himself known to me.

For quite a while afterwards I found it hard to reconcile with what had occurred to me in that little church. There was a scientific reason for the rapture – after fourteen years of enforced inactivity, the endorphins in my brain were starting to wake up again. Maybe they'd been responsible for the epiphany. But in the same breath I knew the incident wasn't something I could so easily explain away and then brush aside. Everything was changing within me. Temptation still reared its ugly head sometimes when I ventured back to London but otherwise I experienced no deep yearning for further dope-befuddlement. It wasn't so bad being straight for a change.

Then it dawned on me – from now on, I had two choices.

Either spend your time constructively or it'll be spent self-destructively. I didn't need to go to any Narcotics Anonymous meeting to learn that. I didn't have the time to recite my old drug misadventures to a roomful of recovering addicts. I knew what I'd done and who I became in the process. Now I needed to just close the door on that old flaky life and get my eyes back on the prize.

What happened next is best kept for another project. In short order, I met the woman who would become my wife in December of 1988. 'I'm going to be your drug now,' she told me not long after our introduction. How can you not respond to a line like that? She lived in Paris and invited me to move in with her. London was bumming me out. Walking its streets stone-cold sober left me feeling more and more isolated. Once you've been homeless in a city, all its inhospitable qualities tend to over-shadow its positive factors anyway – even if it's your birthplace. I needed new horizons to contain me, and Paris aka 'the city of light' seemed ideal. I arrived there with less than £200 to my name but I also had a love to keep me warm, a roof over my head and the innate feeling that Lady Luck was back in my court. Such was the case.

A month after my relocation, I sat down in my new accommodations to put pen to paper. I'd just interviewed Jerry Lee Lewis for the first and only time and had a suitably hellacious encounter to transcribe. Over the past fourteen years, writing had become a truly wretched endeavour for me to undertake. I was always staring at a blank page, grasping in vain for deep thoughts and wise words to fill it with. Inspiration was always tantalisingly out of reach. The wheels in my brain just weren't turning fast enough. But that day my old gift returned, the one I'd briefly possessed back in the early seventies before it got squandered. The words just came to me. I wrote them down as if in a trance. Several hours later, I'd finished a 6,000-word profile. I read it back and my eyes misted over: I had the power again. It had been restored to me. From that point on, I never looked back. Life just kept getting better and better.

It's been twenty years now since I've been living in Paris and my family is still together, we all remain in good health, *la vie est encore belle*. My son James's birth in January 1993 was the cherry on the cake for me. I even followed John Lennon's example and became a house-husband, changing diapers and taking him to parks daily. Forget anything I've described in this book – being around my infant boy is what I'll be flashing back to in the final seconds before life gets sucked out of me.

Jim is sixteen now – with hair growing more than halfway down his back and a room full of computers and guitars. Every morning before setting off to school he psychs himself by playing music – death metal they call it – that sounds like the Lord of Misrule and his minions building shelves in an adjacent building. He has no respect for the old groups I used to knock around with. The seventies have little to tempt him with, or so he claims, and I can't say that I blame him.

I still regularly dig out records from that era and play them for pleasure but they're more likely to be something by Steely Dan or Joni Mitchell than anything punk- or new-wave-related. I can't help resenting the way 'postmodernists' have ceaselessly endeavoured to rewrite history by claiming that the early seventies were empty, worthless times and that the decade only began to flourish with the arrival of Johnny Rotten and his barbarian hordes. That's just a wilful misrepresentation of the facts. But then again,

I may well have happier memories of the first five years simply because they were the ones that neatly corresponded with my rise in personal circumstances whilst the five that followed now represent more of a full-on fall from grace.

All I know is – if a time-travel machine was ever invented and made easily available to the hoi polloi, the seventies would be the last time zone in history I'd want to return to. I harbour no nostalgic yearnings whatsoever for the days of my wayward youth and have been more inclined over the past twenty years to simply distance myself from the feelings and past frequentations of that era. As a result, I remain in contact with only a precious few of the figures that have populated this book.

Apart from Pennie Smith and Nick Logan, I haven't seen or spoken to any of the original *NME* gang in aeons. Some kind of impromptu reunion would probably have occurred had I attended Ian MacDonald's funeral in 2003 but no one invited me or even thought to tell me about it.

As for the Sex Pistols, I've stayed on good terms with Glen Matlock and enjoy the occasional impromptu phone call from Steve Jones but wouldn't be caught dead at one of their reunion shows.

Iggy Pop and I stayed friends throughout the nineties; we shared much in common after all. We'd once been prodigal sons but now we were both clear-headed and work-driven individuals still trying to make full sense of our past shortcomings. But when the noughties struck, we just drifted apart. It happens. Maybe we've just used each other enough for one lifetime.

In 2003 I re-established contact with Jimmy Page. It was great to see him clean and sober and fully focused once more. I'm interested to hear what he'll do next musically. He, Plant and

Jones should definitely try to get the Zep aloft one more time in the studio. There's still unfinished business to be completed there.

Talking of unfinished business, Chrissie Hynde also re-entered my life in '03. She'd turned fifty and had just split from her second husband, and I guess she maybe just wanted to reconnect with some old faces again. At first I was hesitant but then thought better of it and invited her over for a meal. She was still the same impetuous Chrissie but age had now provided her with wisdom and self-awareness too. I really enjoyed being in her company and we became friends again, even exchanging the odd letter and telephone call. Mind you, whether our friendship will still be standing after she reads this book remains a matter for conjecture.

My father passed away in February 2007 at the age of eighty-six. I'd seen him for the last time three months earlier. He told me then that he was in such near-constant physical discomfort he would have preferred to have died three years earlier. He said this without a hint of melodrama, almost matter-of-factly. I looked into his eyes, saw all the pain barely contained behind them and told him I understood. So it wasn't a big shock to my system when the news came through. That word Americans love to throw around – closure – we'd achieved it in the nineteen years prior to his death. Everything we'd needed to say to each other had been said. I knew he'd always loved me and he knew I would always love him back. There were no regrets unaired or thorny issues still unresolved between us. I kept this foremost in my mind during the weeks leading up to and then following his funeral. I only cried once and didn't suffer any semblance of a grief-triggered meltdown. I needed to stay strong and support my mother in her time of sorrow.

In March she and I were driven by a friend to a specific stretch of countryside outside Swindon where the shape of a gigantic white horse that had somehow been etched into a hillside back in ancient times was still plainly visible. My father had often indicated that he wanted his ashes scattered on this spot of land. The sun was high in the sky but there was also a fierce wind bustling up the trees and hedgerows and it sent the contents of the urn I was carrying flying all around me as I emptied his remains out. I stood there and breathed him in one last time. He was inside me now and as time marched on I came to learn a simple truth: the best way to mourn the death of a beloved parent is to endeavour to actively adopt the finest aspects of their personality and then let them live on through you as you struggle to follow their example.

In my case, it'll always be easier said than done. My old man was a paragon of steadfastness, moral rectitude and self-discipline and, as you already gathered, I've been notoriously deficient in all three virtues. And I'll never have his unassailable faith in the existence of God and the kingdom of heaven. But even in my darkest hours I couldn't quite shake off the inner voice of his influence and value system. Sooner or later we all turn into our parents anyway. It's best just to go with the flow of human nature.

I've yet to re-establish any real face-to-face contact with the Rolling Stones. But our destinies still seem to be strangely intertwined. Whilst writing this book, I was contacted by James Fox, who's actually writing Keith Richards's forthcoming autobiography, and sat down with him one afternoon to share my memories of the great man during his vampire years. Apparently Keith has only the dimmest recollection of what transpired in the seventies. It figures.

I don't have that problem though. I may have left the seventies but the seventies never totally left me. Not in my waking hours so much. But when I sleep, they still reappear to torment me anew.

At least once a week, I have the same dream. It's the late seventies again and I am a passenger on a train pulling into King's Cross station. People are laughing at me in the streets outside. They can see I'm strung out and vulnerable. I need to escape. Suddenly I'm backstage at a Rolling Stones concert. It's the usual scene; the superstars and the slaves. Sometimes I get to have a short conversation with the group's two principals, other times I get blanked.

Sudden change of scene. I'm in a small club somewhere watching Iggy Pop misbehave. It's another loveless night with another loveless crowd. One of my *NME* co-workers saunters over and plies me with his sugary condescension. An aggrieved ex-girlfriend is lurking somewhere behind her cold-eyed stare. But I can't stay. I've got to find a place to crash for the night. I go from door to door but no one answers. Finally I open one and walk into a confined space of impenetrable darkness. It feels like being inside a coffin. I start to panic. Then I wake up.

It takes all of ten minutes to reacclimatise myself to ongoing reality. I've developed a mantra to pave the way. 'I've got a beautiful son. I've got a beautiful wife. I've got a beautiful life.' It seems to help.

By the time I'm out of the bed I know who I am again. Once upon a time I was just another dead fop walking. But I changed ranks along the way and now I am a soldier of love.

Soundtrack for the Seventies

These individual songs and entire albums make up the music that meant the most to me during the years I've focused on in this book.

1970

'Dark Star' – the Grateful Dead

'Dark Star' – the 'Live Dead' version released in the UK in January 1970 – was psychedelic rock's crowning glory and last hurrah. Exquisite, other-worldly and drenched in LSD's sense-shifting dream-like otherness, this is nothing less than Coltrane's *A Love Supreme* reimagined as the stoner rock of the gods.

'Facelift' – Soft Machine

This quirky jazz-fusion exercise from *Third* was playing over the sound system of the 1970 Bath Festival at the very moment I inhaled my first marijuana fumes, so it understandably still looms large in my memory. In fact, the whole double album remains one of my most frequently replayed early-seventies recordings.

'Golden Hair' – Syd Barrett

I can't be 100 per cent sure but I'm still fairly certain that being

373

exposed to this beguiling Barrett recasting of a piece of verse from *Ulysses* in early '70 was what actually prompted me to start reading the James Joyce novel.

'Chestnut Mare' – the Byrds

The Byrds were my all-time favourite sixties group but I never forgave McGuinn for sacking David Crosby in 1967 and generally took a dimmer view of their later output. But 'Chestnut Mare' was just too irresistible – their last shot at transcendental greatness.

'Monterey' – Tim Buckley

Like the Grateful Dead, Buckley released no fewer than three great albums in 1970 – *Blue Afternoon*, *Lorca* and *Starsailor*. But the last named was the most startlingly creative of them all and I defy anyone to find a recorded vocal performance as octave-spanningly gymnastic and demonically possessed as the one Buckley delivers on this extraordinary track. Just listen to the way he screeches out the line 'I run with the damned, my darling'. It will make your blood run cold.

If I Could Only Remember My Name – David Crosby

This album instantly sets up a dreamy pothead ambience that re-evokes the mood of its time so completely that hearing it again is like experiencing instant déjà vu.

'When You Dance I Can Really Love' – Neil Young

1970 was Neil Young's breakthrough year and it really took off for him that autumn with the release of the *After the Gold Rush* album. I was a bit ambivalent about some of the record's contents, finding parts of it too fey and whimsical. But 'When You Dance' found Young strapping on an electric guitar and conspiring with Crazy Horse and Jack Nitzsche to create a truly glorious racket that was seldom off my record player that season.

Fun House – the Stooges

The sound of the seventies barbarians baying at the door. Back then, you either felt the power of the Stooges' disruptive music reverberate through the very core of your being – or you didn't.

'Directly from My Heart to You' – the Mothers of Invention

Frank Zappa's musical output post-Mothers mostly gave me the creeps but on his final MOI compilation *Weasels Ripped My Flesh* – released a year after the group's 1969 demise – he released this unforgettably greasy rearrangement of the old Little Richard classic just to convincingly prove that this old outfit – greatly abetted here by violinist Don 'Sugarcane' Harris – could rock out with the best of 'em.

Plastic Ono Band – John Lennon

This, Lennon's last truly inspired set of songs and performances, came down like a jackhammer on the youth culture of the hour when it was released in the winter of 1970. When he wasn't frantically exorcising the demons of his childhood, Lennon used the record to ritually slaughter the whole late-sixties peace-and-love pipe dream still hypnotising the rock landscape. In the final selection 'God' he spelt it out in no uncertain terms: 'The dream is over'; 'I just believe in me / Yoko and me / and that's reality.' From that point on, the whole 'me' decade mindset was officially in session.

1971

'Let It Rock' – the Rolling Stones (*Rarities*)
Sticky Fingers – my all-time favourite Stones album and the record I played most frequently throughout the year under discussion – is amply eulogised in the 1971 chapter but this lesser-known rampage through Chuck Berry's back catalogue – released as a bonus B-side to the 'Brown Sugar' 45 rpm – was what I'd put on first thing every morning in order to wake up and face the day.

Performance – various artists
The deeply spooky and wickedly eclectic Jack Nitzsche-helmed project gets my vote as the greatest film soundtrack recording ever made.

'I'm Eighteen' – Alice Cooper
Alice Cooper's early-seventies mega-success was short-lived but significant if only for this track – the quintet's first global hit – which not only gave glam rock some much-needed hard-rock sneer and rebel clout but also – stylistically and attitude-wise – boldly helped pave the way for the punk explosion that finally came five years after its release.

'Sweet Jane' – the Velvet Underground
This wasn't a hit in 1971 but I'd still hear it everywhere I went that year. Lou Reed sang the words with uncharacteristic gusto but it's his irresistibly circular guitar riff holding the whole thing together that really seals the deal.

'Mandolin Wind' – Rod Stewart
You can't spotlight the most memorable musical moments of 1971 without including something by its 'man of the year' Rod

Stewart, and this hauntingly plaintive folk ballad from *Every Picture Tells a Story* still glistens with everything that was once great about the man.

'Surf's Up' – the Beach Boys
Brian Wilson wrote and recorded this back in 1966 but it took the Beach Boys five more years before they saw the wisdom in actually releasing it. Miraculously this spine-tingling ode to the rise and fall of the sixties' golden wave of spiritual uplift sounded just as divine and unearthly in the seventies as it would have done in the time frame it was written for.

'At the Chime of the City Clock' – Nick Drake
This melancholy, drifting meditation on big-city isolation became the all-purpose soundtrack to my period as a student at London University which began in the October of 1971.

'What's Going On' – Marvin Gaye
Like another of '71's key singles, John Lennon's 'Imagine', 'What's Going On' is an unapologetic musical sermon from the mount to the pop masses, but unlike Lennon's sanctimonious diatribe, it actually works for me. The message is heartfelt, righteous and to the point, the groove, chords and arrangement are all sublime but its most outstanding feature is the prayer-like way Gaye sings to himself in the call-and-response sections, inventing a whole new form of vocal self-expression in the process.

Led Zep IV – Led Zeppelin
Simply their all-time best masterclass recording.

'The Bewlay Brothers' – David Bowie
Ziggy Stardust was still a few months away from being introduced

into the public domain when Bowie released his *Hunky Dory* album late in '71, but anyone who heard the record that winter instantly sensed that he would become one of the decade's leading creative luminaries. This track in particular stopped everyone in their tracks, an unforgettable foray into the realm of fractured surreal songcraft that beguiled and mystified like a darker shade of 'Strawberry Fields Forever'.

1972

'The Bells' – Laura Nyro and LaBelle

The album this comes from – *Gonna Take a Miracle* – was the first record I ever reviewed for the UK press but that's not the reason why I've chosen it. 'The Bells' is a beautiful Marvin Gaye-penned torch song that was first recorded by the Originals for Tamla Motown in '71 and which even reached no. 1 in the US singles chart that year. It's one of Motown's most incandescent late-period productions but Nyro and LaBelle trump the original with a more intimate reading that blends sublime gospel harmonies with a lead vocal that is the very essence of barely contained romantic hysteria. By the time La Nyro gets to the pay-off line 'If you ever leave me, I believe I'll go insane', you're already convinced she means exactly what she's singing.

'Thunder Express' – the MC5 (*The Big Bang!*)

When the Motor City 5 exiled themselves to England in early '72, this was the song they had up their collective sleeves as a possible hit single. Basically a rewrite and update of the classic four-to-the-bar Chuck Berry automobile fetish, 'Thunder Express' never made it into a recording studio but still managed to become the highlight of all their concerts that year. This live version – recorded for a TV show in Paris – totally captures what it was like to be one of those privileged few who actually made up their audience.

Tago Mago – Can
The stoner-rock masterpiece of 1972.

'Siberian Khatru' – Yes (*Close to the Edge*)
Don't laugh. This vibrant ambitious blending of hard-rock light-and-shade with classical music's sweep and sensibility is UK prog's greatest-ever achievement bar none. So good in fact that it almost single-handedly vindicates one of the dodgiest musical hybrids of the past fifty years.

'Do It Again' – Steely Dan
You couldn't escape this track in 1972 for love or money. Every London club DJ played it in seeming rotation until the wee small hours, by which time its sensual groove had every patron swaying and buzzing with hypnotised grins. In many respects, Steely Dan defined the seventies just as potently as David Bowie. But they did it purely on their musical talent.

'Ventilator Blues' – the Rolling Stones
Exile on Main St. was received cautiously by the pop pundits when it first appeared in the late spring of '72. But that didn't hinder its two vinyl albums from taking up dominion on my turntable for most of the summer. Hearing 'Ventilator Blues'' deep, druggy groove always takes me back to that hot and hectic season.

'King Heroin' – James Brown
I first heard this single over at the Stooges' rented house in

Barons Court. Iggy used to play it a lot, nodding sagely at the sentiments being expressed in King James's dramatic soliloquy against 'one of the most deadly menaces in the world today'. Thirty-eight years later it still stands up as the most effective anti-hard-drug statement ever made through the medium of music.

'Glistening Glyndebourne' – John Martyn

Whilst writing this book I was sidetracked and saddened by news of the death of John Martyn. John was a friend of mine during the late seventies, as well as being someone I've always considered a supremely gifted musician. This enchanted instrumental from *Bless the Weather* is just one of many Martyn classics from a decade that never gave him the success and acclaim he deserved. Maybe now that he's passed on, he'll finally get that global iconic stature that so eluded him in life.

'Walk in the Night' – Junior Walker

This loping, elegant instrumental from the Tamla Motown saxophone titan was what often used to be playing in my head when I'd promenade around London's sleepy streets after dark.

'All the Young Dudes' – Mott the Hoople

Ah yes, glam rock. Well, 'Dudes' was the form's very own national anthem that year, its best-written song and most inspired production. Runners-up included Bowie's own 'Suffragette City', Roxy Music's 'Virginia Plain' and a T.Rex B-side called 'Raw Ramp'.

1973

'The Ballad of El Goodo' – Big Star

Big Star's glorious first album and *Raw Power* were the two records I listened to incessantly whenever I had access to a record player during my travels through America that year.

Raw Power – Iggy and the Stooges
Still the greatest, meanest-eyed, coldest-blooded hard-rock tour de force ever summoned up in a recording studio.

'Mother of Pearl' – Roxy Music (*Stranded*)
Diehard fans may argue the point but I've always preferred Roxy Music's recordings after Brian Eno was banished from their midst, specifically this epic meditation on the soul-deadening side effects of living in the 'looking-glass world' of seventies celebrity narcissism. Bryan Ferry is quite right when he refers to it as the best song he ever wrote.

'Call Me' – Al Green
This actually came out as a single in 1973 but I could have just as easily picked earlier Green releases like 'Let's Stay Together'. His music became so omnipresent in the early seventies – particularly in all the clubs – that you could have been forgiven at the time for not fully appreciating just how remarkable the run of singles and albums he made with genius producer, arranger and co-writer Willie Mitchell really were.

'Cracked Actor' – David Bowie
Bowie totally nailed the soul-suckingly decadent vibe of Hollywood circa 1973 in this underrated selection from *Aladdin Sane*.

Clear Spot – Captain Beefheart and the Magic Band
This is – hands down – Beefheart's musical magnum opus. More musically accessible and way better produced than *Trout Mask Replica* but still as weird as all hell, *Clear Spot* is the splendid sound of the Captain at full creative throttle backed by a

Magic Band at their most inspired and – yes – magical.

'The Kiss' – Judee Sill (*Heart Food*)
Like 'Surf's Up', this is the sound of utter perfection and full-on spiritual rapture merging together in the pop-song medium. Beyond exquisite, this is holy, healing music that remains to this day criminally underappreciated.

'Bad Girl' – the New York Dolls
This careening track from their eponymous debut album contains all the approaching-train-wreck bliss of their best live shows.

The Harder They Come – various artists
1973 was the year when reggae reached out beyond its previous UK 'specialist' fan base of Jamaican expats and home-grown skinheads and started appealing to the larger white rock and pop demographic. The Wailers' 'Catch a Fire' and 'Burning' were crucial in spreading the weed-head gospel throughout the British Isles but this Jimmy Cliff-dominated soundtrack album was the key artefact to detonate a full-blown reggae revolution in the pre-punk UK.

Fresh – Sly & the Family Stone
Sly's last recording of consequence before drugs and ego turned him into one of the biggest losers of the late twentieth century.

1974

'Trouble Man' – Marvin Gaye (*Live!*)
Alongside the Temptations' Norman Whitfield-produced 'Papa Was a Rollin' Stone', Marvin Gaye's '73 hit single 'Trouble Man' introduced the world to a new, edgier, gloomier Motown sound for the seventies. A year after the studio version had sat proudly

in the UK top ten, Gaye returned to the song for a special in-concert rendition that shredded the original courtesy of some jaw-dropping vocal gymnastics and a backing band – Gaye's old Snakepit support crew reunited once more – that swings like the proverbial motherfucker.

'I Can't Stand the Rain' – Ann Peebles

Peebles never got to duplicate the worldwide success this sultry, lovesick single briefly brought her in 1974 but I will never forget the indelible impact this record had on taste-makers and music-lovers alike during that year.

Future Days – Can

This is the record that contained the dreamiest and most mind-scrambling musical explorations Can ever managed to conceive together.

Grievous Angel – Gram Parsons

Chrissie Hynde was a big fan of this, Parsons's posthumous final recording, and played it over and over again throughout the last months we lived together.

'Casanova' – Roxy Music

Bryan Ferry's second all-time masterpiece composition was too dark to be considered a plausible single choice for Roxy Music but nonetheless lit up their *Country Life* album with its caution-ary ode to some drug-dependent early-seventies dandy libertine. I wonder who he was referring to.

On the Beach – Neil Young

If you want to know even more about what it felt like to be cast adrift and left to float uncertainly through the spiritual quagmire of the (early) seventies, this album will fill you in.

'I Can Understand It' – Bobby Womack

Womack – one of American soul music's most talented singer/ songwriters – became a bona fide hipster cult item in 1974, with the Stones and Rod Stewart frequently praising his records to the skies and clued-in club DJs playing tracks like this until the grooves had been worn down to a static hiss.

Veedon Fleece – Van Morrison

Let us not be forgetting the prickly Belfast cowboy's mighty contribution to music in the early seventies. *Moondance* and *Tupelo Honey* were also particular favourites of mine during this time frame.

'Guilty' – Randy Newman

This maudlin drug addict's confession from Newman's seventies high point, *Good Old Boys*, really spoke to my personal condition as the decade headed towards its midway stretch.

1975

'Kashmir' – Led Zeppelin

I first heard *Physical Graffiti* in its entirety four months or more before its March '75 release date. Jimmy Page arranged an exclusive listening session at a London recording studio. Afterwards he asked me what I thought. I told him then that the stand-out track was 'Kashmir' and that it would probably go down in history as their greatest-ever recording. He seemed disappointed by this information and claimed to prefer 'Ten Years Gone'. Thirty-five years later though I'll bet he's revised his opinion.

'Fame' – David Bowie

King David's celebrity-bashing disco extravaganza was unavoidable in '75. 'Fame''s co-author John Lennon is lurking somewhere in the mix but the key contributor here – apart from Bowie himself of course – is Carlos Alomar, the Duke's most accomplished guitar foil and riff provider.

Blood on the Tracks – Bob Dylan

The Great One's return to sustained songwriting excellence after eight erratic years was a humongous hit worldwide in early '75. Obliquely centred on Dylan's recent marital conflicts, *Blood* became the perfect record for lovesick fools like me to use as a musical I Ching for the broken-hearted.

The Hissing of Summer Lawns – Joni Mitchell

On this sumptuously disturbing record La Mitchell daringly ditched her old LA neighbourhood of winsome Canyon ladies and free-spirited male troubadours to move into the loveless side of town where the pimps and junkies mingled with the rich and the damned. Her singing voice went down an octave in the process but her songwriting gifts flourished like never before in the new noir setting.

'I Love Music' – the O'Jays

Disco's most euphoric-sounding single was also the high-water mark for Gamble and Huff's prolific production factory out in Philadelphia.

'Roadrunner'/'Pablo Picasso' – the Modern Lovers

Long before these two tracks were available on vinyl, John Cale gave me a cassette tape of studio sessions he'd produced with this oddball Boston outfit, and both 'Roadrunner' and 'Picasso' instantly stood out as dual portents of 'things to come'.

'Cortez the Killer' – Neil Young

The gaunt Canadian dropped the bomb twice in '75, first by finally releasing *Tonight's the Night*, his prophetic meditation on the role of drugs and death in evolving pop culture, and then by unleashing *Zuma* at year's end. 'Cortez' was the highlight of the latter, with Young and a freshly reunited Crazy Horse down-pacing their usual prairie lope until it moved more like the sound of war canoes and their paddles slicing through calm waters in order to destroy ancient civilisations.

'Long Distance Love' – Little Feat

This once sorely underrated LA band were suddenly a hot ticket in '75 – particularly in Britain, which received their first live pre-sentations with rapturous acclaim. Doubtless influenced by this stroke of fate, their leader Lowell George went on to deliver his most soulful composition and vocal performance ever during that same year before succumbing to drug-accelerated flame-out and death at decade's end.

'Any World That I'm Welcome To' – Steely Dan

Something about the nakedness of emotion expressed in this beautiful song – a lonely, oversensitive introvert's simple prayer for acceptance in a more sympathetic universe – really put the spook in me when I first heard it.

'I'm a Hog for You Baby' – Dr. Feelgood

This double-fierce, borderline-obscene, amphetamine-sharp rearrangement of an old Coasters novelty track from the fifties was always the pivotal performance in their live shows in the mid-seventies.

1976

Station to Station – David Bowie

The sessions for this album were so drug-sated that Bowie now claims he can't remember any of the details about recording the six tracks. That's too bad because in my estimation it's his most fascinating work. If you really want to unravel the mysteries lurking in this deeply strange record, read Ian MacDonald's brilliant analysis in the chapter 'Dark Doings' from his 2005 book *The People's Music* (Serpent's Tail).

'I Want You' – Marvin Gaye

The late seventies found Gaye struggling to match the lofty creative standards he'd set for himself earlier in the decade. But this sublime single was another immaculate conception from Motown's greatest-ever God-given vocal talent.

'Blitzkrieg Bop' – the Ramones

The Stooges had already pushed the door marked 'punk rock' ajar at the outset of the seventies, but this track and the group who performed it were the proverbial dynamite stick which blew that door clear off its hinges in '76, opening wide a space in rock culture for the Sex Pistols and the Clash to rampage through.

Metallic KO – Iggy and the Stooges

This hellish live recording is in the list mainly because I was a prime mover in getting it released in the first place. It certainly had a ferocious influence on the emerging punk scene – not all of it good unfortunately. A lot of the violence that took place at London punk shows was directly caused by clueless young people trying to copy the audience mayhem of *Metallic KO*. More macabre audio *vérité* than a conventional rock album, this record now sends an uncomfortably cold chill down my spine whenever I even think about it. Bad karma on black vinyl.

'(Don't Fear) The Reaper' – Blue Oyster Cult

In recent years this has become a global biker anthem like 'Free Bird', as well as the victim of a side-splittingly funny Christopher Walken 'More Cowbell' routine on America's *Saturday Night Live*. Back in '76 though this majestically creepy rumination on looming death hit all the right buttons amongst record buyers and rock critics alike, both of whom couldn't get enough of its ingenious 'Byrds meet Darth Vader' ambience.

'The Boys Are Back in Town' – Thin Lizzy

Full-tilt seventies testosterone rock was what Phil Lynott's boys served up to the masses, and this breakthrough single proved beyond a shadow of a doubt that they were the toughest and tastiest in their field.

'Love of the Common Man' – Todd Rundgren

Rundgren was an oddity throughout the seventies. Early in the decade he looked set to become America's answer to Bowie but – after experimenting with psychedelic drugs – veered away from his more commercial instincts to clumsily embrace prog rock. Result: his fan base never grew beyond a cult. Still, in '76 he released some of his best-ever work on the album *Faithful*, specifically this killer salute to everyman that packed into approximately three minutes everything you needed to hear from his wide-ranging talents.

Hejira – Joni Mitchell

For my money, this remains the most intimate and breathtakingly beautiful album released during the seventies bar none.

The Pretender – Jackson Browne
The haunting title track – inspired by the suicide of Browne's girlfriend – was an unforgettable 'how to survive the seventies' burst of lyrical self-exegesis.

'Two Headed Dog' – Roky Erickson and Bleib Alien
One of the first 'indie'-distributed 45s I ever heard or saw. Mad as a sack of wild cats. Pure cerebral psychosis with a flaming backbeat and demons for guitar picks.

1977

'Watching the Detectives' – Elvis Costello and the Attractions
I remember spending an evening with Nick Lowe and Jake Riviera at their Kensington flat listening to a rough mix of this track – which Lowe had just produced – over and over again. I'd already heard Costello's *My Aim Is True* record and thought it was good. But this was monumental. Still one of the only examples of white blokes playing reggae that hits all the right spots for me.

The Idiot/Lust for Life – Iggy Pop
I've already praised these two Iggy/Bowie sonic groundbreakers sufficiently in the 1977 chapter.

Marquee Moon – Television
Several London punk notables took me to task for raving about this record so extensively in the *NME* that year. They said it was just 'music for old hippies' and that it would never last the test of

time. Thirty-two years later though I see *Marquee Moon* routinely perched in the highest branches of all those 'greatest-ever albums' polls instigated by the media whilst the recorded output of those who castigated them barely gets a mention.

'Joe the Lion' – David Bowie

The album *Heroes* could well have been the creative blueprint for the late-seventies 'new wave' musical hybrid. Everyone from the Human League to Simple Minds drew their core musical cues from its sulphurous contents. But no one ever merged US funk with European avant-pop drama more artfully than the Bromley Alien, and the album's second selection – a skewed homage to performance artist Chris Burden – was uncommonly inspired even by Bowie's exacting standards.

'Bodies' – the Sex Pistols

'Anarchy in the U.K.', 'God Save the Queen' and 'Pretty Vacant' were all brilliant blockbuster singles but the uproariously venomous 'Bodies' best captured the full foul-mouthed, flint-hearted essence of who and what the Sex Pistols really were from my vantage point.

Aja – Steely Dan

It's amazing to think the Sex Pistols' debut album and this sublime collection were released during the same year. The Dan's creative high point was the sonic antithesis of punk and took Donald Fagen and Walter Becker's noble quest to merge penetrating pop songcraft with sophisticated jazz-drenched chords and arrangements and five-star musicianship to a level of accomplishment no one has since come close to matching.

Little Criminals – **Randy Newman**

Greil Marcus really laid into this record via a long *Rolling Stone* review but I actually preferred its sleeker sound to most of Newman's early-seventies output.

The Belle Album – **Al Green**

In the mid-seventies, Green's mighty run of hits was interrupted by the singer's sudden urge to become an ordained preacher. *The Belle Album* was his first self-produced effort and first post-religious-conversion musical statement. Rarely has music promoting the 'I've found God and you should too' message sounded as compelling and persuasive to non-believing ears.

'The Book I Read' – **Talking Heads**

I stopped listening to David Byrne and his pals in the eighties when they opted to concentrate on manufacturing yuppified funk pastiches for white people with no sense of natural rhythm but this overlooked song from their debut album was still one of my favourites from 1977.

New Boots and Panties!! – **Ian Dury and the Blockheads**

Dury truly found his form once he'd disbanded the Kilburns at mid-decade and thrown in his lot with the more musically accomplished Blockheads. This seminal celebration of English eccentricity was one of the decade's stand-out musical statements.

1978–1979

Darkness on the Edge of Town – **Bruce Springsteen and the E Street Band**

For most Europeans, *Darkness* was the place where Springsteen finally rose above all the formative musical influences that had previously defined his recorded output and became an unstoppable rock superpower strictly on his own terms. These eloquent anthems for blue-collar Americans struggling to keep their faith in uncertain times sounded even better on the various live bootlegs that started appearing hot on the heels of this studio album's '78 release date.

Blue Valentine – Tom Waits

Predecessors *Small Change* and *Foreign Affairs* both had their share of stellar moments but *Valentine* was Waits's real 'coming of age' artistic triumph during a decade that never quite knew what to make of his music.

'Too Much Heaven' – the Bee Gees

Considering we almost came to blows back in 1973, you could be forgiven for thinking that I've always felt only contempt for the Bee Gees but – like virtually everyone else in the late seventies – I fell under the spell of their *Saturday Night Fever* contributions such as 'Stayin' Alive' and 'How Deep Is Your Love'. Even more irresistible was this lilting soul ballad from their *Spirits Having Flown* album.

'Tropical Hot Dog Night' – Captain Beefheart

This infectiously demented samba was all the proof I needed to show me that Beefheart had bounced back from his midseventies wilderness years to re-establish his rightful place on the throne as rock's very own King of Weird.

Excitable Boy – Warren Zevon

Zevon started out hell-bent on portraying himself as West Coast rock's very own Hunter S. Thompson and this – his second solo album – still ranks as his most successful and imaginative attempt at spicing up LA-centric, radio-friendly tunesmithery with an authentic 'gonzo' edge.

'Señor' – Bob Dylan

The highlight from '78's otherwise lacklustre *Street-Legal*, 'Señor' is the gloomily compelling sound of Dylan staring down the black hole of despair and betrayal just prior to being touched by the hand of God.

'Domino' – the Cramps

LA's rockabilly renegades outstripped even Roy Orbison's original version of this song by investing it with just the right hint of authentically psychotic swagger.

Rust Never Sleeps – Neil Young

To my ears this remains Young's all-time career peak. Every song is a masterpiece.

'Kid' – the Pretenders

The Pretenders' second single was the one that really brought it home to me that my old flame Chrissie Hynde had developed into a songwriter of consequence.

'Brand New Cadillac' – the Clash

I was never the world's biggest fan of the Clash's various studio recordings but always kept a special place in my heart for their ferocious rendition of the old fifties rocker first recorded by Vince Taylor.

Acknowledgements

Thanks to Kalina Villeroy, Angus Cargill, Lee Brackstone and Richard Thomas.

Index